AKATHISTS, SERVICES, CANONS, AND OTHER PRAYERS

VOLUME I — AKATHISTS

Printed in the United States of America

Publisher's Cataloguing-in-Publication data

Hutchison-Hall, John (Ellsworth).
   Akathists, Services, Canons, and Other Prayers following the
Tradition of the Russian Orthodox Church.
p. cm.
        ISBN-13: 978-0615835235
        ISBN-10: 0615835236
1. Akathists—Texts — English. 2. Orthodox Eastern Church—
Liturgy — Texts.

I. Hutchison-Hall, John (Ellsworth). II john-that-
theologian.com. III. Title.

Library of Congress Control Number: 2013910939
BX375.A55.H88 2013
264.019—dc22

CONTENTS

AKATHIST TO OUR SWEETEST JESUS CHRIST

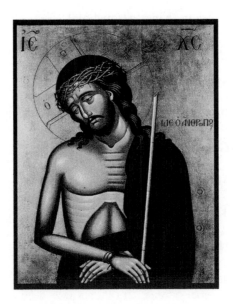

KONTAKION I

TO THEE, the Champion Leader and Lord, the Vanquisher of hell, I Thy creature and servant offer Thee songs of praise, for Thou hast delivered me from eternal death. But as Thou hast unutterable loving-kindness, free me from every danger, as I cry:

Jesus; Son of God, have mercy on me!

OIKOS I

CREATOR of Angels and Lord of Hosts! As of old, Thou didst open ear and tongue to the deaf and dumb, likewise open now my perplexed mind and tongue to the praise of Thy Most Holy Name, that I may cry to Thee:

Jesus; All-Wonderful, Angels' Astonishment!

Jesus; All-Powerful, Forefathers' Deliverance!

Jesus; All-Sweetest, Patriarchs' Exaltation!

Jesus; All-Glorious, Kings' Stronghold!

Jesus; All-Beloved, Prophets' Fulfilment!

Jesus; All-Marvellous, Martyrs' Strength!

Jesus; All-Peaceful, Monks' Joy!

Jesus; All-Gracious, Presbyters' Sweetness!

Jesus; All-Merciful, Fasters' Abstinence!

Jesus; All-Tenderest, Saints' Rejoicing!

Jesus; All-Honourable, Virgins' Chastity!

Jesus; everlasting, Sinners' Salvation!

Jesus; Son of God, have mercy on me!

KONTAKION II

A S when seeing the widow weeping bitterly, O Lord, Thou wast moved with pity, and didst raise her son from the dead as he was being carried to burial, likewise have pity on me, O Lover of men, and raise my soul, deadened by sins, as I cry: ALLELUIA!

OIKOS II

S EEKING to know what passes knowledge, Philip asked: "Lord, show us the Father" and Thou didst answer him: "Have I been so long with you and yet hast thou not known that I am in the Father and the Father in Me?" Likewise, O Inconceivable One, with fear I cry to Thee:

Jesus; Eternal God!

Jesus; All-Powerful King!

Jesus; Long-suffering Master!

Jesus; All-Merciful Saviour!

Jesus; my gracious Guardian!

Jesus; cleanse my sins!

Jesus; take away my iniquities!

Jesus; pardon my unrighteousness!

Jesus; my Hope, forsake me not!

Jesus; my Helper, reject me not!

Jesus; my Creator, forget me not!

Jesus; my Shepherd, lose me not!

Jesus; Son of God, have mercy on me!

KONTAKION III

THOU Who didst endue with power from on high Thy Apostles who tarried in Jerusalem, O Jesus, clothe also me, stripped bare of all good work, with the warmth of Thy Holy Spirit, and grant that with love I may sing to Thee: ALLELUIA!

OIKOS III

IN the abundance of Thy mercy, O Jesus, Thou hast called publicans and sinners and infidels. Now despise me not who am like them, but as precious myrrh accept this song:

Jesus; Invincible Power!

Jesus; Infinite Mercy!

Jesus; Radiant Beauty!

Jesus; Unspeakable Love!

Jesus; Son of the Living God!

Jesus; have mercy on me, a sinner!

Jesus; hear me who was conceived in iniquity!

Jesus; cleanse me who was born in sin!

Jesus; teach me who am worthless!

Jesus; enlighten my darkness!

Jesus; purify me who am unclean!

Jesus; restore me, a prodigal!

Jesus; Son of God, have mercy on me!

KONTAKION IV

HAVING an interior storm of doubting thoughts, Peter was sinking. But beholding Thee, O Jesus, in the flesh walking on the waters, he confessed Thee to be the true God; and receiving the hand of salvation, he cried: ALLELUIA!

OIKOS IV

WHEN the blind man heard Thee, O Lord, passing by on the way, he cried: Jesus, Son of David, have mercy on me! And Thou didst call him and open his eyes. Likewise, enlighten the spiritual eyes of my heart with Thy love as I cry to Thee and say:

Jesus; Creator of those on high!

Jesus; Redeemer of those below!

Jesus; Vanquisher of the powers of hell!

Jesus; Adorner of every creature!

Jesus; Comforter of my soul!

Jesus; Enlightener of my mind!

Jesus; Gladness of my heart!

Jesus; Health of my body!

Jesus; my Saviour, save me!

Jesus; my Light, enlighten me!

Jesus; deliver me from all torments!

Jesus; save me despite my unworthiness!

Jesus; Son of God, have mercy on me!

KONTAKION V

A S of old Thou didst redeem us from the curse of the law by Thy Divinely-shed Blood, O Jesus, likewise rescue me from the snares in which the serpent has entangled us through the passions of the flesh, through lustful suggestions and evil despondency, as we cry to Thee: ALLELUIA!

OIKOS V

S EEING the Creator in human form and knowing Him to be their Lord, the Hebrew children sought to please Him with branches, crying: Hosanna! But we offer Thee a song, saying:

Jesus; True God!

Jesus; Son of David!

Jesus; Glorious King!

Jesus; Innocent Lamb!

Jesus; Wonderful Shepherd!

Jesus; Guardian of my infancy!

Jesus; Nourisher of my youth!

Jesus; Praise of my old age!

Jesus; my Hope at death!

Jesus; my Life after death!

Jesus; my Comfort at Thy Judgment!

Jesus; my Desire, let me not then be ashamed!

Jesus; Son of God, have mercy on me!

KONTAKION VI

IN fulfilment of the words and message of the inspired Prophets, O Jesus, Thou didst appear on earth, and Thou Who art uncontainable didst dwell with men. Thenceforth, being healed through Thy wounds, we learned to sing: ALLELUIA!

OIKOS VI

WHEN the light of Thy truth dawned on the world, devilish delusion was driven away; for the idols, O our Saviour, have fallen, unable to endure Thy strength. But we, who have received salvation, cry to Thee:

Jesus; the Truth, dispelling falsehood!

Jesus; the Light above all lights!

Jesus; the King, surpassing all in strength!

Jesus; God, constant in mercy!

Jesus; Bread of Life, fill me who am hungry!

Jesus; Source of Knowledge, refresh me who am thirsty!

Jesus; Garment of Gladness, clothe my nakedness!

Jesus; Veil of Joy, cover my unworthiness!

Jesus; Giver to those who ask, give me sorrow for my sins!

Jesus; Finder of those who seek, find my soul!

Jesus; Opener to those who knock, open my wretched heart!

Jesus; Redeemer of sinners, wash away my sins!

Jesus; Son of God, have mercy on me!

KONTAKION VII

DESIRING to unveil the mystery hidden from all ages, Thou wast led as a sheep to the slaughter, O Jesus, and as a lamb before its shearer. But as God Thou didst rise from the dead and didst ascend with glory to Heaven, and along with Thyself Thou didst raise us who cry: ALLELUIA!

OIKOS VII

THE Creator has shown us a marvellous Creature, Who took flesh without seed from a Virgin, rose from the tomb without breaking the seal, and entered bodily the Apostles' room when the doors were shut. Therefore, marvelling at this we sing:

Jesus; Uncontainable Word!

Jesus; Inscrutable Intelligence!

Jesus; Incomprehensible Power!

Jesus; Inconceivable Wisdom!

Jesus; Undepictable Deity!

Jesus; Boundless Dominion!

Jesus; Invincible Kingdom!

Jesus; Unending Sovereignty!

Jesus; Supreme Strength!

Jesus; Eternal Power!

Jesus; my Creator, have compassion on me!

Jesus; my Saviour, save me!

Jesus; Son of God, have mercy on me!

KONTAKION VIII

SEEING God wondrously incarnate, let us shun the vain world and set our mind on things divine; for God descended to earth to raise to Heaven us who cry to Him: ALLELUIA!

OIKOS VIII

BEING both below and above, Thou didst never falter, O Thou immeasurable One, when Thou didst voluntarily suffer for us, and by Thy death our death didst put to death, and by Thy Resurrection didst grant life to those who sing:

Jesus; Sweetness of the heart!

Jesus; Strength of the body!

Jesus; Purity of the soul!

Jesus; Brightness of the mind!

Jesus; Gladness of the conscience!

Jesus; Sure Hope!

Jesus; Memory Eternal!

Jesus; High Praise!

Jesus; my most exalted Glory!

Jesus; my Desire, reject me not!

Jesus; my Shepherd, recover me!

Jesus; my Saviour, save me!

Jesus; Son of God, have mercy on me!

KONTAKION IX

THE Angelic Hosts in Heaven glorify unceasingly Thy most holy Name, O Jesus, crying: Holy, Holy, Holy! But we sinners on earth, with our frail voices cry: ALLELUIA!

OIKOS IX

WE see most eloquent orators voiceless as fish when they must speak of Thee, O Jesus our Saviour. For it is beyond their power to tell how Thou art both perfect man and immutable God at the same time. But we, marvelling at this Mystery, cry faithfully:

Jesus; Eternal God!

Jesus; King of Kings!

Jesus; Lord of Lords!

Jesus; Judge of the living and the dead!

Jesus; Hope of the hopeless!

Jesus; Comforter of the mournful!

Jesus; Glory of the poor!

Jesus; condemn me not according to my deeds!

Jesus; cleanse me according to Thy mercy!

Jesus; take from me despondency!

Jesus; enlighten the thoughts of my heart!

Jesus; make me ever mindful of death!

Jesus; Son of God, have mercy on me!

KONTAKION X

WISHING to save the world, O Sunrise of the East, Thou didst come to the dark Occident of our nature, and didst humble Thyself even to the point of death. Therefore, Thy Name is exalted above every name, and from all the tribes of earth and heaven, Thou dost hear: ALLELUIA!

OIKOS X

KING Eternal, Comforter, true Christ! Cleanse us from every stain as Thou didst cleanse the Ten Lepers, and heal us as Thou didst heal the greedy soul of Zacchaeus the publican, that we may cry to Thee with compunction and say:

Jesus; Treasurer Incorruptible!

Jesus; Unfailing Wealth!

Jesus; Strong Food!

Jesus; Inexhaustible Drink!

Jesus; Garment of the poor!

Jesus; Defender of widows!

Jesus; Protector of orphans!

Jesus; Helper of toilers!

Jesus; Guide of pilgrims!

Jesus; Pilot of voyagers!

Jesus; Calmer of tempests!

Jesus; raise me who am fallen!

Jesus; Son of God, have mercy on me!

KONTAKION XI

TENDEREST songs I, though unworthy, offer to Thee, and like the woman of Canaan, I cry to Thee: O Jesus, have mercy on me! For it is not my daughter, but my flesh violently possessed with passions and burning with fury. So grant healing to me, who cry to Thee: ALLELUIA!

OIKOS XI

HAVING previously persecuted Thee Who art the Light that enlightens those who are in the darkness of ignorance, Paul experienced the power of the voice of divine enlightenment, and understood the swiftness of the soul's conversion to God. Likewise, enlighten the dark eye of my soul, as I cry:

Jesus; my All-powerful King!

Jesus; my Almighty God!

Jesus; my Immortal Lord!

Jesus; my most glorious Creator!

Jesus; my most kind Teacher and Guide!

Jesus; my most compassionate Shepherd!

Jesus; my most gracious Master!

Jesus; my most merciful Saviour!

Jesus; enlighten my senses darkened by passions!

Jesus; heal my body scabbed with sins!

Jesus; cleanse my mind from vain thoughts!

Jesus; keep my heart from evil desires!

Jesus; Son of God, have mercy on me!

KONTAKION XII

G RANT me Thy grace, O Jesus, Absolver of all debts, and receive me who repent, as Thou didst receive Peter who denied Thee, and call me who am downcast, as of old Thou didst call Paul who persecuted Thee, and hear me crying to Thee: ALLELUIA!

OIKOS XII

P RAISING Thy Incarnation, we all glorify Thee and, with Thomas, we believe that Thou art our Lord and God, sitting with the Father and coming to judge the living and the dead. Grant that then I may stand at Thy right hand, who now cry:

Jesus; Eternal King, have mercy on me!

Jesus; sweet-scented Flower, make me fragrant!

Jesus; beloved Warmth, make me warm!

Jesus; Eternal Temple, shelter me!

Jesus; Garment of Light, adorn me!

Jesus; Pearl of great price, beam on me!

Jesus; precious Stone, illumine me!

Jesus; Sun of Righteousness, shine on me!

Jesus; holy Light, make me radiant!

Jesus; deliver me from sickness of soul and body!

Jesus; rescue me from the hands of the adversary!

Jesus; save me from the unquenchable fire and from the
other eternal torments!

Jesus; Son of God, have mercy on me!

KONTAKION XIII

O MOST sweet and most generous Jesus! Receive this, our humble prayer, as Thou didst receive the widow's mite and keep Thy faithful people from all enemies, visible and invisible, from foreign invasion, from disease and hunger, from all tribulations and mortal wounds, and deliver from future torments all who cry to Thee: ALLELUIA! *(Thrice)*

And again, Kontakion I and Oikos I are read.

KONTAKION I

TO THEE, the Champion Leader and Lord, the Vanquisher of hell, I, Thy creature and servant, offer Thee songs of praise, for Thou hast delivered me from eternal death. But as Thou hast unutterable loving-kindness, free me from every danger, as I cry:

Jesus; Son of God, have mercy on me!

OIKOS I

CREATOR of Angels and Lord of Hosts! As of old, Thou didst open ear and tongue to the deaf and dumb, likewise open now my perplexed mind and tongue to the praise of Thy Most Holy Name, that I may cry to Thee:

Jesus; All-Wonderful, Angels' Astonishment!

Jesus; All-Powerful, Forefathers' Deliverance!

Jesus; All-Sweetest, Patriarchs' Exaltation!

Jesus; All-Glorious, Kings' Stronghold!

Jesus; All-Beloved, Prophets' Fulfilment!

Jesus; All-Marvellous, Martyrs' Strength!

Jesus; All-Peaceful, Monks' Joy!

Jesus; All-Gracious, Presbyters' Sweetness!

Jesus; All-Merciful, Fasters' Abstinence!

Jesus; All-Tenderest, Saints' Rejoicing!

Jesus; All-Honourable, Virgins' Chastity!

Jesus; everlasting, Sinners' Salvation!

Jesus; Son of God, have mercy on me!

PRAYERS TO OUR LORD JESUS CHRIST

O ALL-WISE and All-gracious Lord, Our Saviour, Who didst enlighten all the ends of the world by the radiance of Thy Coming, and Who didst call us into Thy Holy Church through the promise of the inheritance of incorruptible and eternal good! Graciously look down on us, Thy worthless servants, and remember not our iniquities, but according to Thy infinite mercies forgive all our sins. For though we transgress Thy holy will, we do not deny Thee, Our God and Saviour. Against Thee alone do we sin, yet Thee alone do we serve, in Thee alone do we believe, to Thee alone do we come, and Thy servants only do we wish to be. Remember the infirmity of our nature and the temptations of the adversary and the worldly enticements and seducements which surround us on all sides, and against which, according to Thy word, we can do nothing without Thy help. Cleanse us and save us! Enlighten our minds that we may firmly believe in Thee, our only Saviour and Redeemer! Inspire our hearts that we may wholly love Thee, our only God and Creator! Direct our steps that we may stumblingly walk in the light of Thy commandments! Yea, our Lord and Creator, show us Thy great and abundant kindness, and make us live all the days of our life in holiness and truth, that at the time of Thy glorious Second Coming, we may be worthy to hear Thy gracious call into Thy Heavenly Kingdom. Grant us, Thy sinful and unprofitable servants, to receive Thy Kingdom, and that in the enjoyment of its ineffable beauty; we may ever glorify Thee, together with Thy Eternal Father, and Thy Ever-living Divine Spirit unto the ages of ages. AMEN.

SWEETEST Lord Jesus, strong Son of God, Who didst shed Thy precious Blood and die for love of my love, I am ready to die for love of Thy love. Sweetest Jesus, my Life, and my All, I love and adore Thee. Thee only do I wish for my Spouse, as Thou dost wish me for Thy bride. I give myself to Thee. I surrender myself to Thee. O Jesus, Thou Whose heart is ever turned to me, heal my heart, that I may feel the sweetness of Thy love, that I may taste no sweetness but Thee, seek no love but Thee, love no beauty but Thee. I have no desire but to please Thee and to do Thy will. Teach me to repent, and to take up the Cross daily and follow Thee with joy. Teach me to pray with faith and love. Thyself pray in me, that with Thee I may love my enemies and pray for them. Jesus, Thou art life in my death, strength in my weakness, light in my darkness, joy in my sorrow, courage in my faint-heartedness, peace in my agitation, obedience in my prayer, glory in my dishonour, and deliverance from my dishonour. Glory and thanks to Thee Jesus my Saviour and Healer. AMEN.

AKATHIST: "GLORY TO GOD FOR ALL THINGS"

This Akathist, also called the "Akathist of Thanksgiving," was composed by Protopresbyter Gregory Petrov shortly before his death in a prison camp in 1940. The title is from the words of Saint John Chrysostom as he was dying in exile. It is a song of praise from amidst the most terrible sufferings.

KONTAKION I

EVERLASTING King, Thy will for our salvation is full of power. Thy right arm controls the whole course of human life. We give Thee thanks for all Thy mercies, seen and unseen, for eternal life, for the heavenly joys of the Kingdom which is to be. Grant mercy to us who sing Thy praise, both now and in the time to come. Glory to Thee, O God, from age to age.

OIKOS I

I WAS born a weak, defenceless child, but Thine angel spread his wings over my cradle to defend me. From birth until now, Thy love hast illumined my path, and has wondrously guided me towards the light of eternity; from birth until now the generous gifts of Thy providence hath been marvellously showered upon me. I give Thee thanks, with all who have come to know Thee, who call upon Thy name.

Glory to Thee for calling me into being;

Glory to Thee, showing me the beauty of the universe;

Glory to Thee, spreading out before me heaven and earth;

Like the pages in a book of eternal wisdom;

Glory to Thee for Thine eternity in this fleeting world;

Glory to Thee for Thy mercies, seen and unseen;

Glory to Thee through every sigh of my sorrow;

Glory to Thee for every step of my life's journey;

For every moment of glory;

Glory to Thee, O God, from age to age.

KONTAKION II

O LORD, how lovely it is to be Thy guest. Breeze full of scents; mountains reaching to the skies; waters like boundless mirrors, reflecting the sun's golden rays and the scudding clouds. All nature murmurs mysteriously, breathing the depth of tenderness. Birds and beasts of the forest bear the imprint of Thy love. Blessed art thou, mother earth, in thy fleeting loveliness, which wakens our yearning for happiness that will last for ever, in the land where, amid beauty that grows not old, the cry rings out: ALLELUIA!

OIKOS II

THOU hast brought me into life as into an enchanted paradise. We have seen the sky like a chalice of deepest blue, where in the azure heights the birds are singing. We have listened to the soothing murmur of the forest and the melodious music of the streams. We have tasted fruit of fine flavour and the sweet-scented honey. We can live very well on Thine earth. It is a pleasure to be Thy guest.

Glory to Thee for the Feast Day of life;

Glory to Thee for the perfume of lilies and roses;

Glory to Thee for each different taste of berry and fruit;

Glory to Thee for the sparkling silver of early morning dew;

Glory to Thee for the joy of dawn's awakening;

Glory to Thee for the new life each day brings;

Glory to Thee, O God, from age to age.

KONTAKION III

IT IS the Holy Spirit who makes us find joy in each flower, the exquisite scent, the delicate colour, the beauty of the Most High in the tiniest of things. Glory and honour to the Spirit, the Giver of Life, who covers the fields with their carpet of flowers, crowns the harvest with gold, and gives to us the joy of gazing at it with our eyes. O be joyful and sing unto Him: ALLELUIA!

OIKOS III

HOW glorious art Thou in the springtime, when every creature awakes to new life and joyfully sings Thy praises with a thousand tongues. Thou art the Source of Life, the Destroyer of Death. By the light of the moon, nightingales sing, and the valleys and hills lie like wedding garments, white as snow. All the earth is Thy promised bride awaiting her spotless husband. If the grass of the field is like this, how gloriously shall we be transfigured in the Second Coming after the Resurrection! How splendid our bodies, how spotless our souls!

> Glory to Thee, bringing from the depth of the earth an endless variety of colours, tastes, and scents;
>
> Glory to Thee for the warmth and tenderness of the world of nature;
>
> Glory to Thee for the numberless creatures around us;
>
> Glory to Thee for the depths of Thy wisdom, the whole world a living sign of it;
>
> Glory to Thee; on my knees, I kiss the traces of Thine unseen hand;
>
> Glory to Thee, enlightening us with the clearness of eternal life;
>
> Glory to Thee for the hope of the unutterable, imperishable beauty of immortality;

Glory to Thee, O God, from age to age.

KONTAKION IV

HOW filled with sweetness are those whose thoughts dwell on Thee; how life-giving Thy holy Word. To speak with Thee is more soothing than anointing with oil; sweeter than the honeycomb. To pray to Thee lifts the spirit, refreshes the soul. Where Thou art not, there is only emptiness; hearts are smitten with sadness; nature, and life itself, become sorrowful; where Thou art, the soul is filled with abundance, and its song resounds like a torrent of life: ALLELUIA!

OIKOS IV

WHEN the sun is setting, when quietness falls like the peace of eternal sleep, and the silence of the spent day reigns, then in the splendour of its declining rays, filtering through the clouds, I see Thy dwelling-place: fiery and purple, gold and blue, they speak prophet-like of the ineffable beauty of Thy presence, and call to us in their majesty. We turn to the Father.

Glory to Thee at the hushed hour of nightfall;

Glory to Thee, covering the earth with peace;

Glory to Thee for the last ray of the sun as it sets;

Glory to Thee for sleep's repose that restores us;

Glory to Thee for Thy goodness even in the time
of darkness;

When the entire world is hidden from our eyes;

Glory to Thee for the prayers offered by a trembling soul;

Glory to Thee for the pledge of our reawakening;

On that glorious last day, that day which hath no evening;

Glory to Thee, O God, from age to age.

KONTAKION V

THE dark storm clouds of life bring no terror to those in whose hearts Thy fire is burning brightly. Outside is the darkness of the whirlwind, the terror, and howling of the storm, but in the heart, in the presence of Christ, there is light and peace, silence: ALLELUIA!

OIKOS V

I SEE Thine heavens resplendent with stars. How glorious art Thou radiant with light! Eternity watches me by the rays of the distant stars. I am small, insignificant, but the Lord is at my side. Thy right arm guides me wherever I go.

> Glory to Thee, ceaselessly watching over me;
>
> Glory to Thee for the encounters Thou dost arrange
>   for me;
>
> Glory to Thee for the love of parents, for the faithfulness
>   of friends;
>
> Glory to Thee for the humbleness of the animals which
>   serve me;
>
> Glory to Thee for the unforgettable moments of life;
>
> Glory to Thee for the heart's innocent joy;
>
> Glory to Thee for the joy of living;
>
> Moving and being able to return Thy love;
>
> Glory to Thee, O God, from age to age.

KONTAKION VI

HOW great and how close art Thou in the powerful track of the storm! How mighty Thy right arm in the blinding flash of the lightning! How awesome Thy majesty! The voice of the Lord fills the fields; it speaks in the rustling of the trees. The voice of the Lord is in the thunder and the downpour. The voice of the Lord is heard above the waters. Praise be unto Thee in the roar of mountains ablaze. Thou dost shake the earth like a garment; Thou dost pile up to the sky the waves of the sea. Praise be unto Thee, bringing low the pride of man. Thou dost bring from his heart a cry of Penitence: ALLELUIA!

OIKOS VI

When the lightning flash has lit up the camp dining hall, how feeble seems the light from the lamp. Thus dost Thou, like the lightning, unexpectedly light up my heart with flashes of intense joy. After Thy blinding light, how drab, how colourless, how illusory all else seems. My soul clings to Thee.

Glory to Thee, the highest peak of men's dreaming;

Glory to Thee for our unquenchable thirst for communion with God;

Glory to Thee, making us dissatisfied with earthly things;

Glory to Thee, turning on us Thy healing rays;

Glory to Thee, subduing the power of the spirits of darkness, and dooming to death every evil;

Glory to Thee for the signs of Thy presence for the joy of hearing Thy voice and living in Thy love;

Glory to Thee, O God, from age to age.

KONTAKION VII

In the wondrous blending of sounds it is Thy call we hear; in the harmony of many voices, in the sublime beauty of music, in the glory of the works of great composers: Thou leadest us to the threshold of paradise to come, and to the choirs of angels. All true beauty has the power to draw the soul towards Thee, and to make it sing in ecstasy: ALLELUIA!

OIKOS VII

THE breath of Thy Holy Spirit inspires artists, poets, and scientists. The power of Thy supreme knowledge makes them prophets and interpreters of Thy laws, who reveal the depths of Thy creative wisdom. Their works speak unwittingly of Thee. How great art Thou in Thy creation! How great art Thou in man!

Glory to Thee, showing Thine unsurpassable power in the laws of the universe;

Glory to Thee, for all nature is filled with Thy laws;

Glory to Thee for what Thou hast revealed to us in Thy mercy;

Glory to Thee for what Thou hast hidden from us in Thy wisdom;

Glory to Thee for the inventiveness of the human mind;

Glory to Thee for the dignity of man's labour;

Glory to Thee for the tongues of fire that bring inspiration;

Glory to Thee, O God, from age to age.

KONTAKION VIII

HOW near Thou art in the day of sickness. Thou Thyself visitest the sick; Thou Thyself bendest over the sufferer's bed. His heart speaks to Thee. In the throes of sorrow and suffering, Thou bringest peace and unexpected consolation. Thou art the comforter. Thou art the love which watches over and heals us. To Thee we sing the song: ALLELUIA!

OIKOS VIII

WHEN in childhood I called upon Thee consciously for the first time, Thou didst hear my prayer, and Thou didst fill my heart with the blessing of peace. At that moment I knew Thy goodness and knew how blessed are those who turn to Thee. I started to call upon Thee night and day; and now even now I call upon Thy name.

Glory to Thee, satisfying my desires with good things;

Glory to Thee, watching over me day and night;

Glory to Thee, curing affliction and emptiness with the healing flow of time;

Glory to Thee, no loss is irreparable in Thee, Giver of eternal life to all;

Glory to Thee, making immortal all that is lofty and good;

Glory to Thee, promising us the longed-for meeting with our loved ones who have died;

Glory to Thee, O God, from age to age.

KONTAKION IX

WHY is it that on a Feast Day the whole of nature mysteriously smiles? Why is it that then a heavenly gladness fills our hearts; a gladness far beyond that of earth and the very air in church and in the altar becomes luminous? It is the breath of Thy gracious love. It is the reflection of the glory of Mount Tabor. Then do heaven and earth sing Thy praise: ALLELUIA!

OIKOS IX

WHEN Thou didst call me to serve my brothers and filled my soul with humility, one of Thy deep, piercing rays shone into my heart; it became luminous, full of light like iron glowing in the furnace. I have seen Thy face, face of mystery and of unapproachable glory.

Glory to Thee, transfiguring our lives with deeds of love;

Glory to Thee, making wonderfully sweet the keeping of Thy commandments;

Glory to Thee, making Thyself known where man shows mercy on his neighbour;

Glory to Thee, sending us failure and misfortune that we may understand the sorrows of others;

Glory to Thee, rewarding us so well for the good we do;

Glory to Thee, welcoming the impulse of our heart's love;

Glory to Thee, raising to the heights of heaven every act of love in earth and sky;

Glory to Thee, O God, from age to age.

KONTAKION X

NO ONE can put together what has crumbled into dust, but Thou canst restore a conscience turned to ashes. Thou canst restore to its former beauty a soul lost and without hope. With Thee, there is nothing that cannot be redeemed. Thou art love; Thou art Creator and Redeemer. We praise Thee, singing: ALLELUIA!

OIKOS X

REMEMBER, my God, the fall of Lucifer full of pride, and keep me safe with the power of Thy Grace; save me from falling away from Thee. Save me from doubt. Incline my heart to hear Thy mysterious voice every moment of my life. Incline my heart to call upon Thee, present in everything.

Glory to Thee for every happening;

Every condition Thy providence has put me in;

Glory to Thee for what Thou speakest to me in my heart;

Glory to Thee for what Thou revealest to me, asleep
or awake;

Glory to Thee for scattering our vain imaginations;

Glory to Thee for raising us from the slough of our
passions through suffering;

Glory to Thee for curing our pride of heart by humiliation;

Glory to Thee, O God, from age to age.

KONTAKION XI

ACROSS the cold chains of the centuries, I feel the warmth of Thy breath; I feel Thy blood pulsing in my veins. Part of time has already gone, but now Thou art the present. I stand by Thy Cross; I was the cause of it. I cast myself down in the dust before it. Here is the triumph of love, the victory of salvation. Here the centuries themselves cannot remain silent, singing Thy praises: ALLELUIA!

OIKOS XI

BLESSED are they that will share in the King's Banquet: but already on earth Thou givest me a foretaste of this blessedness. How many times with Thine own hand hast Thou held out to me Thy Body and Thy Blood, and I, though a miserable sinner, have received this Mystery, and have tasted Thy love, so ineffable, so heavenly.

Glory to Thee for the unquenchable fire of Thy Grace;

Glory to Thee, building Thy Church, a haven of peace in a
tortured world;

Glory to Thee for the life-giving water of Baptism in
which we find new birth;

Glory to Thee, restoring to the penitent purity white
as the lily;

Glory to Thee for the cup of salvation and the bread of
eternal joy;

Glory to Thee for exalting us to the highest heaven;

Glory to Thee, O God, from age to age.

KONTAKION XII

HOW often have I seen the reflection of Thy glory in the faces of the
dead. How resplendent they were, with beauty and heavenly joy.
How ethereal, how translucent their faces. How triumphant over suffering
and death, their felicity and peace. Even in the silence, they were calling
upon Thee. In the hour of my death, enlighten my soul, too, that it may
cry out to Thee: ALLELUIA!

OIKOS XII

WHAT sort of praise can I give Thee? I have never heard the song
of the Cherubim, a joy reserved for the spirits above. But I
know the praises that nature sings to Thee. In winter, I have beheld how
silently in the moonlight the whole earth offers Thee prayer, clad in its
white mantle of snow, sparkling like diamonds. I have seen how the
rising sun rejoices in Thee, how the song of the birds is a chorus of
praise to Thee. I have heard the mysterious mutterings of the forests
about Thee, and the winds singing Thy praise as they stir the waters. I
have understood how the choirs of stars proclaim Thy glory as they
move forever in the depths of infinite space. What is my poor worship!
All nature obeys Thee, I do not. Yet while I live, I see Thy love, I long
to thank Thee, and call upon Thy name.

Glory to Thee, giving us light;

Glory to Thee, loving us with love so deep, divine,
and infinite;

Glory to Thee, blessing us with light, and with the host of
angels and saints;

Glory to Thee, Father all-holy, promising us a share in
Thy Kingdom;

Glory to Thee, Holy Spirit, life-giving Sun of the world
to come;

Glory to Thee for all things, Holy and most merciful Trinity;

Glory to Thee, O God, from age to age.

KONTAKION XIII

LIFE-GIVING and merciful Trinity, receive our thanksgiving for all
Thy goodness. Make us worthy of Thy blessings, so that, when
we have brought to fruit the talents Thou hast entrusted to us, we
may enter into the joy of our Lord, forever exulting in the shout of
victory: ALLELUIA! *(Thrice)*

And again, Oikos I and Kontakion I are read.

OIKOS I

I WAS born a weak, defenceless child, but Thine angel spread his wings
over my cradle to defend me. From birth until now, Thy love has
illumined my path, and has wondrously guided me towards the light of
eternity; from birth until now, the generous gifts of Thy providence have
been marvellously showered upon me. I give Thee thanks, with all who
have come to know Thee, who call upon Thy name.

Glory to Thee for calling me into being;

Glory to Thee, showing me the beauty of the universe;

Glory to Thee, spreading out before me heaven and earth
like the pages in a book of eternal wisdom;

Glory to Thee for Thine eternity in this fleeting world;

Glory to Thee for Thy mercies, seen and unseen;

Glory to Thee through every sigh of my sorrow;

Glory to Thee for every step of my life's journey for every
     moment of glory;

Glory to Thee, O God, from age to age.

KONTAKION I

EVERLASTING King, Thy will for our salvation is full of power. Thy right arm controls the whole course of human life. We give Thee thanks for all Thy mercies, seen and unseen. For eternal life, for the heavenly Joys of the Kingdom which is to be. Grant mercy to us who sing Thy praise, both now and in the time to come. Glory to Thee, O God, from age to age.

AKATHIST TO THE LIFE-BEARING TOMB
AND THE RESURRECTION OF
THE LORD JESUS CHRIST

KONTAKION I

To the chosen Champion Leader risen from the dead, a hymn of victory do we sing unto Thee, O Christ Eternal King, for Thou hast risen from the tomb: and we being delivered from everlasting corruption, bring joyous acclamations unto Thine honourable tomb crying out:

Rejoice; life-bearing tomb whence Christ hath risen!

OIKOS I

An Archangel came down from heaven to roll away the stone from before Thy tomb at Thy resurrection, O Christ God, and to announce Thy rising unto the Myrrh-bearers saying: Go ye and tell His disciples that He is risen from the dead. And they, wondering at the strange word of the angel, cried unto Thy life-bearing tomb these praises:

> Rejoice; life-bearing tomb wherein Christ lay as dead and whence He arose upon the third day!

> Rejoice; for He arose from thee and hath granted us resurrection!

> Rejoice; for as a bridegroom from the bridal-chamber so didst Christ come forth from thee, leading hell captive!

> Rejoice; for in His rising the dead of all ages have arisen!

> Rejoice; for by thee hath Peter the chief Apostle known the resurrection!

> Rejoice; for by Christ's lying within thee hath all the earth been hallowed!

> Rejoice; life-bearing tomb whence Christ hath risen!

KONTAKION II

WHEN Mary Magdalene and the other Mary came unto Thy tomb to anoint Thy Body, O Christ God, they found an angel sitting upon the stone and he said unto them: Be ye not afraid for I know that ye seek the Crucified; He is not here but is risen as He said unto you. And when they had announced the resurrection to the disciples then did all sing as unto the Creator and Master of All, the angels hymn: ALLELUIA!

OIKOS II

THEIR thoughts storming within their minds, Thy disciples, O Christ, knew not the scripture that it was fitting for Thee to rise from the dead: therefore, they did not believe the Myrrh-bearers' joyous announcement of Thy rising: but Peter ran unto Thy tomb and stooping down beheld the linen clothes laid by themselves and the napkin which had been about Thy divine Head, and rightly believed together with the rest of the disciples and, therefore, rejoicing, cried such praises unto Thy life-bearing tomb:

Rejoice; life-bearing tomb, for by thee was wrought the salvation of the whole world!

Rejoice; for thou art venerated by all creation!

Rejoice; for coming unto thee from the North and from the sea the faithful glorify Christ!

Rejoice; for from the West and from the East all magnify the resurrection within thee!

Rejoice; for thou wast couch and repose unto the King of kings!

Rejoice; for by thee the assembly of the Jews was put to shame!

Rejoice; life-bearing tomb whence Christ hath risen!

KONTAKION III

THE sentries, that vain guard placed about Thy tomb, O Christ, heard the mighty earthquake and the Angel proclaiming the good news of Thy resurrection to the Myrrh-bearers and, quaking with fear became as dead men, and rushing headlong into the city told the high-priest and the elders the things that had come to pass, but in their great unrighteousness they thought to conceal Thy resurrection but were not able, and rather taught all to sing: ALLELUIA!

OIKOS III

THE Arimathean who from fear of the Jews had secretly been Thy disciple, O Christ, did beg Thy divine body from Pilate and then, too, did Nicodemus come bearing a mixture of myrrh and aloes and did anoint Thine incorruptible body, and, having wrapped it in a winding sheet with spices, did lay Thee in a new tomb wherein no other had yet been placed but Thou only, O Lord, that Thou mightest sanctify the substance of the earth. But when they had learned of Thy resurrection from the dead, they shouted praises unto Thy life-bearing tomb:

Rejoice; life-bearing tomb, for the mysteries of salvation have been performed within thee!

Rejoice; for by thee the resurrection hath been made known unto the whole world!

Rejoice; sure and certain knowledge of the resurrection!

Rejoice; for Christ coming forth from thee hath led captivity captive, and brought human nature unto God the Father!

Rejoice; for although as man He was laid within thee, as God did He arise with glory!

Rejoice; for thou didst, hold within thyself Him Who holdeth all creation!

Rejoice; life-bearing tomb whence Christ hath risen!

KONTAKION IV

WHEN the Myrrh-bearers came unto Thy disciples, O Christ God, announcing Thy resurrection, they were filled with joy and went into Galilee to the mount, as Thou hadst commanded them; and seeing Thee, very God, in the flesh and not an apparition, they worshiped God, crying: ALLELUIA!

OIKOS IV

THIS knowledge remained unknown to the Jews who neither understood the prophecies nor sought to understand Thy resurrection, O Christ: how Thou couldst come forth from Thy tomb without breaking the seals thereof. Wherefore do they slander and jeer at Thy rising, but we, marvelling at the mystery, bring praises to Thy life-bearing tomb, saying:

Rejoice; life-bearing tomb, for Christ from thee hath risen
and raised up the dead!

Rejoice; for through thee hell is known and stripped bare!

Rejoice; for the naked Adam is once more clothed in a
divinely-woven garment!

Rejoice; for the earth, polluted by Abel's fratricidal blood, is
hallowed again, by Christ's abiding in thee!

Rejoice; for when the Angel had rolled away the stone from
before thee, the Myrrh-bearers came to know of
Christ's resurrection!

Rejoice; for when Christ had arisen from thee, the news
of this resurrection did spread throughout the
whole world!

Rejoice; life-bearing tomb whence Christ hath risen!

KONTAKION V

ON the eighth day after Thy resurrection, Thou, O Lord, didst come
unto Thy disciples, although the doors were closed, and bestow the
gifts of the Holy Spirit upon them. And then Thou didst say unto Thy
disciple Thomas, "Come hither and touch Me!" and he, at the touch,
knew Thee as being truly risen and not an apparition. Wherefore together
with the other disciples did he cry unto Thee: ALLELUIA!

OIKOS V

WE see the council of the Jews, the falsely-wise orators, mute as fish
and unable to speak about Thy resurrection, O Christ, and not
understanding the prophecies, how it was meet for Thee, the God of all, to
rise from the dead. But we, marvelling at the mystery of Thy resurrection,
cry out unto Thy life-bearing tomb:

Rejoice; life-bearing tomb, for Pilate's foolish watchmen
were terrified when Christ came forth from thee!

Rejoice; for He Who arose from thee broke not the seals
upon the grave!

Rejoice; O truly rich tomb, for thou didst hold within thyself
Christ the Life-giver, Who bestoweth life upon all!

Rejoice; for when Christ arose from thee the heavens
did rejoice!

Rejoice; for then the things of earth did teach the
resurrection to all!

Rejoice; life-bearing tomb whence Christ hath risen!

KONTAKION VI

WHEN after Thy resurrection Thou, O Christ, didst reveal thyself to Thy disciples at the sea of Tiberius and command them to cast the net on the right side of the ship, and then did Thy beloved disciple, recognizing Thee, O God, from the mighty draught of fishes, say unto Peter, "It is the Lord!" And as soon as they had come to land, they saw a fire and fish thereupon and bread, and in the giving of bread, they did know Thee and as to the risen God did shout: ALLELUIA!

OIKOS VI

THE women made their way unto Thy tomb in the deep dawn, O Christ God, and though they found not Thy sought-for body, O Jesus, they discerned not Thy rising, but straightway saw an Angel standing before them, who asked them, "Why seek ye the living among the dead? He is not here, but is risen." And seeing Thy resurrection with great gladness they cried out these praises unto Thy life-bearing tomb:

Rejoice; life-bearing tomb, for by Christ's abiding within thee
the nether regions were seized with great fear!

Rejoice; for then with trembling did hell give up the dead
which it had held down through the ages!

Rejoice; for by Christ's rising we are all restored to newness
of life!

Rejoice; for by Christ's rising from thee Thomas was taught
to say, "My Lord and my God!"

Rejoice; for in Christ's rising all creation hath found joy!

Rejoice; too, O Arimathean, for within thine own garden
thou hast acquired so great a treasure!

Rejoice; life-bearing tomb whence Christ hath risen!

KONTAKION VII

THE sun at Thy passion, O Christ, unable to bear the raging frenzy of
the lawless, did hide its light and the veil of the temple was rent, and
when Thou wast laid in the life-bearing tomb the earth was shaken as
though wanting to swallow up the unlawful, but Thou as God didst rise in
glory and with Thyself didst raise up Adam, the father of us all.
Wherefore, unto our truly risen God to we sing: ALLELUIA!

OIKOS VII

AFTER Thy resurrection, O Christ, Thou didst reveal Thyself unto
Luke and Cleopas along the way and didst accompany them as they
discussed together those things that had happened unto Thee, O Master
of all, and Thou wast scorned by them as being but a stranger in
Jerusalem. But Thou as God didst open unto them the prophecies
concerning Thyself and thus wast known by them in the breaking of the
bread, whence with great joy they turned back to Jerusalem and told the
good news of Thy resurrection and appearance unto Thy disciples.
Wherefore, all together, they did worship and sing praises unto Thy life-
bearing tomb:

Rejoice; life-bearing tomb, for thou hast received within
thyself Christ, the heavenly bread, given as food for all!

Rejoice; for thou wast able to contain Christ as a
sleeping king!

Rejoice; for heaven and earth were filled with glad tidings
when Christ arose from thee!

Rejoice; for by thee the Jews were brought to disgrace!

Rejoice; for no longer are the unlawful able to slander
Christ's resurrection!

Rejoice; for through thee the Apostles' choir was filled
with joy!

Rejoice; life-bearing tomb whence Christ hath risen!

KONTAKION VIII

MANKIND together with all the Angels doth stand in wonder before Thy great care for us — Thou Who as God art inaccessible and yet as an approachable man art seen by all; Thou Who wast crucified and buried and Who didst rise in glory, and therefore, unto Thee as Creator and Master doth sing: ALLELUIA!

OIKOS VIII

IN Thy resurrection, O Christ, Thou didst show forth the new creation, for, just as in Thy birth from the Virgin, Thou didst not destroy the seal upon the tomb. Therefore, we honour Thy Passion, we glorify Thy Burial, in faith we worship Thy glorious Resurrection and offer hymns of thanksgiving unto Thy tomb, saying:

Rejoice; life-bearing tomb, for Christ is risen from thee and
hath renewed the whole world!

Rejoice; for the stone that was rolled away from thee hath
shattered the gates and door-posts of hell!

Rejoice; for the sun of the whole world hath shone forth
from thee!

Rejoice; for when Christ lay within thee the nether regions
were shaken asunder!

Rejoice; for those dead whom hell of old did seize, it hath
unwillingly given back alive!

Rejoice; thou lightning flash which did hide the divine pearl
within thyself!

Rejoice; life-bearing tomb whence Christ hath risen!

KONTAKION IX

THE Apostles, those God-bearing heralds of Thy resurrection,
were sent out into the whole world and they did preach Thee, the
true God; they taught all the faithful to sing unto Thee, the Creator
and Master: ALLELUIA!

OIKOS IX

AFTER THY rising from the grave, Mary Magdalene came unto the
tomb while it was still dark and saw the stone taken away from the
tomb. She, therefore, went quickly to the disciples, saying, "They have
taken away the Lord out of the sepulchre!" Then Peter, that disciple of
burning faith, ran with John to the tomb and peering within saw the
garments lying together and, coming to the knowledge of Thy resurrection,
began to shout praises to Thy life-bearing tomb:

Rejoice; life-bearing tomb, for when Christ was shut within
thee He shone forth light upon the nether regions!

Rejoice; for when the stone was removed from thee the
stony-hearted nations began to sing, "Christ is
truly risen!"

Rejoice; for within thee God did pass three days asleep in
the flesh!

Rejoice; for by His rising hath He awakened those who
through the ages have been asleep!

Rejoice; for coming forth from thee, He hath bestowed
resurrection upon all!

Rejoice; for as a bright sun shining forth from thee hath He
enlightened the whole world!

Rejoice; life-bearing tomb whence Christ hath risen!

KONTAKION X

THE earth grew frightened and fell silent, seeing Thee its Creator lying
in a small tomb, and hell, trembling with fear before Thy power,
gave up its dead preparing for Thee Thy rising to the Father from Whom
Thou wast never separate. Wherefore do we sing unto Thee: ALLELUIA!

OIKOS X

MARY Magdalene with most ardent faith in Thee, O Jesus Christ,
came very early unto Thy tomb, O Saviour, and was granted the
vision of an angel telling her, "He is not here, but is risen." Furthermore,
Thou didst Thyself appear to her as God, therefore she was sent as the
bearer of good news to announce to Thy disciples Thy rising to the
Father. Thy disciples were thereby filled with joy and together with the
Myrrh-bearers offered praises unto Thy life-bearing tomb, crying:

Rejoice; life-bearing tomb, thou opening of the gates of
paradise!

Rejoice; for of Him Who lay within thee doth hell
unwillingly speak truly, saying, "It were better
for me had I never seized the Son of Mary!"

Rejoice; for He Who arose from thee hath led hell captive
and filled the heavenly Jerusalem!

Rejoice; for as one who sleepeth hast thou held within
thyself the very Lamb, the Son of God!

Rejoice; for according to the prophecy Christ did sleep
within thee and as a lion did take His rest and
who hath stirred Him up?

Rejoice; for from thee He raised Himself by His own power!

Rejoice; life-bearing tomb whence Christ hath risen!

KONTAKION XI

WHEN the Saviour stood before His disciples, granting them peace,
He also gave them the power to forgive sins and to baptize in the
name of the Father, and of the Son, and of the Holy Spirit, and to preach
His resurrection from the dead; and they did go forth and teach all nations
to cry unto the risen God: ALLELUIA!

OIKOS XI

AFTER Thy rising from the dead, O Christ, appearing unto Thy
disciples Thou didst say unto Simon Peter, "Simon, son of Jonas,
lovest thou Me?" And after his threefold declaration of his love for Thee,
Thou didst establish him as the first leader of Thy Church and all the
faithful, having known Thee the risen God, cried out praises to Thy life-
bearing tomb:

Rejoice; life-bearing tomb, for in coming forth from thee
hath Christ made us a path up to heaven!

Rejoice; for, placed within thee, Christ hath raised up
the dead of all the ages!

Rejoice; for unto the resurrected hath He given eternal life!

Rejoice; for the Cross and Resurrection are glorified in thee!

Rejoice; for by thee the sentries learned of the resurrection!

Rejoice; for thou art the fountain of divine knowledge!

Rejoice; life-bearing tomb whence Christ hath risen!

KONTAKION XII

G LORIFYING Thy Passion, we honour Thy divine providence for us and we worship Thy divine resurrection. Glorifying Thine all-glorious ascension from earth unto the heavenly Father, we pray: Take not Thine all-holy Spirit away from us, so that we may all sing unto Thee as Creator and Master: ALLELUIA!

OIKOS XII

T HOU the radiance of the Father didst go unto the Mount of Olives and then a most bright cloud did lift Thee up, as Thy disciples looked on, O Almighty One, and Thine angels said unto Thine Apostles, "Ye men of Galilee, why stand ye gazing up into heaven? Him Whom ye see taken up from you shall come again in the flesh." And they returned to Jerusalem with joy, praising Thee, the true God, and offering praises unto Thy life-bearing tomb, wherein Thou wast laid and on the third day didst rise:

> Rejoice; life-bearing tomb, for from thee hath Christ, the
> ineffable light, shone forth, and enlightened the
> whole world!

> Rejoice; for the Myrrh-bearers did hear, "Rejoice!"
> when Christ arose from thee!

> Rejoice; for thou hast been the resting-place of the King of
> kings and Lord of lords!

> Rejoice; for thou hast held the sustainer of all creation!

> Rejoice; for the most wise Jews were made fools by thee, for
> they could not speak against the resurrection!

> Rejoice; for the choir of the Apostles hath found joy
> through thee!

> Rejoice; life-bearing tomb whence Christ hath risen!

KONTAKION XIII

O MOST holy and life-bearing tomb of Christ, thou the enrichment of the whole world! Standing before thee as the bearer of life we pray unto Christ our God Who lay within thee and rose in glory on the third day, that He deliver His inheritance from famine, pestilence, earthquake and flood and from every mortal wound, that He grant peace unto Orthodox Christians and subdue under their feet those who strive against them, that we may all sing unto Thee, our Creator and Master: ALLELUIA, ALLELUIA, ALLELUIA! *(Three times.)*

And again, Oikos I and Kontakion I are read.

OIKOS I

A N Archangel came down from heaven to roll away the stone from before Thy tomb at Thy resurrection, O Christ God, and to announce Thy rising unto the Myrrh-bearers saying: Go ye and tell His disciples that He is risen from the dead. And they, wondering at the strange word of the angel, cried unto Thy life-bearing tomb these praises:

Rejoice; life-bearing tomb wherein Christ lay as dead and
    whence He arose upon the third day!

Rejoice; for He arose from thee and hath granted
    us resurrection!

Rejoice; for as a bridegroom from the bridal-chamber so did
    Christ come forth from thee, leading hell captive!

Rejoice; for in His rising the dead of all ages have arisen!

Rejoice; for by thee hath Peter the chief Apostle known
    the resurrection!

Rejoice; for by Christ's lying within thee hath all the earth
    been hallowed!

Rejoice; life-bearing tomb whence Christ hath risen!

KONTAKION I

To the chosen Champion Leader risen from the dead, a hymn of victory do we sing unto Thee, O Christ Eternal King, for Thou hast risen from the tomb: and we being delivered from everlasting corruption, bring joyous acclamations unto Thine honourable tomb crying out:

Rejoice; life-bearing tomb whence Christ hath risen!

Akathist to the Divine Passion of Christ

Kontakion I

SUPREME Ruler and Lord of Heaven and earth, seeing Thee, the Immortal King, hanging on the Cross, all creation was changed, Heaven was horrified, and the foundations of the earth were shaken. But we, unworthy as we are, offer Thee thankful adoration for Thy Passion on our behalf, and with the robber we cry to Thee:

> Jesus; Son of God, remember us when Thou comest into
> Thy Kingdom!

Oikos I

IN completing the choirs of angels, Thou didst not take on the angelic nature, but being the Eternal God, for my sake Thou becamest man, and Thou didst restore to life men who were dead through sin with Thy Life-giving Body and Blood. Therefore, in gratitude for Thine amazing love, we humbly cry to Thee:

> Jesus; God, Eternal Love, Who was pleased to save us who are born of earth!

> Jesus; Infinite Mercy, Who didst come down here to us fallen creatures!

> Jesus; Who was clothed in our flesh and didst destroy the dominion of death by Thy death!

> Jesus; Who dost deify us with Thy Divine Mysteries!

> Jesus; Who hast redeemed the whole world by Thy Cross and Passion!

> Jesus; Son of God, remember us when Thou comest into Thy Kingdom!

KONTAKION II

SEEING THEE in the Garden of Gethsemane struggling in prayer till Thou didst sweat blood, an angel appeared and strengthened Thee when our sins weighed upon Thee like a heavy burden. For, having taken lost Adam on Thy shoulders, Thou didst bring him to the Father by bending Thy knees and praying. For this, I sing to Thee with faith and love: ALLELUIA!

OIKOS II

THE Jews did not know the incredible truth of Thy voluntary Passion. Therefore, when Thou didst say to those who were seeking Thee at night with lanterns: I AM HE, even though they fell to the ground, yet afterwards they bound Thee and led Thee to the judgment hall. But we fall down before Thee on the Way of the Cross and cry with love:

> Jesus; Light of the world, hated by evil and worldly people!

Jesus; Who dwellest in unapproachable Light, seized by
the realms of darkness!

Jesus; Immortal Son of God, condemned to death by a son
of perdition!

Jesus; in Whom there is nothing false, falsely kissed by
the traitor!

Jesus; Who givest Thyself freely to all, sold for a sum
of silver!

Jesus; Son of God, remember us when Thou comest in
Thy Kingdom!

KONTAKION III

B Y the power of Thy divinity Thou didst foretell to Thy disciple his
threefold denial. But even though after this he denied Thee with an
oath, yet when he saw Thee, His Lord and Master, in the high priest's
court his heart was touched, and he went out and wept bitterly. Look,
then, also upon me, O Lord, and strike my hard heart, that with my tears I
may wash away my sins and sing to Thee: ALLELUIA!

OIKOS III

H AVING true power as High Priest for ever, after the order of
Melchizedek, Thou didst stand before the criminal high priest
Caiaphas. O Lord and Master of all, who didst accept torture from Thy
slaves, accept from us these prayers and praises:

Jesus; Priceless One Who was bought for a price; adopt me
into Thine eternal inheritance!

Jesus; desire of all nations, denied from fear by Peter,
reject me not a sinner!

Jesus; Innocent Lamb, torn by cruel scourges, rescue me
from mine enemies!

Jesus; High Priest, Who hast entered the Holy of Holies
   with Thy Blood, cleanse me from fleshly impurity!

Jesus; bound, Who hast power to bind and to loose,
   absolve my grievous sins!

Jesus; Son of God, remember us when Thou comest into
   Thy Kingdom!

KONTAKION IV

BREATHING a storm of murderous thoughts, the Jews having
listened to the voice of the father of lies and manslayer from time
immemorial, the devil, rejected Thee, the right Way, the Truth, and
the Life. But we confess Thee to be Christ, the power of God, in
Whom are hidden all the treasures of wisdom and knowledge, and
we cry: ALLELUIA!

OIKOS IV

HAVING heard Thy meek and gentle words, Pilate delivered Thee up
to be crucified as deserving death, even though he himself bore
witness that he had found not a single fault in Thee. Then he washed his
hands, but defiled his heart. And wondering at the mystery of Thy
voluntary Passion, with compunction we cry to Thee:

Jesus; Son of God, and Son of the Virgin, tortured by the
   sons of iniquity!

Jesus; mocked and stripped, Who givest the flowers of the
   field their beauty and bedecks the sky with clouds!

Jesus; covered with wounds, Who satisfied the hunger of five
   thousand men with five loaves of bread!

Jesus; King of all, who instead of a tribute of love and
   gratitude receivest cruel tortures!

Jesus; Who art wounded all the day long for our sake, heal
   the wounds of our souls!

Jesus; Son of God, remember us when Thou comest into
    Thy Kingdom!

KONTAKION V

THOU wast all arrayed in Thy divine blood, O Thou Who coverest
Thyself with light as with a garment. I know, indeed I know with
the Prophet why Thy garments are purple. I, Lord, it is I who wounded
Thee with my sins. So to Thee Who was wounded for my sake I
thankfully cry: ALLELUIA!

OIKOS V

FORESEEING THEE in spirit covered with shame and wounds, the
divinely inspired Isaiah cried in horror: We have seen Him, and He
had no form or beauty. And we, seeing thee on the Cross, with faith and
amazement cry:

    Jesus; enduring dishonour, Who hast crowned man with
        glory and honour!

    Jesus; on Whom angels cannot gaze, slapped in the face!

    Jesus; Who was struck on the head with a reed, bow my
        head in humility!

    Jesus; Whose bright eyes were darkened with blood, turn
        away my eyes from beholding vanity!

    Jesus; Who from head to feet hadst not part whole, make
        me perfectly whole and healthy!

    Jesus; Son of God, remember us when Thou comest into
        Thy Kingdom!

KONTAKION VI

PILATE proved a preacher of Thine innocence, when he told the
people that he found nothing in Thee deserving death. But the Jews,
like wild beasts that have seen blood, gnashed their teeth at Thee and

cried: Crucify, crucify Him! We, however, kiss Thy most pure wounds and cry: ALLELUIA!

OIKOS VI

THOU wast a spectacle and marvel to men and angels, and to Pilate who said of Thee: Behold the Man! Come, then, let us worship Jesus Who suffered abuse for our sake, as we cry:

Jesus; Creator and Judge of all, judged and tortured by
Thy creatures!

Jesus; Giver of Wisdom, Who gavest no answer to foolish
questions!

Jesus; Healer of those wounded by sin, grant me the healing
of repentance!

Jesus; Shepherd Who was struck; strike the demons that
cause me temptation!

Jesus; crushed in body, crush my heart with Thy fear!

Jesus; Son of God, remember us when Thou comest into
Thy Kingdom!

KONTAKION VII

WISHING to deliver mankind from slavery to the enemy, Thou didst humble Thyself before Thine enemies, O Jesus, and like a lamb that is dumb Thou wast led to the slaughter, and didst endure wounds all over, that having healed the whole man, he might cry: ALLELUIA!

OIKOS VII

Wonderful patience didst Thou show when, after the sentence of the unjust judge, the soldiers reviled Thee and inflicted cruel wounds on Thy Most-pure Body, so that it was purple with blood from head to foot. Therefore, with tears we cry to Thee:

Jesus; Lover of mankind, crowned with thorns by mankind!

Jesus; impassable in Thy Divinity, enduring thy Passion to
     free us from our passions!

Jesus; my Saviour, save me who deserve all sufferings!

Jesus; forsaken by all, my Strength, strengthen me!

Jesus; my Joy, from all insults gladden me!

Jesus; Son of God, remember us when Thou comest into
     Thy Kingdom!

KONTAKION VIII

STRANGE and wonderful it was when Moses and Elias appeared to
Thee on Tabor and spoke of Thy death which Thou wast about to
accomplish in Jerusalem, that having beheld Thy glory there and seen our
salvation here, they might cry: ALLELUIA!

OIKOS VIII

EVERYWHERE persecuted by the Jews on account of the great
multitude of my sins, Thou didst endure my shame and torment.
For some say that Thou art opposed to Caesar, others accuse Thee of
being a criminal while some cry: Take Him, take Him, and crucify Him.
So to Thee, our Lord, condemned by all and led to crucifixion, from the
depth of our souls we say:

Jesus; unjustly condemned, our Judge, condemn us not
     according to our deeds!

Jesus; Who was exhausted on the way under Thy Cross, my
     Power, forsake me not in the hour of my sorrow
     and suffering!

Jesus; Who didst cry for help to the Father, mine Exemplar,
     strengthen me in my weakness!

Jesus; Who didst accept dishonour, my Glory, deprive me
               not of Thy glory!

Jesus; radiant image of the Father's Being, transfigure
               my dark and impure life!

Jesus; Son of God, remember us when Thou comest into
               Thy Kingdom!

KONTAKION IX

ALL nature was confounded at the sight of Thee hanging on the Cross: in the heavens the sun hid his rays, the earth quaked, the veil of the Temple was torn, the rocks split, and hell gave up her dead. But we worship on the place where Thy most pure feet stood, crying: ALLELUIA!

OIKOS IX

ELOQUENT orators, even if they speak much, cannot render sufficient gratitude for Thy Divine Passion, O Lover of mankind. But our souls and bodies, our hearts and all our members with compunction cry to Thee:

Jesus; Who wast nailed to the Cross, nail down and annul
               the handwriting of our sins!

Jesus; Who stretchest out Thy hands from the Cross to all,
               draw me to Thyself, for I too have gone astray!

Jesus; Door of the sheep, pierced in Thy side, lead me
               through Thy wounds into Thy bridal chamber!

Jesus; crucified in the flesh, crucify my flesh with its passions
               and desires!

Jesus; Who didst end Thy life in agony, grant that my heart
               may know nothing but Thee crucified!

Jesus; Son of God, remember us when Thou comest into
               Thy Kingdom!

KONTAKION X

DESIRING to save the world, Thou didst heal the blind, the lame, the lepers, the deaf and the dumb, and didst drive out evil spirits. But the foolish Jews, breathing envy and malice, nailed Thee to the Cross, not knowing how to sing: ALLELUIA!

OIKOS X

JESUS Eternal King, Thou sufferest in every limb for my intemperance and incontinence, that Thou mightest make the whole of me pure, giving us a pattern in everything that we might follow in Thy steps and cry:

> Jesus; unfathomable Love, Who didst not charge with sin those who crucified Thee!

> Jesus; Who didst pray earnestly with crying and tears in the garden, teach us also to pray!

> Jesus; Who hast fulfilled all prophecy in Thyself, fulfil our heart's desire for goodness!

> Jesus; Who didst surrender Thy spirit into thy Father's hands, in the hour of my death receive my spirit!

> Jesus; Who didst not prevent the division of Thy garments, separate my soul from my body gently!

> Jesus; Son of God, remember us when Thou comest into Thy Kingdom!

KONTAKION XI

TENDEREST songs did Thine immaculate Mother offer to Thee, saying: Even though Thou sufferest on the Cross, yet I know Thee from the womb to be begotten of the Father before the morning star, for I see that all creation is suffering with Thee. Thou surrenderest Thy spirit to the Father. Receive also my spirit and forsake me not as I cry: ALLELUIA!

OIKOS XI

LIKE a light-receiving lamp the immaculate Virgin stood at Thy Cross burning with love and torn with a mother's sorrow for Thee, the true Sun of Righteousness that was setting in the grave, and with Her accept these prayers of our heart:

> Jesus; Who was lifted up on the Tree that with Thyself
> Thou mightest lift us fallen creatures to Thy Father!

> Jesus; Who didst give the Ever-Virgin as a mother to the
> virgin Apostle that Thou mightest teach us purity
> and virginity!

> Jesus; Who didst entrust Thy Mother to Thy disciple, the
> Theologian, commit us all to Her maternal protection!

> Jesus; Conqueror of the world and hell, conquer the
> unbelief, the pride of life, and the lust of the
> eyes that lurks within us!

> Jesus; Destroyer of the power of death, deliver me from
> eternal death!

> Jesus; Son of God, remember us when Thou comest into
> Thy Kingdom!

KONTAKION XII

GRANT me Thy Grace, O Jesus my God. Receive me as Thou didst receive Joseph and Nicodemus; that I may offer to Thee my soul like a clean shroud, may anoint Thy most pure body with the fragrant spices of virtue, and may have Thee in my heart as in a tomb, as I cry: ALLELUIA!

OIKOS XII

PRAISING Thy voluntary Crucifixion, we worship Thy Passion, O Christ. We believe with the centurion that Thou art truly the Son of

God Who art coming on the clouds with power and great glory. Put us not then to shame, who are redeemed by Thy blood, and thus cry aloud:

> Jesus; long-suffering, by the lamentation of Thy Virgin
>   Mother rescue us from eternal weeping!

> Jesus; forsaken by all, forsake me not in the hour
>   of my death!

> Jesus; with Mary Magdalene who touched Thy feet,
>   receive me!

> Jesus; condemn me not with the traitor and those who
>   crucified Thee!

> Jesus; bring me with the good thief into Paradise!

> Jesus; Son of God, remember us when Thou comest into
>   Thy Kingdom!

KONTAKION XIII

O JESUS CHRIST, Lamb of God, Who takest away the sins of the world, accept this small act of thanksgiving offered to Thee with all our soul, and heal us by Thy saving Passion from all sickness of soul and body. Protect us by Thy Cross from enemies visible and invisible, and forsake us not at the end of our life, that saved by Thy death from eternal death, we may unceasingly cry to Thee: ALLELUIA! *(Thrice)*

And again, Oikos I and Kontakion I are read.

OIKOS I

IN completing the choirs of angels, Thou didst not take on the angelic nature, but being the Eternal God, for my sake Thou becamest man, and Thou didst restore to life men who were dead through sin with Thy Life-giving Body and Blood. Therefore, in gratitude for Thine amazing love, we humbly cry to Thee:

Jesus; God, Eternal Love, Who was pleased to save us who are born of earth!

Jesus; Infinite Mercy, Who didst come down here to us fallen creatures!

Jesus; Who was clothed in our flesh and didst destroy the dominion of death by Thy death!

Jesus; Who dost deify us with Thy Divine Mysteries!

Jesus; Who hast redeemed the whole world by Thy Cross and Passion!

Jesus; Son of God, remember us when Thou comest into Thy Kingdom!

KONTAKION I

SUPREME Ruler and Lord of Heaven and earth, seeing Thee, the Immortal King, hanging on the Cross, all creation was changed, Heaven was horrified, and the foundations of the earth were shaken. But we, unworthy as we are, offer Thee thankful adoration for Thy Passion in our behalf, and with the robber we cry to Thee:

Jesus; Son of God, remember us when Thou comest into Thy Kingdom!

PRAYER TO THE LORD JESUS CRUCIFIED

LORD JESUS CHRIST, Son of the Living God, Creator of Heaven and earth, Saviour of the world, Behold I who am unworthy and of all men most sinful, humbly bow the knee of my heart before the glory of Thy majesty and praise Thy Cross and Passion, and offer thanksgiving to Thee, the King and God of all, that Thou wast pleased to bear as man all labours and hardships, all temptations and tortures, that Thou mightest be our Fellow-sufferer and Helper, and a Saviour to all of us in all our sorrows, needs, and sufferings.

I know, O all-powerful Lord, that all these things were not necessary for Thee, but for us men and for our salvation Thou didst endure Thy Cross and Passion that Thou mightest redeem us from all cruel bondage to the enemy.

What, then, shall I give in return to Thee, O Lover of mankind, for all that Thou hast suffered for me, a sinner? I cannot say, for soul and body and all blessings come from Thee, and all that I have is Thine, and I am Thine. Yet I know that love is repaid only by love. Teach me, then, to love and praise Thee.

TRUSTING solely in Thine infinite compassion and mercy, O Lord, I praise Thine unspeakable patience, I magnify Thine unutterable exhaustion, I glorify Thy boundless mercy, I adore Thy purest Passion, and most lovingly kissing Thy wounds, I cry: Have mercy on me a sinner, and cause that Thy holy Cross may not be fruitless in me, that I may participate here with faith in Thy sufferings and be vouchsafed to behold also the glory of Thy Kingdom in Heaven. AMEN.

AKATHIST TO OUR LADY OF ALL PROTECTION

KONTAKION I

O CHOSEN by the pre-eternal God, Queen of Heaven and earth higher than all creation, who hast in days past entered praying into the Church of the Blachernae we, offering Thee with thanksgiving due veneration, flee with faith and compunction under Thy shining vestment for we lie in darkness. And Thou who hast invincible power dost set us free from every affliction that we may cry to Thee:

Hail! Our Joy, protect us from every ill by Thy precious veil.

OIKOS I

ARCHANGELS and angels, with John the Forerunner, John the Theologian, and the choir of all the saints, were present with Thee, their Queen, in the Church of the Blachernae and hearing Thy moving supplication for the whole world, they cried out with wonder as follows:

Hail! O pre-eternal good will of God the Father Who
    has no beginning of days.

Hail! Timeless and most pure who contained God the Son.

Hail! Thou chosen dwelling-place of God the all-holy Spirit.

Hail! Thou never-ceasing wonder of the angelic hosts
    on high.

Hail! Thou all-threatening terror of the dark forces of hell.

Hail! Thou whom the many-eyed cherubim meet in the air.

Hail! Thou to whom the six-winged seraphim
    ascribe praises.

Hail! Thou whose most precious veil we born on earth
    thankfully venerate.

Hail! Our Joy, protect us from every ill by Thy
    precious Veil.

KONTAKION II

SAINT Andrew with Epiphanios having seen Thee inside the Church praying God in the air for all Christians, acknowledged Thee to be the Mother of Christ our God Who ascended into heaven and falling to the ground they joyfully venerated Thine all-precious veil, crying: ALLELUIA!

OIKOS II

THOU, O Theotokos Virgin art knowledge unknowable in defence of Orthodox people. Therefore, our enemies know not how strong is the prayer of the Mother of God: while we well aware of Thine all-mighty protection cry to Thee with tender feeling:

Hail! Most merciful Comforter of all the afflicted and heavy laden.

Hail! Never sleeping Guide of all those who have strayed and gone blind.

Hail! Thou who by Thy supplication dost swiftly appease the wrath of God rightly poured out on us.

Hail! Thou who by an all-powerful behest dost tame our evil passions.

Hail! Strong waker of sleeping consciences.

Hail! Easy overcomer of sinful practices.

Hail! Thou for whose sake hell groans and the spirits of evil tremble.

Hail! Thou for whose sake the gates of paradise are opened to all.

Hail! Our Joy, protect us from every ill by Thy precious veil.

KONTAKION III

POWER from on high overshadows those who run for refuge with faith and reverence to Thy precious protection: for to Thee alone, O all holy and all pure only Mother of God is it given that every petition of Thine be fulfilled. Therefore, the faithful of all ages glorify Thee and Thy Son, crying: ALLELUIA!

OIKOS III

O LADY, having a never-failing wealth of mercy, Thou dost stretch the hand of help to all the ends of the earth: and dost give healing to the sick, relief to the suffering, sight to the blind, and to all everything that is expedient for them as they cry aloud in thanksgiving:

Hail! Indestructible fortress and bulwark of Orthodox kingdoms.

Hail! Principle adornment of holy churches and altars.

Hail! Truest guard of holy monasteries.

Hail! Vigilant Helper of stout-hearted city governors.

Hail! Unconquerable Leader of Christian captains and armies.

Hail! Holy mirror of justice for judges who take no bribes.

Hail! Perfect knowledge for teachers and those who bring up children.

Hail! Blessing of pious homes and families.

Hail! Our Joy, protect us from every ill by Thy precious veil.

KONTAKION IV

O LADY, Thou dost help us held fast by a storm of many afflictions: for Thou dost stand before the altar of the Lord, lifting Thine hands and praying that the Lord of glory look down on our unworthy prayer and hearken to the petitions of those who call upon Thy holy Name crying to Thy Son: ALLELUIA!

OIKOS IV

T HE LORD GOD heard Joshua, son of Nun, praying and He commanded the sun to stand still until he defeat the enemy. The

Lord Jesus now hears Thy supplication, O chosen dwelling of the Holy Spirit. Therefore, we sinners, putting our trust in Thy protection, make bold to say to Thee, Mother of God:

> Hail! Thou who art lit by the Sun of the mind and who dost enlighten us with the light that never sets.

> Hail! Thou who hast illumined the whole earth by the brightness of Thy most pure soul.

> Hail! Thou who hast made glad the whole heavens by the purity of Thy body.

> Hail! Protector and Provider of the holy monasteries of Christ.

> Hail! Thou who art the strength and understanding of the pastors of the Church.

> Hail! Guide of God-fearing monks and nuns.

> Hail! Untroubled rest of the pious aged.

> Hail! Secret gladness of pure virgins and widows.

> Hail! Our Joy, protect us from every ill by Thy precious veil.

KONTAKION V

WHEN Moses who saw God lifted his arms while the battle with Amalek raged, Israel overcame and when he let his hands fall, Amalek was victorious and strengthened by those who hold up his arms, Israel defeated the enemy: and Thou, O Mother of God, having raised Thine hands in supplication, even though no man hold them up, dost always conquer the enemies of Christ and art an invincible shield for us who cry: ALLELUIA!

OIKOS V

THE assemblies of saints when they had seen Thee in the air inside the church of the Blachernae stretching Thy hands in prayer to Thy Son and God, sang Thee a song in thanksgiving with the archangels and angels: while we, our hands fortified by Thee made stronger than the arms of Moses, cry aloud with compunction:

Hail! Thou whose love and mercy towards us alone hold up Thine hands for us.

Hail! Thou before Whom our enemies, visible and invisible, cannot stand.

Hail! Thou who drivest away the dark hordes of our passions and lusts.

Hail! Thou who holdest in Thine hand without being consumed, the divine fire of Christ and who with it dost set us in our coldness aflame.

Hail! Thou who crownest with a fair crown of chastity those who fight against the flesh.

Hail! Thou perpetual Converser with those who strive in fasting and silent prayer.

Hail! Thou speedy Comforter of those who fall from despair and sadness.

Hail! Thou who dost by grace provide us with humility and patience.

Hail! Our Joy, protect us from every ill by Thy precious veil.

KONTAKION VI

SAINT Roman the Melodist, appeared as an unfailing proclaimer of Thy grace and mercy when he had received from Thee in a dream a paper roll to swallow: for thereby made wise, he began to sing with skill in

Thine honour and to write praises for the saints, calling out with faith: ALLELUIA!

OIKOS VI

O VIRGIN, Maid of God, who hast shone forth the Dawn from the true Sun of righteousness, enlightening all with the wisdom of Thy God and Son and who leadest all to knowledge of the truth those who cry to Thee:

Hail! Thou who hast given birth to Christ in the flesh, Power of God, and wisdom of God.

Hail! Thou who hast confounded the foolish wisdom of this world, and who hast guided those blinded by it on the way of truth.

Hail! Preserver of our holy faith and teacher of Orthodox dogma.

Hail! Uprooter of impious heresies and corrupting divisions.

Hail! Thou who well knowest secret and unforeseen difficulties and dost tell those whom it is proper about them.

Hail! Thou who puttest to shame false seers and vain divining.

Hail! Thou who in the hour of perplexity dost put a good thought in our hearts.

Hail! Thou who dost turn us from perilous purposes and senseless desires.

Hail! Our Joy, protect us from every ill by Thy precious veil.

KONTAKION VII

THE all-seeing, long-suffering Lord, wishing to manifest the unsearchable deep of His mercies and love for mankind, chose Thee alone to be His Mother, and made Thee into an invincible defence for His people: that even though one of them appear worthy of condemnation by the righteous judgement of God, yet all the more shall he be preserved for repentance by Thy mighty protection, crying: ALLELUIA!

OIKOS VII

O LORD, Thou hast shown in Thine all-pure Mother, how wonderful are Thy works when Her most marvellous veil was revealed in Her hand shining brighter than the rays of the sun and with it, She protected the people in the Church of Blachernae: for hearing of such a sign of Her defence, held by fear and joy, all say:

Hail! Thou veil not made by hand of man that is spread over the whole world like a cloud.

Hail! Thou who dost hold in Thine hands the banner of Thy Son, the pre-eternal Bishop.

Hail! Thou who hast thereby made manifest a new mercy and new grace in the Orthodox Church.

Hail! Pillar of cloud who protects all of us in the world from temptations and scandals.

Hail! Pillar of fire amidst the darkness, showing us all the path of salvation.

Hail! Visible strength of manifest strivers for godliness.

Hail! Secret Giver of understanding to the secret servants of God in this world.

Hail! Thou who also leavest not without Thy grace and protection me who am stripped of all good works.

Hail! Our Joy, protect us from every ill by Thy precious veil.

KONTAKION VIII

ANGELS sang Thy praises when Thou didst appear in wondrous wise from heaven in the Church of the Blachernae and apostles gave Thee glory. The choir of holy Bishops and monks and the band of holy women extolled Thee, the Forerunner with John the Divine venerated Thee, and the people present in the Church cried aloud with joy: ALLELUIA!

OIKOS VIII

THE LORD Who reigns over all things above and below, when He had seen Thee, His Mother, standing in the Church and praying with tender feeling to Him, said: Ask, O my Mother, because I shall never turn from Thee but will fulfil all Thy petitions and teach all to sing to Thee in thanksgiving:

Hail! Ark of the law in which is kept the sanctification of all mankind.

Hail! All-holy Jar in which the bread of eternal life is preserved for those who hunger for righteousness.

Hail! All-golden Vessel in which the flesh and blood of the divine Lamb are prepared for us.

Hail! Thou who dost receive in Thine all-powerful arms those forsaken by the physicians.

Hail! Thou who dost raise from their bed of sickness those crippled in body but not in spirit and faith.

Hail! Thou who givest a new and better understanding to those who are perishing from infirmity of mind.

Hail! Thou who dost wisely trip us up on the stubborn path of sin and passion.

Hail! Thou who dost turn to mercy the cruelty of our
    unrepentant hearts.

Hail! Our Joy, protect us from every ill by Thy precious veil.

KONTAKION IX

The whole assembly of angels offers Thee praises, Thou true
Mother of God and Defender of all who run to Thee,
knowing how with Thine unfailing protection Thou dost rejoice the
righteous, protect and deliver the poor, and pray for all the faithful
crying: ALLELUIA!

OIKOS IX

THE wordy orators, become as dumb fish, are at a loss as to how to
praise as is due, the great feast of Thine all-precious protection: for
all the things said by them about Thee suffice not to number Thy mercies
alone. And we, seeing Thy good works without number, cry with
gladness:

Hail! Thou who dost guard us from the deadly plague in
    which all perish.

Hail! Thou who dost preserve cities and villages from
    sudden earthquakes.

Hail! Thou who dost lead us out with Thy strong arm from
    flood and drowning.

Hail! Thou who by the dew of Thy prayers dost deliver us
    from the kindling of fire.

Hail! Thou who dost provide against hunger of soul and
    body by the Bread of life.

Hail! Thou who dost lead away from our heads the blows of
    lightning and thunder.

Hail! Thou who dost save us from the attacks of strangers and
secret murderers.

Hail! Thou who dost guard us with peace and love against
family quarrels and the enmities of those of our
own blood.

Hail! Our Joy, protect us from every ill by Thy precious veil.

KONTAKION X

WISHING to save mankind from the error of the enemy, the Lord
Who loves mankind gave us on earth Thee His Mother to be our
help, protection, and defence, for Thee to be the Comforter of those that
sorrow, the Joy of the afflicted, the Defender of the injured, and to raise all
from the depth of sin, singing: ALLELUIA!

OIKOS X

"O KING of heaven," spoke the all-pure Queen in prayer as she
stood with the angels, "do Thou accept every man praying to
Thee, and calling upon my name for help, that he go not away from my
face empty and unheard." Hearing this most good supplication, the
assemblies of the saints cried in thanksgiving:

Hail! Thou who crownest with blessed fruits the
husbandmen pure in hand and heart.

Hail! Succour and righteous Rewarder for all those who
honestly trade.

Hail! Reprover before all nations of those who keep not
their oaths and whose gains are unjust.

Hail! Unexpected Helper of those in distress in their travels
by land and water.

Hail! Thou who makest glad with the fruits of faith and the
spirit childless couples.

Hail! Unseen Tutor of motherless orphans.

Hail! Strong Defender of those in captivity and exile.

Hail! Ever-watchful Guardian of those sitting in bonds
and prison.

Hail! Our Joy, protect us from every ill by Thy precious veil.

KONTAKION XI

HEARING a most moving song and attending to Thy prayer for us, we beg Thee, O Virgin Theotokos, look not away from the voices of Thy servants for we run to Thee in assaults and affliction and in our distress we pour out our tears before Thee, crying: ALLELUIA!

OIKOS XI

SEEING Thee in the air inside the Blachernae Church burning in prayer as a candle aflame with light, I gave voice together with a multitude of people there present: how can this be that the Mother of my Lord has come to me? And Saint Andrew with Epiphanios prayed warmly to Thee, crying:

Hail! Abundant Giver of all spiritual and bodily gifts.

Hail! True Advocate of sinners who have started to repent.

Hail! Perpetual Champion of those fighting with enemy
passions and intents.

Hail! Invisible Tamer of cruel and bestial masters.

Hail! Secret Rest and Consolation of humble and
suffering servants.

Hail! Most longed-for Fulfiller of blessed marriages.

Hail! Swift and painless relief of mothers in childbirth.

Hail! Our only Help in the hour of death.

Hail! Our Joy, protect us from every ill by Thy
precious Veil.

KONTAKION XII

A SK Thy Son to give us divine grace; stretch towards us a helping
hand; ward off from us every enemy and adversary and give our
lives peace that we parish not grievously without repentance, but accept
us, O our Protector, in the eternal mansions, that, rejoicing we may cry
to Thee: ALLELUIA!

OIKOS XII

S INGING the praises of Thy mighty protection, we praise Thee for
Thou art to us all our firm Advocate and we venerate Thee who
dost pray for us: for we believe and we trust that Thou wilt beg of Thy
Son and God eternal and temporal good things for all who cry thus
to Thee with love:

Hail! Strong Defence of the whole inhabited earth.

Hail! Sanctification of all the earthly and heavenly elements.

Hail! Thou Blessing of all the seasons of the year.

Hail! Thou Conqueror of all assaults and temptations that
come from the world, the flesh, and the devil.

Hail! Unhoped for Reconciliation of those who are at
daggers drawn.

Hail! Amendment without their knowledge of unrepentant
sinners.

Hail! Thou who dost not turn away those despised and
forsaken by all.

Hail! Thou who dost pluck from the pit of destruction those that
indeed despair.

Hail! Our Joy, protect us from every ill by Thy precious veil.

KONTAKION XIII

O ALL-PRAISED Mother, Most pure Lady, Virgin, Theotokos, to Thee do I lift up the eyes of my soul and body, to Thee do I stretch forth my hands grown feeble and I cry from the depth of my heart: look down on the faith and humility of my soul; shelter me with Thy almighty protection, that I be saved from all assault and distress, and in the hour of my death, be by me, O Thou all-blessed, and deliver me from the torment prepared for me because of my sins, that, venerating Thee, I may ever cry: ALLELUIA! *(Thrice.)*

And again, Oikos I and Kontakion I are read,
followed by two prayers to the Holy Virgin.

OIKOS I

A RCHANGELS and angels, with John the Forerunner, John the Theologian, and the choir of all the saints, were present with Thee, their Queen, in the Church of the Blachernae and hearing Thy moving supplication for the whole world, they cried out with wonder as follows:

Hail! O pre-eternal good will of God the Father Who has no
beginning of days.

Hail! Timeless and most pure who contained God the Son.

Hail! Thou chosen dwelling-place of God the all-holy Spirit.

Hail! Thou never-ceasing wonder of the angelic hosts
on high.

Hail! Thou all-threatening terror of the dark forces of hell.

Hail! Thou whom the many-eyed cherubim meet in the air.

Hail! Thou to whom the six-winged seraphim ascribe
praises.

Hail! Thou whose most precious veil we born on earth thankfully venerate.

Hail! Our Joy, protect us from every ill by Thy precious Veil.

KONTAKION I

O CHOSEN by the pre-eternal God, Queen of heaven and earth higher than all creation, who hast in days past entered praying into the Church of the Blachernae we, offering Thee with thanksgiving due veneration, flee with faith and compunction under Thy shining vestment for we lie in darkness. And Thou who hast invincible power dost set us free from every affliction that we may cry to Thee:

Hail! Our Joy, protect us from every ill by Thy precious veil.

FIRST PRAYER

O ALL-HOLY Virgin, Mother of the Lord of the hosts on high, Thou Queen of heaven and earth and almighty Defender of our country, accept from us Thine unworthy servants this song of praise and thanksgiving and bring our prayer up to the throne of Thy God and Son, that He be merciful towards our unrighteousness, and extend His grace to those who honour Thy name and venerate with faith and love Thy wonder-working ikon. For we are not worthy to be forgiven by Him hadst Thou, O Lady, not made Him merciful towards us, for all things from Him are possible to Thee. Therefore, we run to Thee as Thou art our swift and undoubted Protector. Hear us who pray to Thee: overshadow us with Thine almighty veil and ask from Thy God and Son zeal and vigilance for our shepherds, wisdom and strength for the souls of those who govern our cities, righteousness and impartiality for our judges, understanding and humility for our leaders, love and concord for the married, obedience for our children, patience for those who have been offended, the fear of God for those that offend, stout-heartedness for the afflicted, restraint for those that rejoice, and for all of us the spirit of understanding and godliness, the spirit of mercy and meekness, the spirit of chastity and truth. Yea, O all-holy Lady, be merciful towards Thy feeble people: gather together the dispersed, guide on the right way those that have gone astray, uphold old age, make the young pure, bring up the children and look down upon all of us with the care of Thy merciful protection. Raise us from the depth of sin and enlighten the eyes of our hearts to see salvation. Be merciful to us both here and yonder, during our wandering in the land of this earth and at the Last Judgement of Thy Son: and make our fathers and brothers who have departed this life live the eternal life with the angels and all the saints. For Thou, O Lady, art the glory of those in heaven and the trust of those on earth. After God, Thou art the hope and Defender of all who flee to Thee with faith. We then pray to Thee and to Thee as our almighty Helper, do we commend ourselves and one another, now and ever, and unto the ages of ages. AMEN.

SECOND PRAYER TO OUR LADY

O MY most blessed Queen, my all-holy hope, Receiver of orphans and Defender of the strangers, Helper of those in poverty, Protector of the sick, behold my distress, behold my affliction. On all sides am I held by temptation, and there is none to defend me. Help me then as I am weak, feed me as I am a pilgrim, guide me as I have strayed, heal and save me as I lie without hope. For I have no other help, nor advocate nor comforter, save Thee, O Mother of all the afflicted and heavy laden. Look down then on me, a sinner lying in sickness, and protect me with Thine all-holy Veil, that I be delivered from all the ills surrounding me and may ever praise Thy Name that all men sing. AMEN.

Akathist in Praise of God's Creation

Kontakion I

INCORRUPTIBLE Lord, Thy right hand controls the whole course
of human life, according to the decrees of Thy Providence for
our salvation.

WE give Thee thanks for all Thy blessings, known and unknown:
for our earthly life and for the heavenly joys of Thy kingdom
which is to come. Henceforth extend Thy mercies towards us as we sing:

Glory to Thee, O God, from age to age!

Oikos I

I WAS born a weak, defenceless child, but Thine angel, spreading his
radiant wings, guarded my cradle. From my birth, Thy love hast

illumined my paths, and hast wondrously guided me towards the light of eternity. From my first day until now, the generous gifts of Thy providence have been wonderfully showered upon me. I give Thee thanks, and with all those who have come to know Thee, I exclaim:

Glory to Thee for calling me into being!

Glory to Thee for spreading out before me the beauty of the universe!

Glory to Thee for revealing to me through heaven and earth the eternal book of wisdom!

Glory to Thine eternity within this fleeting world!

Glory to Thee for Thy mercies, seen and unseen!

Glory to Thee for every sigh of my sorrow!

Glory to Thee for every step in my life's journey, for every moment of joy!

Glory to Thee, O God, from age to age!

KONTAKION II

O LORD, how lovely it is to be Thy guest: Breeze full of scent; mountains reaching to the skies; Waters like a boundless mirror, reflecting the sun's golden rays and the scudding clouds. All nature murmurs mysteriously, breathing depths of tenderness, Birds, and beasts bear the imprint of Thy love, blessed art Thou, mother earth, in Thy fleeting loveliness, Which wakens our yearning for happiness that will last for ever in the land where, amid beauty that grows not old, rings out the cry: ALLELUIA!

OIKOS II

THOU brought me into this life as into an enchanted paradise. We have seen the sky, like a deep blue cup ringing with birds in the azure heights. We have listened to the soothing murmur of the forest and the sweet-sounding music of the waters. We have tasted fragrant fruit of fine flavour and sweet-scented honey. How pleasant is our stay with Thee on earth: it is a joy to be Thy guest.

Glory to Thee for the feast-day of life!

Glory to Thee for the perfume of lilies and roses!

Glory to Thee for each different taste of berry and fruit!

Glory to Thee for the sparkling silver of early morning dew!

Glory to Thee for each smiling, peaceful awakening!

Glory to Thee for eternal life in us, a messenger of heaven!

Glory to Thee, O God, from age to age!

KONTAKION III

In the strength of the Holy Spirit each flower gives out its scent — sweet perfume, delicate colour, beauty of the whole universe revealed in the tiniest thing. Glory and honour to God the Giver of life, who covers the fields with their carpet of flowers, crowns the plains with harvest of gold and the blue of corn-flowers, and our souls with the joy of contemplating him. O be joyful and sing to him: ALLELUIA!

OIKOS III

HOW glorious Thou art in the triumph of spring, when every creature awakes to new life and joyfully sings Thy praises with a thousand tongues: Thou art the source of life, the conqueror of death. By the light of the moon nightingales sing: the plains and the woods put on their wedding garment, white as snow. All the earth is Thy promised bride awaiting her bridegroom who does not know decay. If the grass of the field is clothed like this, how gloriously shall we be transfigured in the coming age of the resurrection: how radiant our bodies, how resplendent our souls!

Glory to Thee, bringing from the darkness of the earth an
endless variety of colours, tastes, and scents!

Glory to Thee for the warmth and tenderness of the world of
nature!

Glory to Thee for surrounding us with thousands of Thy
works!

Glory to Thee for the depth of Thy wisdom: of which the
whole world is a living sign!

Glory to Thee: on my knees, I kiss the traces of Thine
unseen hand!

Glory to Thee for setting before us the dazzling light of
eternal life!

Glory to Thee for the hope of the unutterable, imperishable
beauty of immortality!

Glory to Thee, O God, from age to age!

KONTAKION IV

HOW filled with sweetness are those whose thoughts dwell upon
Thee: how life-giving Thy holy Word; to speak with Thee is more
soothing than anointing with oil, sweeter than the honeycomb. Praying to
Thee refreshes us and gives us wings: our hearts overflow with warmth; a
majesty filled with wisdom permeates nature and all of life! Where Thou
art not, there is only emptiness. Where Thou art, the soul is filled with
abundance, and its song resounds like a torrent of life: ALLELUIA!

OIKOS IV

WHEN over the earth the light of the setting sun fades away, when
the peace of eternal sleep and the quiet of the declining day reign
over all, I see Thy dwelling-place like tents filled with light, reflected in the
shapes of the clouds at dusk: fiery and purple, gold and blue, they speak

prophet-like of the ineffable beauty of Thy heavenly court, and solemnly call: let us go unto the Father!

Glory to Thee in the quiet hour of evening!

Glory to Thee, covering the world with deep peace!

Glory to Thee for the last ray of the setting sun!

Glory to Thee for the rest of blissful sleep!

Glory to Thee for Thy mercy in the midst of darkness, when the whole world has parted company with us!

Glory to Thee for the tender emotion of a soul moved to prayer!

Glory to Thee for the pledge of our awakening on the day which has no evening!

Glory to Thee, O God, from age to age!

KONTAKION V

THE storms of life frighten not those whose hearts are ablaze with the light of Thy flame. Outside is the darkness of the whirlwind, the terror, and howling of the storm. But in their souls reign quiet and light. Christ is there, and the heart sings: ALLELUIA!

OIKOS V

I SEE Thy heaven glowing with stars. How rich Thou art, how much light is Thine! Eternity watches me by the rays of the distant stars: I am small, insignificant, but the Lord is with me, his loving hand protects me wherever I go!

Glory to Thee for the trouble Thou takest for me at all times!

Glory for the people Thy Providence gave me to meet!

Glory to Thee for the love of my dear ones, the faithfulness
of friends!

Glory to Thee for the gentleness of the animals which
serve me!

Glory to Thee for the light-filled moments of life!

Glory to Thee for the radiant joy in my heart!

Glory to Thee for the joy of living, moving and seeing!

Glory to Thee, O God, from age to age!

KONTAKION VI

HOW great and how close Thou art in the powerful track of the
storm; how mighty Thy right arm in the blinding flash of the
lightning; how awesome is Thy greatness! The voice of the Lord is over
the fields and amid the rustling forests, the voice of the Lord is in the birth
of thunder and of rain, the voice of the Lord is over the many waters.
Praise to Thee in the roar of mountains ablaze. Thou shaketh the earth
like a garment. Thou pile up to the sky the waves of the sea. Praise to
Thee, bringing low the pride of man, bringing from his heart the cry of
repentance: ALLELUIA!

OIKOS VI

WHEN the lightning flash has lit up the feasting-hall, how feeble
seems the light of the lamps. Likewise, amidst the strongest joys
of my existence, Thou suddenly flashed in my soul. After Thy blinding
light, how drab, dull, and unreal seemed all those joys! Passionately, my
soul would run after Thee!

Glory to Thee, the Goal in whom mankind's highest dreams
come true!

Glory to Thee, for our unquenchable thirst for communion
with God!

Glory to Thee, making us dissatisfied with earthly things!

Glory to Thee, clothing us with the finest rays of Thy light!

Glory to Thee, destroying the power of the spirits of
darkness, dooming all evil to destruction!

Glory to Thee for the joy of hearing Thy voice, for the
happiness of Thy presence and of living in Thy love!

Glory to Thee, O God, from age to age!

KONTAKION VII

IN the wondrous blending of sounds it is Thy call we hear. In the
harmony of many voices, stirred by the musical tones, dazzled by art's
creativeness, we learn from Thee the splendour of melody and song, and
receive a foretaste of the coming kingdom. All true beauty draws the
soul towards Thee in powerful invocation, and makes it sing
triumphantly: ALLELUIA!

OIKOS VII

THE outpouring of the Holy Spirit enlightens the thoughts of artists,
poets, and scientists. Their great minds receive from Thee
prophetic insights into Thy laws, and reveal to us the depth of Thy creative
wisdom. Unwittingly, their works speak of Thee; how great Thou art in all
Thou hast created, how great Thou art in man!

Glory to Thee, showing Thine unfathomable might in the
laws of the universe!

Glory to Thee, for all nature is permeated by Thy laws!

Glory to Thee for what Thou hast revealed to us in Thy
goodness!

Glory to Thee for all that remains hidden from us in Thy
wisdom!

Glory to Thee for the inventiveness of the human mind!

Glory to Thee for the invigorating effort of work!

Glory to Thee for the tongues of fire which bring inspiration!

Glory to Thee, O God, from age to age!

KONTAKION VIII

HOW near Thou art in the days of sickness; Thou Thyself visit the sick; Thou bend over the sufferer's bed: his heart speaks unto Thee. With Thy peace, Thou enlighten the soul burdened with affliction and pain: Thou send unexpected help. Thou comfort, Thou art Love, bringing trial and salvation, and to Thee we sing the hymn: ALLELUIA!

OIKOS VIII

WHEN in childhood I called upon Thee consciously for the first time, Thou heard my prayer and sacred peace came down into my soul. Then I understood that Thou art good; blessed are those who turn unto Thee. Unceasingly, I started to call upon Thee, and now I call upon Thy Name!

Glory to Thee, satisfying my desires with good things!

Glory to Thee, watching over me day and night!

Glory to Thee, calming tribulations and bereavement with the healing flow of time!

Glory to Thee, no loss is irreparable when Thou art there; to all Thou givest eternal life!

Glory to Thee, making immortal all that is lofty and good, promising to welcome the dead!

Glory to Thee, O God, from age to age!

KONTAKION IX

WHY is it that on a feast day the whole of nature mysteriously smiles? Why doth a marvellous lightness then fill our hearts, to which nothing earthly can be compared? The very air in the altar and in God's house becomes luminous. It is the breath of grace, the reflection of the glory of Mount Tabor; heaven and earth then sing this praise: ALLELUIA!

OIKOS IX

WHEN Thou inspire me to serve my neighbour, and maketh humility shine in my soul, one of Thy deep-piercing rays of light falls into my heart: it then becomes glowing, like iron in the furnace. I have seen Thy Face, mysterious and elusive!

Glory to Thee, transfiguring our lives with deeds of love!

Glory to Thee, making wonderfully sweet each one of
   Thy commandments!

Glory to Thee, clearly present in fragrant compassion!

Glory to Thee, sending us failures and afflictions to make us
   sensitive to other people's sufferings!

Glory to Thee, promising high rewards for precious
   good deeds!

Glory to Thee, welcoming the impulse of our heart's love!

Glory to Thee, for raising love above everything on earth
   or in heaven!

Glory to Thee, O God, from age to age!

KONTAKION X

NO one can put together what has crumbled into dust, but Thou can heal men whose conscience has become twisted; Thou givest the soul its former beauty, which long ago it hath lost without a hope of change. With Thee, nothing is hopeless. Thou art Love. Thou art the creator and the redeemer of all things. We praise Thee with this song: ALLELUIA!

OIKOS X

MY GOD, Thou knowest the fall of proud Lucifer. Save me through the power of Thy grace; do not allow me to fall away from Thee, do not allow me to doubt Thee. Sharpen my ear, that at every minute of my life, I may hear Thy mysterious voice; and I call upon Thee, who art everywhere present!

Glory to Thee for providential circumstances!

Glory to Thee for helpful forebodings!

Glory to Thee for the teaching of Thy secret voice!

Glory to Thee, for revelations Thou givest us in dreams
        or awake!

Glory to Thee for scattering our vain imaginations!

Glory to Thee, freeing us from the fire of passions
        through suffering!

Glory to Thee, who for our salvation, brings down proudness
        of heart!

Glory to Thee, O God, from age to age!

KONTAKION XI

BEYOND the icy sequence of the ages, I feel the warmth of Thy divine Breath; I hear the throbbing of Thy blood. Thou art already near: part of time has already gone by. I see Thy Cross: it is there for my sake. My spirit is but dust before Thy Cross: here is the triumph of love and redemption, here throughout the ages unceasingly rises the praise: ALLELUIA!

OIKOS XI

B LESSED is he who will share Thy mystical supper in Thy kingdom; but even here on earth Thou hath granted me this blessedness. How many times, with Thy divine hand, Thou offered me Thy Body and Thy Blood; whilst I, a great sinner, received these sacred Gifts and felt Thine ineffable and supernatural love!

> Glory to Thee for the inconceivable and life-giving power of grace!

> Glory to Thee, who established Thy Church as a haven of peace for a tormented world!

> Glory to Thee for giving us new birth in the life-giving waters of baptism!

> Glory to Thee, restoring to those who repent purity white as the unstained lily!

> Glory to Thee, unfathomable abyss of forgiveness!

> Glory to Thee for the cup of life, for the bread of eternal joy!

> Glory to Thee, who raisest us to heaven!

> Glory to Thee, O God, from age to age!

KONTAKION XII

M ORE than once have I seen the reflection of Thy glory in the faces of the dead. What beauty, what heavenly joy shone in them! How light their features, now made spiritual! This was the triumph of happiness and peace found once again; in their silence, they were calling upon Thee. At the hour of my death, illumine also my soul which calls unto Thee: ALLELUIA!

OIKOS XII

HOW poor is my praise before Thee! I have not heard the song of the Cherubim, a joy reserved to the souls on high, but I know the praises nature sings unto Thee. In winter, I see how in the moonlit silence the whole earth offers Thee prayer, wrapped in its white mantle of snow, sparkling like diamonds. I see the rising sun rejoice in Thee, and I hear the chorus of birds raise a hymn of glory. I hear the forest mysteriously rustling in Thy honour, the winds sing of Thee, the waters murmur and the processions of stars proclaim Thee as they move in harmony for ever in the depths of infinite space. What is my poor worship? All nature obeyeth Thee, I do not; yet while I live, I see Thy love. I long to thank Thee, pray to Thee, and call upon Thy Name!

> Glory to Thee, who has shown us the light!
>
> Glory to Thee, who loved us with a deep unfathomable and divine love!
>
> Glory to Thee, who blesses us with the light, with a host of angels and saints!
>
> Glory to Thee, Father most holy, revealing us Thy kingdom in Thy commandments!
>
> Glory to Thee, Holy Spirit, life-giving Sun of the world to come!
>
> Glory to Thee for all things, divine and most merciful Trinity!
>
> Glory to Thee, O God, from age to age!

KONTAKION XIII

LIFE-GIVING and most merciful Trinity, receive our thanksgiving for all Thy kindnesses; make us worthy of Thy blessings, so that, when we have brought a profit from the talents Thou hast entrusted unto us, we may enter into the eternal joy of our Lord, singing the triumphal hymn: ALLELUIA! *(Thrice.)*

And again, Oikos I and Kontakion I are read.

OIKOS I

I WAS born a weak, defenceless child, but Thine angel, spreading his radiant wings, guarded my cradle. From my birth, Thy love hast illumined my paths, and hast wondrously guided me towards the light of eternity. From my first day until now, the generous gifts of Thy providence have been wonderfully showered upon me. I give Thee thanks, and with all those who have come to know Thee, I exclaim:

Glory to Thee for calling me into being!

Glory to Thee for spreading out before me the beauty of
the universe!

Glory to Thee for revealing to me through heaven and
earth the eternal book of wisdom!

Glory to Thine eternity within this fleeting world!

Glory to Thee for Thy mercies, seen and unseen!

Glory to Thee for every sigh of my sorrow!

Glory to Thee for every step in my life's journey, for every
moment of joy!

Glory to Thee, O God, from age to age!

KONTAKION I

INCORRUPTIBLE Lord, Thy right hand controls the whole course of human life, according to the decrees of Thy Providence for our salvation.

WE give Thee thanks for all Thy blessings, known and unknown: for our earthly life and for the heavenly joys of Thy kingdom which is to come. Henceforth extend Thy mercies towards us as we sing:

Glory to Thee, O God, from age to age!

AKATHIST FOR THE REPOSE OF THOSE WHO HAVE FALLEN ASLEEP

KONTAKION I

O THOU Who by Thy inscrutable Providence didst prepare the world for eternal beatitude and Who appointest times and seasons and the manner of our end: Forgive, O Lord, those who have died in past ages all their sins, receive them into the realms of light and joy, hasten to open Thy Fatherly arms to them, and hear us who celebrate their memory and sing:

> O Lord of unutterable Love, remember Thy servants who have fallen asleep.

OIKOS I

O THOU Who savest Adam and the whole human race from eternal perdition, Thou didst send Thy Son into the world, O Good God, and by His Cross and Resurrection Thou hast granted us also eternal life. Trusting to Thy infinite mercy, we look for the deathless Kingdom of Thy Glory, we implore Thee to grant it to those who have fallen asleep, and we pray:

> Gladden, O Lord, souls wearied by the storms of life,
>> that earth's sorrows and signings may not bury
>> them in oblivion.

> Hear them, O Lord, in Thy bosom, as a mother responds
>> to her children, and say to them: Your sins are
>> forgiven you.

> Receive them, O Lord, into Thy calm and blessed haven that
>> they may rejoice in Thy divine glory.

> O Lord of unutterable Love, remember Thy servants who
>> have fallen asleep.

KONTAKION II

E NLIGHTENED by the illumination of the Most High, Saint Macarius heard a voice from a pagan skull: "When you pray for those suffering in Hell, there is relief for the heathen." O wonderful power of Christian prayer, by which even the infernal regions are illumined! Both believers and unbelievers receive comfort when we cry for the whole world: ALLELUIA!

OIKOS II

S AINT Isaac the Syrian once said: "A merciful heart is one that burns with love for men and animals and for the whole of creation, and at all times offers prayers with tears that they may be purified and kept." Likewise, we all boldly ask the Lord for help for all the dead from the beginning of time and cry:

Send down to us, O Lord, the gift of fervent prayer for the
dead.

Remember, O Lord, all who have charged us, unworthy as
we are, to pray for them, and pardon the sins they
have forgotten.

Remember, O Lord, all who have been buried without
prayer.

Receive, O Lord, into Thy dwellings all who have died of
sorrow or joy by a sudden or untimely death.

O Lord of unutterable Love, remember Thy servants who
have fallen asleep.

KONTAKION III

WE are to blame for the calamities in the world, for the sufferings of
dumb creatures, and for the diseases and torments of innocent
children, for through the fall of man the beatitude and beauty of all
creation has been marred. O Christ our God, greatest of innocent
Sufferers! Thou alone canst forgive all. Forgive, then, all and everything,
and grant to the world its primordial prosperity, that the living and the
dead may rejoice and cry: ALLELUIA!

OIKOS III

O GLAD Light, Redeemer of the world, embracing the whole universe
with Thy love: behold, Thy cry from the Cross for Thy enemies is
heard: "Father, forgive them." In the name of Thy all-forgiving love, we
make bold to pray to our Heavenly Father for the eternal repose of Thy
enemies and ours.

FORGIVE, O Lord, those who have shed innocent blood, those who
have sown our path of life with sorrows, those who have waded to
prosperity through the tears of their neighbours.

CONDEMN not, O Lord, those who persecute us with slander and malice. Repay with mercy those whom we have wronged or offended through ignorance, and grant that our prayer for them may be holy through the sacrament of reconciliation.

> O Lord of unutterable Love, remember Thy servants who
> have fallen asleep.

KONTAKION IV

SAVE, O Lord, those who have died in grievous sufferings, those who were murdered, those buried alive, those who were drowned or burned, those who were torn by wild beasts, those who died of hunger or cold, from exposure in storms, or by falling from heights, and grant them all eternal joy for the sorrow of their death. May the time of their suffering be blessed as a day of redemption, for which they sing: ALLELUIA!

OIKOS IV

RECOMPENSE with the compassion of Thy infinite love, O Lord, all who have died in the full flush of their youth, who received on earth the thorny crown of suffering, who never experienced earthly joy.

> Grant recompense to those who died from overwork,
> through exploitation or sweated labour.

> Receive, O Lord, into the bridal halls of Paradise boys
> and girls, and grant them joy at the marriage
> supper of Thy Son.

> Comfort and console the grief of parents over their
> dead children.

> Give rest, O Lord, to all who have no one to offer prayer for
> them to Thee, their Creator, that their sins may vanish in
> the dazzling light of Thy forgiveness.

> O Lord of unutterable Love, remember Thy servants who
> have fallen asleep.

KONTAKION V

THOU hast given us death as a last prodigy to bring us to our senses and to repentance, O Lord. In its threatening light, earthly vanity is exposed, carnal passions and sufferings become subdued, in submissive reason is humbled. Eternal justice and righteousness opens to our gaze, and then the godless and those burdened with sins confess on their deathbed Thy real and eternal existence and cry to Thy mercy: ALLELUIA!

OIKOS V

O FATHER of all consolation and comfort, Thou brightenest with the sun, delightest with fruits, and gladdenest with the beauty of the world both Thy friends and enemies. And we believe that even beyond the grave Thy loving kindness, which is merciful even to all rejected sinners, does not fail.

We grieve for hardened and wicked blasphemers of
    Thy Holiness.

May Thy saving and gracious will be over them. Forgive, O
    Lord, those who have died without repentance.

Save those who have committed suicide in the darkness
    of their mind, that the flame of their sinfulness
    may be extinguished in the ocean of Thy grace.

O Lord of unutterable Love, remember Thy servants who
    have fallen asleep.

KONTAKION VI

TERRIBLE is the darkness of a soul separated from God, the torments of conscience, the gnashing of teeth, the unquenchable fire, and the undying worm. I tremble at the thought of such a fate, and I pray for those suffering in Hell as for myself. May our song descend upon them as refreshing dew as we sing: ALLELUIA!

OIKOS VI

THY light, O Christ our God, has shone upon those sitting in the darkness and shadow of death and those in Hell who cannot cry to Thee. Descend into the infernal regions of the earth, O Lord, and bring out into the joy of grace Thy children who have been separated from Thee by sin but who have not rejected Thee. For they suffer cruelly. Have mercy on them. For they sinned against Heaven and before Thee, and their sins are infinitely grievous, and Thy mercy is infinite.

Visit the bitter misery of souls separated from Thee.

Have mercy, O Lord, on those who hated the truth out of ignorance.

May Thy love be to them not a consuming fire but the coolness of Paradise:

O Lord of unutterable Love, remember Thy servants who have fallen asleep.

KONTAKION VII

ENDEAVOURING to give help by Thy might power to Thy servants who have fallen asleep, Thou hast appeared to their loved ones, O Lord, in mysterious visions clearly inspiring them to pray, that they may remember the departed, and do good works and labours of faith and love for them, crying: ALLELUIA!

OIKOS VII

THE universal Church of Christ unceasingly offers prayers every hour for the departed throughout the world, for the sins of the world are washed away by the most pure Blood of Thy divine crown, and the souls of those who have fallen asleep are translated from death to life and from earth to Heaven by the power of the prayers offered for them at God's altars.

May the intercession of the Church for the dead, O Lord, be
a ladder to Heaven.

Have mercy on them, O Lord, through the intercession of
the most holy Mother of God and all the Saints.

Forgive them their sins for the sake of Thy faithful who cry
day and night to Thee.

For the sake of innocent children, O Lord, have mercy on
their parents, and by the tears of their mothers, forgive
the sins of their children.

For the sake of the prayers of innocent sufferers and the
blood of martyrs, spare and have mercy on sinners.

Receive, O Lord, our prayers and alms as a memorial of
their virtues.

O Lord of unutterable Love, remember Thy servants who
have fallen asleep.

KONTAKION VIII

THE whole world is a sacred and common graveyard, for in every
place is the dust of our fathers and brothers. O Christ our God,
Who alone unchangeably lovest us, forgive all who have died from the
beginning till now, that they may sing with infinite love: ALLELUIA!

OIKOS VIII

THE day is coming, as a burning furnace, the great and terrible day of
the Last Judgment, when the secrets of men will be revealed and the
books of conscience will be torn apart. "Be reconciled with God!" cries
the Apostle Paul. "Be reconciled before that terrible day."

Help us, O Lord, to fill up with the tears of the living what
was lacking in the dead.

May the sound of the Angel's trumpet, O Lord, be to them
the glad announcement of their salvation and the
joyful manumission of their freedom at the hour
of Thy judgment.

Crown with glory those who have suffered for Thee, O Lord,
and cover the sins of the weak with Thy goodness.

O Lord, Who knowest all by name, remember those who
have sought salvation in the monastic life. Remember
the blessed pastors with their spiritual children.

O Lord of unutterable Love, remember Thy servants who
have fallen asleep.

KONTAKION IX

BLESS swiftly passing time. For every hour, every moment brings
eternity nearer. A new sorrow, a new grey hair are heralds of the
coming world, witnesses of earthly corruption, for all is passing (they tell
us) and the Eternal kingdom draws near, where there is no sorrow, no
sighing, no tears, but joyful singing: ALLELUIA!

OIKOS IX

JUST as a tree loses its leaves after a time, so our days after a certain
number of years come to an end. The festival of youth fades, the lamp
of joy goes out, the alienation and dispossession of old age approaches.

Friends and relations die. Where are you, young
merrymakers?

Their tombs are silent, but their souls are in Thy hand.

Let us think how they watch us from the spiritual world.

O Lord, Who art the brightest Sun, illumine and warm the
abodes of those who have fallen asleep.

May the time of our bitter separation pass forever.

Grant us a joyful meeting in Heaven.

Grant that all may be one with Thee, O Lord.

Restore to the departed, O Lord, the purity of childhood,
and the genial spirit of youth, and may eternal life be
to them a Paschal Festival.

O Lord of unutterable Love, remember Thy servants who
have fallen asleep.

KONTAKION X

SHEDDING silent tears at the graves of our relatives, we pray with hope,
and cry expectantly: Tell us, O Lord, that their sins are forgiven. Give
our spirit a secret assurance of it, that we may sing: ALLELUIA!

OIKOS X

LOOKING back, I see the whole of our past life. What a vast multitude
of people have departed from the first day until now! And many of
them have done me good. In gratitude for what I owe them, with love I
cry to Thee:

Grant heavenly glory, O Lord, to my parents and those near
and dear to me who watched over my cradle in
childhood, and reared and educated me.

Glorify, O Lord, in the presence of the Holy Angels all who
have told me the glad tidings of salvation and have
taught me what is right and good, just and true by the
holy example of their lives.

Fill with delight, O Lord, those who fed me on hidden
manna in the days of my sorrow and affliction.

Recompense and save all benefactors and all who have
helped others personally and by prayer.

O Lord of unutterable Love, remember Thy servants who
have fallen asleep.

KONTAKION XI

O DEATH, where is thy sting? Where is the gloom and terror that
held sway in the past? From now on thou art the longed for
means of inseparable union with God. Oh, the great peace of the
mystical Sabbath! We long to die and to be with Christ, cries the
Apostle. Therefore, we too look upon death as the gateway to eternal
life, and cry: ALLELUIA!

OIKOS XI

THE dead will rise and those who are in the graves will stand up, and
those who are alive on earth will exult when they stand with their
spiritual bodies, radiantly glories and incorrupt. Dry bones; hear the word
of the Lord:

"I will lay sinews upon you, and will bring up flesh upon you,
and will spread skin upon you, and will put my Spirit
into you, and ye shall live"

Rise out of the ancient past, you who are redeemed by the
Blood of the Son of God, restored to life by His
death, for the light of the Resurrection has dawned
upon you.

Open to them now, O Lord, the whole abyss of Thy
perfections.

Thou hast shone upon them with the light of the sun and
moon, that they may see the glory of the radiant choirs
of Angels,

Thou hast delighted them with the magnificence of the
heavenly lights of East and West, that they may
also see the never-setting light of Thy Divinity.

O Lord of unutterable Love, remember Thy servants who
    have fallen asleep.

KONTAKION XII

FLESH and blood will not inherit the Kingdom of God. While we live
in the flesh, we are separated from Christ. And if we die, we live for
eternity. For our corruptible body must put on incorruption, and this
mortal nature must shine with immortality, that in the light of the eternal
day we may sing: ALLELUIA!

OIKOS XII

WE expect to meet the Lord, we expect the clear dawn of the
Resurrection, we expect the rousing from their tombs of our dead
relatives and acquaintances and their restoration to the most holy beauty of
life. And we rejoice in the coming transfiguration of all creation, and cry
to our Creator:

O Lord, Who didst create the world for the triumph of joy
    and goodness, Who hast restored us to holiness from
    the depths of sin, grant that the dead may reign in the
    new creation, and may shine as heavenly lights in the
    day of their glory.

May the Divine Lamb be their perpetual light.

Grant, O Lord, that we too may celebrate with them a
    deathless Passover.

Unite the dead and the living in unending joy.

O Lord of unutterable Love, remember Thy servants who
    have fallen asleep.

KONTAKION XIII

O MOST merciful and eternal Father, Whose will it is that all should
be saved, Who didst send Thy Son to the lost and didst pour out

Thy Life-giving Spirit: Have mercy on our relatives and those who are near and dear to us who have fallen asleep, and on all who have died throughout the ages; forgive and save them, and by their intercession visit us, that with them we may shout to Thee, our God and Saviour, the song of victory: ALLELUIA! *(Thrice.)*

And again, Oikos I and Kontakion I are read.

OIKOS I

O THOU Who savest Adam and the whole human race from eternal perdition, Thou didst send Thy Son into the world, O Good God, and by His Cross and Resurrection Thou hast granted us also eternal life. Trusting to Thy infinite mercy, we look for the deathless Kingdom of Thy Glory, we implore Thee to grant it to those who have fallen asleep, and we pray:

> Gladden, O Lord, souls wearied by the storms of life, that
> earth's sorrows and signings may not bury them
> in oblivion.

> Hear them, O Lord, in Thy bosom, as a mother responds
> to her children, and say to them: Your sins are
> forgiven you.

> Receive them, O Lord, into Thy calm and blessed haven that
> they may rejoice in Thy divine glory.

> O Lord of unutterable Love, remember Thy servants who
> have fallen asleep.

KONTAKION I

O THOU Who by Thy inscrutable Providence didst prepare the world for eternal beatitude and Who appointest times and seasons and the manner of our end: Forgive, O Lord, those who have died in past ages all their sins, receive them into the realms of light and joy, hasten to open Thy Fatherly arms to them, and hear us who celebrate their memory and sing:

O Lord of unutterable Love, remember Thy servants who
have fallen asleep.

PRAYER FOR THOSE WHO HAVE FALLEN ASLEEP

O GOD of spirits and all flesh, Who hast trampled down death, overthrown the devil, and given life to Thy world: Give rest, O Lord, to the souls of Thy servants who have fallen asleep, Patriarchs, Metropolitans, Archbishops, Bishops, Priests and Deacons, Monks and Nuns, and all who have served Thee in Thy Church; the founders of this Holy Temple and all Churches and Monasteries, and all Orthodox forefathers, fathers, brothers and sisters who lie here and everywhere; officers and men of the armies and navies who have laid down their lives for their Faith and country, all the faithful killed in civil wars, all who were drowned, burned, frozen to death, torn by wild beasts, all who died suddenly without repentance and had no time to be reconciled with the Church and with their enemies; all who took their own lives in a moment of mental unbalance; all who have asked us to pray for them, and those who have no one to pray for them, and all who died without a Christian burial, *(names)*, in a place of light, in a place of refreshment, in a place of repose, whence all suffering, sorrow, and sighing have fled away. Forgive every sin committed by them in thought, word, and deed, for Thou art the good God and Lover of men. For there is no one who lives without sinning. Thou alone art without sin, and Thy righteousness is eternal righteousness, and Thy Word is Truth. For Thou art the Resurrection, the Life, and the Repose of Thy servants who have fallen asleep *(names)*, O Christ our God, and to Thee we send up glory, with Thy Eternal Father, and Thy Holy and Good and Life-giving Spirit, both now and ever, and to the ages of ages. AMEN.

AKATHIST TO OUR MOST HOLY LADY
THE MOTHER OF GOD

KONTAKION I

QUEEN of the Heavenly Host, Defender of our souls, we thy servants offer to thee songs of victory and thanksgiving, for thou, O Mother of God, hast delivered us from dangers. But as thou hast invincible power, free us from conflicts of all kinds that we may cry to thee:

Rejoice; unwedded Bride!

OIKOS I

AN Archangel was sent from Heaven to say to the Mother of God: Rejoice! And seeing Thee, O Lord, taking bodily form, he was amazed and with his bodiless voice, he stood crying to her such things as these:

Rejoice; thou through whom joy will flash forth!

Rejoice; thou through whom the curse will cease!

Rejoice; revival of fallen Adam!

Rejoice; redemption of the tears of Eve!

Rejoice; height hard to climb for human thoughts!

Rejoice; depth hard to contemplate even for the eyes of Angels!

Rejoice; thou who art the King's throne!

Rejoice; thou who barest Him Who bears all!

Rejoice; star that causest the Sun to appear!

Rejoice; womb of the divine incarnation!

Rejoice; thou through whom creation becomes new!

Rejoice; thou through whom the Creator becomes a babe!

Rejoice; unwedded Bride!

KONTAKION II

AWARE that she was living in chastity, the holy Virgin said boldly to Gabriel: "Thy strange message is hard for my soul to accept. How is it thou speakest of the birth from a seedless conception?" And she cried: ALLELUIA!

OIKOS II

SEEKING to know what passes knowledge, the Virgin cried to the ministering spirit: "Tell me, how can a son be born from a chaste womb?" Then he spoke to her in fear, only crying aloud thus:

Rejoice; initiate of God's ineffable will!

Rejoice; assurance of those who pray in silence!

Rejoice; prelude of Christ's miracles!

Rejoice; crown of His dogmas!

Rejoice; heavenly ladder by which God came down!

Rejoice; bridge that conveys us from earth to heaven!

Rejoice; wonder of angels blazed abroad!

Rejoice; wound of demons bewailed afar!

Rejoice; thou who ineffably gavest birth to the Light!

Rejoice; thou who didst reveal thy secret to none!

Rejoice; thou who surpassest the knowledge of the wise!

Rejoice; thou who givest light to the minds of the faithful!

Rejoice; unwedded Bride!

KONTAKION III

THE power of the Most High then overshadowed the Virgin for conception, and showed her fruitful womb as a sweet meadow to all who wish to reap salvation, as they sing: ALLELUIA!

OIKOS III

PREGNANT with the Divine indwelling, the Virgin ran to Elizabeth, whose unborn babe at once recognized her embrace, rejoiced, and with leaps of joy as songs, cried to the Mother of God:

Rejoice; scion of an undying Shoot!

Rejoice; field of untainted fruit!

Rejoice; thou who labourest for Him Whose labour is love!

Rejoice; thou who givest birth to the Father of our life!

Rejoice; cornland yielding a rich crop of mercies!

Rejoice; table bearing a wealth of forgiveness!

Rejoice; thou who revivest the garden of delight!

Rejoice; thou who preparest a haven for souls!

Rejoice; acceptable incense of intercession!

Rejoice; purification of the whole world!

Rejoice; favour of God to mortals!

Rejoice; access of mortals to God!

Rejoice; unwedded Bride!

KONTAKION IV

SUSTAINING from within a storm of doubtful thoughts, the chaste Joseph was troubled. For knowing thee to have no husband, he suspected a secret union, O Immaculate One. But when he learned that thy conception was of the Holy Spirit, he exclaimed: ALLELUIA!

OIKOS IV

THE shepherds heard Angels carolling Christ's incarnate Presence, and running like sheep to their shepherd, they beheld him as an innocent Lamb fed at Mary's breast, and they sang to her and said:

Rejoice; mother of the Lamb and the Shepherd!

Rejoice; fold of spiritual sheep!

Rejoice; defence against invisible enemies!

Rejoice; key to the gates of Paradise!

Rejoice; for the things of Heaven rejoice with the earth!

Rejoice; for the things of earth join chorus with the Heavens!

Rejoice; never-silent voice of the Apostles!

Rejoice; invincible courage of the martyrs!

Rejoice; firm support of faith!

Rejoice; radiant blaze of grace!

Rejoice; thou through whom hell was stripped bare!

Rejoice; thou through whom we are clothed with glory!

Rejoice; unwedded Bride!

KONTAKION V

HAVING sighted the divinely moving star, the Wise Men followed its light and held it as a lamp by which they sought a powerful King. And as they approached the Unapproachable, they rejoiced and shouted to Him: ALLELUIA!

OIKOS V

THE sons of the Chaldees saw in the hands of the Virgin Him Who with His hand made man. And knowing Him to be the Lord although He had taken the form of a servant, they hastened to worship Him with their gifts and cried to her who is blessed:

Rejoice; mother of the never-setting Star!

Rejoice; dawn of the mystic Day!

Rejoice; thou who didst extinguish the furnace of error!

Rejoice; thou who didst enlighten the initiates of the Trinity!

Rejoice; thou who didst banish from power the
      inhuman tyrant!

Rejoice; thou who hast shown us Christ as the Lord and
Lover of men!

Rejoice; thou who redeemest from pagan worship!

Rejoice; thou who dost drag from the mire of works!

Rejoice; thou who hast stopped the worship of fire!

Rejoice; thou who hast quenched the flame of the passions!

Rejoice; guide of the faithful to chastity!

Rejoice; joy of all generations!

Rejoice; unwedded Bride!

KONTAKION VI

TURNED God-bearing heralds, the Wise Men returned to Babylon.
They fulfilled Thy prophecy and to all preached Thee as the Christ,
and they left Herod as a trifler, who could not sing: ALLELUIA!

OIKOS VI

BY shining in Egypt the light of truth, Thou didst dispel the darkness
of falsehood, O Saviour. For, unable to endure Thy strength,
its idols fell; and those who were freed from their spell cried to the
Mother of God:

Rejoice; uplifting of men!

Rejoice; downfall of demons!

Rejoice; thou who hast trampled on the delusion of error!

Rejoice; thou who hast exposed the fraud of idols!

Rejoice; sea that has drowned the spiritual Pharaoh!

Rejoice; rock that has refreshed those thirsting for Life!

Rejoice; pillar of fire guiding those in darkness!

Rejoice; shelter of the world broader than a cloud!

Rejoice; sustenance replacing Manna!

Rejoice; minister of holy delight!

Rejoice; land of promise!

Rejoice; thou from whom flows milk and honey!

Rejoice; unwedded Bride!

KONTAKION VII

WHEN Simeon was about to depart this life of delusion, Thou wast brought as a Babe to him. But he recognized Thee as also perfect God, and marvelling at Thy ineffable wisdom, he cried: ALLELUIA!

OIKOS VII

THE Creator showed us a new creation when He appeared to us who came from Him. For He sprang from an unsown womb and kept it chaste as it was, that seeing the miracle we might sing to her and say:

Rejoice; flower of incorruption!

Rejoice; crown of continence!

Rejoice; flashing symbol of the resurrection!

Rejoice; mirror of the life of the Angels!

Rejoice; tree of glorious fruit by which the faithful are nourished!

Rejoice; bush of shady leaves by which many are sheltered!

Rejoice; thou who bearest the Guide of those astray!

Rejoice; thou who givest birth to the Redeemer of captives!

Rejoice; pleader before the Just Judge!

Rejoice; forgiveness of many sinners!

Rejoice; robe of freedom for the naked!

Rejoice; love that vanquishes all desire!

Rejoice; unwedded Bride!

KONTAKION VIII

SEEING the Child Exile, let us be exiles from the world and transport our minds to Heaven. For the Most High God appeared on earth as lowly man, because He wished to draw to the heights those who cry to Him: ALLELUIA!

OIKOS VIII

WHOLLY present was the infinite Word among those here below, yet in no way absent from those on high; for this was a divine condescension and not a change of place. And His birth was from a God-possessed Virgin who heard words like these:

Rejoice; container of the uncontainable God!

Rejoice; door of solemn mystery!

Rejoice; doubtful report of unbelievers!

Rejoice; undoubted boast of the faithful!

Rejoice; all-holy chariot of Him Who rides on the Cherubim!

Rejoice; all-glorious temple of Him Who is above the Seraphim!

Rejoice; thou who hast united opposites!

Rejoice; thou who hast joined virginity and motherhood!

Rejoice; thou through whom sin has been absolved!

Rejoice; thou through whom Paradise is opened!

Rejoice; key to the Kingdom of Christ!

Rejoice; hope of eternal blessings!

Rejoice; unwedded Bride!

KONTAKION IX

ALL angel-kind was amazed at the great act of Thy incarnation; for they saw the inaccessible God as a man accessible to all, dwelling with us and hearing from all: ALLELUIA!

OIKOS IX

WE see most eloquent orators dumb as fish before thee, O Mother of God. For they dare not ask: How canst thou bear a Child and yet remain a Virgin? But we marvel at the mystery, and cry with faith:

Rejoice; receptacle of the Wisdom of God!

Rejoice; treasury of His Providence!

Rejoice; thou who showest philosophers to be fools!

Rejoice; thou who constrainest the learned to silence!

Rejoice; for the clever critics have made fools of themselves!

Rejoice; for the writers of myths have died out!

Rejoice; thou who didst break the webs of the Athenians!

Rejoice; thou who didst fill the nets of the fishermen!

Rejoice; thou who drawest us from the depths of ignorance!

Rejoice; thou who enlightenest many with knowledge!

Rejoice; ship of those who wish to be saved!

Rejoice; haven for sailors on the sea of life!

Rejoice; unwedded Bride!

KONTAKION X

WISHING to save the world, the Ruler of all came to it spontaneously. And though as God He is our Shepherd, for us He appeared to us as a Man; and having called mankind to salvation by His own Perfect Manhood, as God He hears: ALLELUIA!

OIKOS X

THOU art a wall to virgins and to all who run to thee, O Virgin Mother of God. For the Maker of heaven and earth prepared thee, O Immaculate One, and dwelt in thy womb, and taught all to call to thee:

Rejoice; pillar of virginity!

Rejoice; gate of salvation!

Rejoice; founder of spiritual reformation!

Rejoice; leader of divine goodness!

Rejoice; for thou didst regenerate those conceived in shame!

Rejoice; for thou gavest understanding to those robbed of
their senses!

Rejoice; thou who didst foil the corrupter of minds!

Rejoice; thou who gavest birth to the Sower of chastity!

Rejoice; bride-chamber of a virgin marriage!

Rejoice; thou who dost wed the faithful to the Lord!

Rejoice; fair mother and nurse of virgins!

Rejoice; betrother of holy souls!

Rejoice; unwedded Bride!

KONTAKION XI

EVERY hymn falls short that aspires to embrace the multitude of Thy many mercies. For if, we should offer to Thee, O Holy King, songs numberless as the sand, we should still have done nothing worthy of what Thou hast given to us who shout to Thee: ALLELUIA!

OIKOS XI

WE see the Holy Virgin as a flaming torch appearing to those in darkness. For having kindled the Immaterial Light, she leads all to divine knowledge; she illumines our minds with radiance and is honoured by our shouting these praises:

Rejoice; ray of the spiritual Sun!

Rejoice; flash of unfading splendour!

Rejoice; lightning that lights up our souls!

Rejoice; thunder that stuns our enemies!

Rejoice; for thou didst cause the refulgent Light to dawn!

Rejoice; for thou didst cause the ever-flowing river to
gush forth!

Rejoice; living image of the font!

Rejoice; remover of the stain of sin!

Rejoice; laver that washes the conscience clean!

Rejoice; bowl for mixing the wine of joy!

Rejoice; aroma of the fragrance of Christ!

Rejoice; life of mystical festivity!

Rejoice; unwedded Bride!

KONTAKION XII

WHEN He Who forgives all men their past debts wished to restore us to favour, of His own will He came to dwell among those who had fallen from His grace; and having torn up the record of their sins, He hears from all: ALLELUIA!

OIKOS XII

WHILE singing to thy Child, we all praise thee as a living temple, O Mother of God. For the Lord Who holds all things in His hand dwelt in thy womb, and He sanctified and glorified thee, and taught all to cry to thee:

Rejoice; tabernacle of God the Word!

Rejoice; saint greater than the saints!

Rejoice; ark made golden by the Spirit!

Rejoice; inexhaustible treasury of Life!

Rejoice; precious diadem of pious kings!

Rejoice; adorable boast of devoted priests!

Rejoice; unshaken tower of the Church!

Rejoice; impregnable wall of the Kingdom!

Rejoice; thou through whom we obtain our victories!

Rejoice; thou before whom our foes fall prostrate!

Rejoice; healing of my body!

Rejoice; salvation of my soul!

Rejoice; unwedded Bride!

KONTAKION XIII

O ALL-PRAISED Mother who didst bear the Word, holiest of all the Saints, accept this our offering, and deliver us from all offense, and redeem from future torment those who cry in unison to thee: ALLELUIA! *(Thrice.)*

And again, Oikos I and Kontakion I are read.

OIKOS I

AN Archangel was sent from Heaven to say to the Mother of God: Rejoice! And seeing Thee, O Lord, taking bodily form, he was amazed and with his bodiless voice, he stood crying to her such things as these:

Rejoice; thou through whom joy will flash forth!

Rejoice; thou through whom the curse will cease!

Rejoice; revival of fallen Adam!

Rejoice; redemption of the tears of Eve!

Rejoice; height hard to climb for human thoughts!

Rejoice; depth hard to contemplate even for the eyes
of Angels!

Rejoice; thou who art the King's throne!

Rejoice; thou who bearest Him Who bears all!

Rejoice; star that causest the Sun to appear!

Rejoice; womb of the divine incarnation!

Rejoice; thou through whom creation becomes new!

Rejoice; thou through whom the Creator becomes a babe!

Rejoice; unwedded Bride!

KONTAKION I

QUEEN of the Heavenly Host, Defender of our souls, we thy servants offer to thee songs of victory and thanksgiving, for thou, O Mother of God, hast delivered us from dangers. But as thou hast invincible power, free us from conflicts of all kinds that we may cry to thee:

Rejoice; unwedded Bride!

PRAYER TO OUR MOST HOLY LADY THE MOTHER OF GOD

MY most gracious Queen, my hope, Mother of God, shelter of orphans, and intercessor of travellers, strangers and pilgrims, joy of those in sorrow, protectress of the wronged; see my distress, see my affliction! Help me, for I am helpless. Feed me, for I am a stranger and pilgrim. Thou knowest my offence; forgive and resolve it as thou wilt. For I know no other help but thee, no other intercessor, no gracious consoler but thee, O Mother of God, to guard and protect me throughout the ages. AMEN.

AKATHIST TO THE THEOTOKOS, JOY OF ALL WHO SORROW

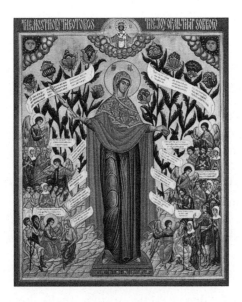

KONTAKION I

To Thee, the champion leader, do we Thy servants dedicate a hymn of victory and thanksgiving, as ones who have been delivered from eternal death by the Grace of Christ our God Who was born of Thee and by Thy maternal mediation before Him. As Thou dost have invincible might, free us from all misfortunes and sorrowful circumstances who cry aloud:

> Rejoice; O Virgin Theotokos, full of Grace, Joy of all
> who sorrow!

OIKOS I

An archangel was sent from Heaven to declare unto the Theotokos: Rejoice, announcing the divine Incarnation of Christ, Who desired to be born of Her, the Joy of the whole world which was languishing in sorrow.

Wherefore, heavy laden with sins, but having obtained the hope of salvation in Thee, we cry out unto Thee with compunction:

Rejoice; goodwill of God toward sinners!

Rejoice; strong help for those who repent before the
Lord God!

Rejoice; restoration of fallen Adam!

Rejoice; redemption of the tears of Eve!

Rejoice; Thou that dost remove the stain of sin!

Rejoice; laver that dost wash the conscience clean!

Rejoice; Thou that didst bear the Redeemer Who freely
cleanseth us of our transgressions!

Rejoice; all-wondrous reconciliation of all with God!

Rejoice; bridge that dost truly lead us from death to life!

Rejoice; Thou that savest the world from the flood of sin!

Rejoice; heavenly ladder by which the Lord descended
to us!

Rejoice; cause of deification for all!

Rejoice; O Virgin Theotokos, full of Grace, Joy of all
who sorrow!

KONTAKION II

BEHOLDING the streams of wonders which pour forth from Thy holy icon, O most blessed Mother of God, in that Thou art the good helper of them that pray, the support of the oppressed, the hope of the hopeless, the consolation of them that grieve, the nourisher of the hungry, the raiment of the naked, the chastity of virgins, the guide of strangers, the assistance of them that labour, the restoration of sight for the blind, the clear hearing of the deaf, and the healing of the sick, in Thee do we thankfully chant unto God: ALLELUIA!

OIKOS II

SEEKING to understand the incomprehensible reason for the bitter sorrows that assail us, in need of consolation we flee to Thee, O Mother and Virgin. And in that Thou art good, teach us to see in them the merciful providence of Thy good Son for the salvation of our souls and the cleansing of our many transgressions, that we may joyfully cry unto Thee:

Rejoice; calm haven of the tempest-tossed!

Rejoice; sure confirmation of them in doubt!

Rejoice; only mother of loving-kindness!

Rejoice; ready helper of them in misfortunes
and temptations!

Rejoice; Thou that dost wash away the sorrows of our sins!

Rejoice; Thou that healest the grief of our spiritual infirmity!

Rejoice; Thou that dost teach us to disdain the vain joys of
this world!

Rejoice; Thou that leadest our minds from the world to that
which transcendeth it!

Rejoice; Thou that drawest us from the love of things earthly
to the heavenly love of God!

Rejoice; Thou that grantest us consolation and a life of
Grace amid our very sorrows!

Rejoice; pledge of eternal blessings!

Rejoice; mediatress of everlasting joy!

Rejoice; O Virgin Theotokos, full of Grace, Joy of all
who sorrow!

KONTAKION III

WITH power from on high, do Thou strengthen me, who am
afflicted in body and soul, O good Lady, and vouchsafe me
Thy visitation and provident care, dispelling the gloom of despondency
and sorrow which enfold me, that saved by Thee I may unceasingly cry
out to God: ALLELUIA!

OIKOS III

O THOU that hast an ineffable wealth of loving-kindness, that dost
stretch forth the hand of Thine assistance unto all that sorrow, that
curest infirmities and healest the passions: disdain not even me, O blessed
Lady, as I lie upon the bed of mine affliction and cry unto Thee:

Rejoice; priceless treasury of mercy!

Rejoice; sole hope of the despairing!

Rejoice; healing of my body!

Rejoice; salvation of my soul!

Rejoice; unfailing strength of the infirm!

Rejoice; aid and strengthening of the disabled!

Rejoice; Thou that quickly assuagest the wrath of God by
Thy supplication!

Rejoice; Thou that dost tame our passions by the power of
Thy prayers!

Rejoice; sight for the blind and hearing for the deaf!

Rejoice; feet for the lame, speech for the dumb!

Rejoice; visitation of good cheer for the sick!

Rejoice; for through Thee are Grace-filled healings granted
to the infirm, according to the measure of their faith!

Rejoice; O Virgin Theotokos, full of Grace, Joy of all
who sorrow!

KONTAKION IV

A TEMPEST of many misfortunes and temptations doth beset me, and no longer can I endure its ragings. But as Thou art the merciful mother of my Saviour and God, lift up Thy hands to Thy Son, beseeching Him to regard the bitter sorrow of my heart and to raise me up from the abyss of despair, who cry unto Him: ALLELUIA!

OIKOS IV

O MOST holy Virgin and Mother, hearing the prophecy of the righteous Simeon: A sword shall pierce through Thine own soul; Thou didst keep all these sayings in Thy heart, understanding that the joy of a mother's heart over her children can be accompanied with much grief in this world. Wherefore, as one tried in everything and able to commiserate with a mother's sorrows, we cry unto Thee:

Rejoice; Thou that didst bear the Saviour Christ, the Joy of
the world!

Rejoice; Thou that deliverest the world from sorrows!

Rejoice; Thou that didst endure the blasphemies and slanders
hurled at Thy Son!

Rejoice; Thou that didst suffer together with Him through
His suffering!

Rejoice; consolation of the sorrows of mothers!

Rejoice; gracious preservation of their children!

Rejoice; speedy help amid misfortunes!

Rejoice; correction of the erring!

Rejoice; nourishment of infants!

Rejoice; guidance of the young!

Rejoice; mother of the orphaned!

Rejoice; help of widows!

Rejoice; O Virgin Theotokos, full of Grace, Joy of all
who sorrow!

KONTAKION V

B EHOLDING the divinely-flowing blood of Thy Son poured forth upon the Cross of our salvation, as the handmaiden of the Lord Who didst humbly subject Thyself to the will of the Father Who is in the heavens, Thou didst give us an example of endurance and of patience, that amid the furnace of temptations and present misfortunes we may cry aloud to God: ALLELUIA!

OIKOS V

B EHOLDING Thee crucified with Him in Thy heart and standing with His beloved disciple by the Cross, Thy Son and God did say: Woman, behold Thy son, and to His disciple: Behold thy mother, thereby giving Thee as sons all that believe in Him. And having in Thee a good mother, placing all our hope in Thee amid our sorrow, as partakers of the sorrows and sufferings of Thy Son, we cry to Thee:

Rejoice; mother of the Christian race!

Rejoice; Thou that didst adopt us at the Cross of Thy Son!

Rejoice; Thou that didst unite God with mankind!

Rejoice; Thou that didst join the faithful to the Lord!

Rejoice; ewe that didst bear the Lamb that taketh away the
sin of the world!

Rejoice; cup that drawest joy for us from the Fountain
    of Immortality!

Rejoice; surety of the salvation of sinners!

Rejoice; search for the perishing!

Rejoice; unexpected joy of sinners!

Rejoice; raising up of all the fallen!

Rejoice; healer of all infirmities!

Rejoice; alleviation of every sorrow!

Rejoice; O Virgin Theotokos, full of Grace, Joy of all
    who sorrow!

KONTAKION VI

O MOTHER of God, all the ends of the earth proclaim Thy mercies, for by Thy sacred protection Thou dost shelter the whole Christian race for which Thou dost supplicate Christ our Saviour and dost deliver from all misfortune Thy pious and God-fearing servants who faithfully cry out to God: ALLELUIA!

OIKOS VI

BEHOLDING the radiant Grace which shineth forth from Thy most wondrous icon, O Mother of God, falling down before it with tears, we beseech Thee: disperse the clouds of temptations which have come upon us, that we may cry out to Thee with joy:

Rejoice; Thou that bearest the supplications of the faithful
    unto Thy Son and God!

Rejoice; Thou that thyself dost pray for us at the throne of
    Thy Son!

Rejoice; intercessor before God that dost save the world
    from calamities!

Rejoice; help of the Christian race, given us by God!

Rejoice; tree of goodly shade, whereby many are sheltered!

Rejoice; tree bearing radiant fruit, whereby the faithful
are nourished!

Rejoice; shelter of the world, more spacious than a cloud!

Rejoice; land of promise whence milk and honey floweth!

Rejoice; radiant cloud, unceasingly illuminating the faithful!

Rejoice; pillar of fire, guiding the elect to their heavenly
inheritance!

Rejoice; field that yieldest an abundance of compassion!

Rejoice; bestower of every blessing!

Rejoice; O Virgin Theotokos, full of Grace, Joy of all
who sorrow!

KONTAKION VII

DESIRING to produce streams of wonders from Thine icon, "The Joy of All Who Sorrow," Thou, O Lady, didst command the ailing Euphemia to have a moleben served before it, and having received healing, to proclaim to all the mercies bestowed through this icon, that the source of gracious healings be not hid from those in need. Wherefore, we hide not Thy good deeds, but thankfully glorifying God, we cry unto Him: ALLELUIA!

OIKOS VII

THY temple, in which we bow down before Thy wonder-working icon, is shown to be a new pool of Siloam, surpassing the one of old, O Most-pure Lady; for health of body is given not once a year and only to the first-come, but Thou dost always heal every ailment and every disease of soul and body of them that hasten to Thee with faith and love. Wherefore we cry unto Thee:

Rejoice; font wherein our sorrows are drowned!

Rejoice; cup whereby we partake of joy and salvation!

Rejoice; rock that givest drink to them that thirst for life!

Rejoice; tree that dost sweeten the salty waters of the sea of life!

Rejoice; inexhaustible fountain of life-giving waters!

Rejoice; laver that dost wash away the stain of sin!

Rejoice; sweetening of our sorrows!

Rejoice; assuagement of our sorrows!

Rejoice; healing of our afflictions!

Rejoice; deliverance from misfortune!

Rejoice; trampling down of demons!

Rejoice; humiliation of enemies!

Rejoice; O Virgin Theotokos, full of Grace, Joy of all who sorrow!

KONTAKION VIII

STRANGERS and pilgrims are we upon this earth, in the words of the Apostle: enduring perils at the hands of enemies, perils at the hands of relatives, perils at the hands of false brethren, in much want and sorrow. And in that Thou art the good Directress, O Lady, do Thou grant us remission of our transgressions before the end, that we may unceasingly cry unto God: ALLELUIA!

OIKOS VIII

OUR whole life on earth is painful and filled with grief because of false accusations, reproaches, insults, and various other misfortunes and temptations, for the flesh is weak and our spirit faileth. Therefore, to Thee do we flee, O Mother of God, falling down before Thine all-pure icon. Fill our sorrowful hearts with joy and gladness, that we may cry unto Thee:

Rejoice; guide that dost direct us to the heavenly fatherland!

Rejoice; queen of Heaven and earth Who dost open unto us the gates of Paradise!

Rejoice; merciful one that hast mercy upon us!

Rejoice; steward that orderest well our life!

Rejoice; fleece bedewed, which Gideon didst foresee!

Rejoice; blessed womb which didst contain the uncontainable God of all!

Rejoice; bush that burned and yet remained unconsumed!

Rejoice; unassailable wall!

Rejoice; life-giving fountain!

Rejoice; never-fading bloom!

Rejoice; softening of the hearts of the wicked!

Rejoice; compunction of the good!

Rejoice; O Virgin Theotokos, full of Grace, Joy of all who sorrow!

KONTAKION IX

EVERY sweetness of life in this world partaketh of sorrow: glory endureth not, wealth passeth, beauty and health fade away, and friends and neighbours are taken away by death. Wherefore, sweeten our sorrows, Thou cause of every good thing, bestowing Thine incorruptible joy upon us that cry out to God: ALLELUIA!

OIKOS IX

THE most eloquent orators know not with what words to console the sorrowful; but do Thou Thyself, O Lady, speak consolation to our hearts, dispersing the cloud of our sorrow and the gloom of despair with the rays of Thy Grace, that we may cry out to Thee:

Rejoice; Thou that hast made glad all Christians that have confidence in Thee!

Rejoice; joy and tranquillity of the world!

Rejoice; bestower of divine goodness!

Rejoice; hope of eternal blessings!

Rejoice; ship of them that wish to be saved!

Rejoice; harbour for the voyages of life!

Rejoice; faithful preserver of them that, after God, do trust in Thee!

Rejoice; vesture of them that are stripped of boldness!

Rejoice; preserver and confirmation for all!

Rejoice; fortification and sacred refuge of all the faithful!

Rejoice; help of them that faithfully pray to Thee!

Rejoice; radiant knowledge of Grace!

Rejoice; O Virgin Theotokos, full of Grace, Joy of all
who sorrow!

KONTAKION X

DESIRING to save the human race from eternal torment and unending
sorrow, the Lord Who loveth mankind dwelt in Thine ever-virgin
womb, and gave Thee, His own mother, to the perishing as a
help, protection, and defence, that Thou mightest be the consolation
of the grieving, the rejoicing of the sorrowful, the hope of the despairing,
releasing them from eternal torment by Thine intercession, and leading
to heavenly gladness all that faithfully cry to Thy Son and our
God: ALLELUIA!

OIKOS X

THOU art the bulwark of virgins, O Virgin Theotokos, and of all that
flee to Thy protection. Wherefore do we beseech Thee: help,
protect, and preserve from temptations, afflictions, and misfortunes all the
orphans and helpless ones who cry out to Thee with love:

Rejoice; pillar of virginity!

Rejoice; chosen vessel of purity and chastity!

Rejoice; special crowning of them that by chastity make war
upon the flesh!

Rejoice; bestower of eternal rejoicing upon them that
mourn profitably in monasticism!

Rejoice; Thou that dost quench the flame of the passions!

Rejoice; Thou that dost dispel the darkness of temptations!

Rejoice; guide to chastity!

Rejoice; rampart of purity!

Rejoice; reformation of mankind!

Rejoice; Thou by whom we are raised up from the fall!

Rejoice; steadfast affirmation of the Faith!

Rejoice; pleasing incense of prayer!

Rejoice; O Virgin Theotokos, full of Grace, Joy of all
    who sorrow!

KONTAKION XI

WE, Thy servants, offer Thee a hymn of compunction, O
Theotokos, for Thou art the all-powerful helper of our race.
Assuage the pains of those who flee to Thee; appease the wrath of
God which hath been justly aroused against us because of our sins; deliver
us from every bitter pain and sorrow, who cry through Thee to
God: ALLELUIA!

OIKOS XI

O LADY, Thy most honoured icon, a light-bearing lamp lit by the
ember of the Grace of God, hath appeared unto us for our
sanctification and consolation. And we, honouring it with love and falling
down before it with faith, cry out to Thee:

Rejoice; Thou that by Thy mighty assistance dost deliver us
    from all calamities!

Rejoice; Thou that dost defend us from earthquake
    and flood!

Rejoice; Thou that dost provide for us against hunger of
    body and soul!

Rejoice; Thou that dost extinguish the fire by the dew of
    Thy prayers!

Rejoice; Thou that dost save us from deadly pestilence!

Rejoice; mighty helper in battles!

Rejoice; Thou that defendest us from the invasions
  of foreigners!

Rejoice; Thou that dost preserve us from civil strife!

Rejoice; easy passage of them that sail upon the water!

Rejoice; good guide of them that travel!

Rejoice; liberation of captives!

Rejoice; speedy deliverance from the righteous wrath of God
  that threateneth us!

Rejoice; O Virgin Theotokos, full of Grace, Joy of all
  who sorrow!

KONTAKION XII

WISHING to give a pledge of Grace to mankind, Thou didst reveal Thy healing icon to us, O Mother of God, from which streams of wonders are poured forth for them that approach with faith - infirmities are healed and sorrows assuaged. Wherefore do we cry in Thee unto God: ALLELUIA!

OIKOS XII

LAUDING Thy mercies and wonders, O Theotokos, we all praise Thee as our steadfast mediatress, and we bow down with compunction before Thee that prayest for us, and we implore: lift up Thy hands to Thy Son, that always in this life and after our death His mercy may continually be upon us that cry out to Thee:

Rejoice; our unashamed hope in life and after our repose!

Rejoice; Thou that dost grant a peaceful end of this life to
  them that trust in Thee!

Rejoice; our hope and defence on the Day of Judgment!

Rejoice; supplication of the just Judge!

Rejoice; deliverance from everlasting Gehenna!

Rejoice; hope of eternal salvation!

Rejoice; key to the Kingdom of Christ!

Rejoice; portal of Paradise!

Rejoice; bridge leading to the heavens!

Rejoice; refuge and good intercessor for all repentant sinners!

Rejoice; joy of the angels!

Rejoice; glory and consolation of all the righteous!

Rejoice; O Virgin Theotokos, full of Grace, Joy of all who sorrow!

KONTAKION XIII

O ALL-HYMNED, divinely favoured Mother, Thou that didst bear Christ the King, our God, to the joy of Heaven and earth: hearken unto the voice of Thy sorrowing servants and having received this our small supplication, deliver us from every affliction, sorrow, and temptation; heal our infirmities, destroy vicious slanders, drive far from us every evil and enemy, and deliver from future torment them that cry in Thee: ALLELUIA! *(Thrice.)*

And again, Oikos I and Kontakion I are read.

OIKOS I

A N archangel was sent from Heaven to declare unto the Theotokos: Rejoice, announcing the divine Incarnation of Christ, Who desired to be born of Her, the Joy of the whole world which was languishing in sorrow. Wherefore, heavy laden with sins, but having obtained the hope of salvation in Thee, we cry out to Thee with compunction:

Rejoice; goodwill of God toward sinners!

Rejoice; strong help for those who repent before the
Lord God!

Rejoice; restoration of fallen Adam!

Rejoice; redemption of the tears of Eve!

Rejoice; Thou that dost remove the stain of sin!

Rejoice; laver that dost wash the conscience clean!

Rejoice; Thou that didst bear the Redeemer Who freely
cleanseth us of our transgressions!

Rejoice; all-wondrous reconciliation of all with God!

Rejoice; bridge that dost truly lead us from death to life!

Rejoice; Thou that savest the world from the flood of sin!

Rejoice; heavenly ladder by which the Lord descended
to us!

Rejoice; cause of deification for all!

Rejoice; O Virgin Theotokos, full of Grace, Joy of all
who sorrow!

KONTAKION I

To Thee, the champion leader, do we Thy servants dedicate a hymn of victory and thanksgiving, as ones who have been delivered from eternal death by the Grace of Christ our God Who was born of Thee and by Thy maternal mediation before Him. As Thou dost have invincible might, free us from all misfortunes and sorrowful circumstances who cry aloud:

Rejoice; O Virgin Theotokos, full of Grace, Joy of all
who sorrow!

FIRST PRAYER

O LADY most holy and Theotokos, Thou that art more exalted than the Cherubim and more honourable than the Seraphim, O divinely-chosen Maiden, Joy of all who sorrow; grant consolation even unto us that are sunk in sorrow, for apart from Thee we have no refuge or assistance. Thou alone are the Mediatress of our joy and, in that Thou art the Mother of God and Mother of mercy, standing at the throne of the All-holy Trinity, Thou art able to help us, for none that doth flee to Thee departeth ashamed. Therefore, hearken now in the day of our sorrow unto us who fall down before Thine icon and supplicate Thee with tears: drive away from us the sorrows and griefs that assail us in this temporal life, and by Thine omnipotent intercession may we not be deprived of eternal and never-ending joy in the Kingdom of Thy Son and our God. AMEN.

SECOND PRAYER

O MY most blessed Queen, O Theotokos my hope, guardian of orphans and intercessor for strangers, Joy of the sorrowful, Protectress of the oppressed; Thou beholdest my misfortune, Thou seest my sorrow. Help me, for I am infirm; feed me, for I am a stranger. Thou knowest mine offense: do Thou loose it, as Thou dost will, for I have none other help but Thee, nor any other intercessor save Thee, O Mother of God. Do Thou preserve and protect me unto the ages of ages. AMEN.

THIRD PRAYER

O MOST holy Virgin, Mother of the Lord of the hosts on high, Queen of Heaven and earth, almighty intercessor of our city and country: receive this hymn of praise and thanksgiving from us, Thine unworthy servants, and bear our prayers to the throne of God, Thy Son, that He may be merciful towards our unrighteousness and extend His Grace to them that honour Thine All-honourable name and bow down before Thy wonder-working icon with faith and love. For we are not worthy to be pitied by Him. Wherefore we flee to Thee as our undoubted and speedy intercessor: hearken Thou unto us that supplicate Thee. Overshadow us with Thine almighty protection, and request of God Thy Son: zeal and vigilance concerning souls for our pastors, wisdom and strength for civil authorities, justice and equity for judges; knowledge and humility for them that teach; love and concord between husbands and wives, obedience for children; patience for the oppressed; fear of God for the oppressors; strength of spirit for the sorrowful; moderation for the joyful; and for all of us: the spirit of understanding and piety, the spirit of mercy and meekness, the spirit of purity and righteousness. Yea, O most holy Lady, take pity on Thine afflicted people: gather the dispersed, guide to the right path them that are astray, support the aged, teach the young sober-mindedness, nourish the infants, and look down with the gaze of Thy merciful assistance upon us all. Raise us up from the abyss of sin and open the eyes of our hearts to the vision of salvation. Take pity on us here and now - both in the land of our earthly sojourn and at the dread judgment of Thy Son. Cause our fathers and brethren who have passed from this life in faith and repentance to abide in eternal life with the angels and all the saints, for Thou, O Lady, art the glory of them in Heaven and the hope of them upon the earth. After God, Thou art our hope and the helper of all that flee to Thee with faith. Therefore, to Thee do we pray, and as to an all-powerful helper, to Thee do we commend ourselves and each other and all our life, now and ever, and unto the ages of ages. AMEN.

AKATHIST TO THE THEOTOKOS, NURTURER OF CHILDREN

KONTAKION I

VICTORIOUS Leader and Good Nurturer of the Christian race, we Thy servants, delivered from evil, sing out grateful thanks to Thee. But as Thou hast invincible might deliver my children from all dangers that with tears I may cry to Thee:

> Raise my children *(names)*, to be made worthy of the
>   Kingdom of Heaven, and make them heirs of eternal
>   blessings.

OIKOS I

I ntercede with Thy Son and God, O most Holy One, that an angel from heaven be sent to my children, just as to Thee was sent a most mighty protector, the Archangel Gabriel; and vouchsafe me to cry to Thee thus:

Raise my children to be earthly angels.

Raise my children to be heavenly men.

Raise my children to be Thy servants.

Raise my children to cry out to Thee:

"Rejoice, O Full of Grace, the Lord is with Thee!"

Raise my children *(names)*, O Lady, to be made worthy of
the Kingdom of Heaven and make them heirs of
eternal blessings.

KONTAKION II

A S thou seest my maternal entreaty for my children, begging help of Thee alone; do Thou take them under Thine honourable and compassionate protection, that we may cry to God: ALLELUIA!

OIKOS II

S END my children understanding, that they may know how to serve Thee well; fill their hearts with heavenly wisdom and grant that they may love it alone and scorn the things of the world. Do not hinder my lips from crying such things as these:

Raise my children to be wise as serpents and as innocent
as doves.

Raise my children to have knowledge of good but not of sin.

Raise my children to be wise against the snares of the devil.

Raise my children to order their lives wisely, following the
examples of the saints.

Raise my children, nourishing them with the milk of the
hidden wisdom of God, that they may seek it all of
their lives.

Raise my children *(names)*, O Lady, to be made worthy of
the Kingdom of Heaven and make them heirs of
eternal blessings.

KONTAKION III

M AY the power of the Most High overshadow my
children through Thine unceasing intercession before Thy
Son, and on account of this, having come to know Thy maternal
compassion towards all who run to God with faith, may they cry
to God: ALLELUIA!

OIKOS III

H AVING received my children from God, I do not desire to behold
them dwelling in eternal torment, but rather to see them written in
the Book of Life and made inheritors of eternal life. For Thy sake, O
Most Pure Virgin, incline Thine ear to my supplication, as I cry to Thee:

Raise my children to flee eternal torment.

Raise my children to inherit life eternal.

Raise my children to pass the course of their life
in Repentance.

Raise my children to labour to acquire the grace of the
Holy Spirit.

Raise my children to exert effort to attain the Kingdom
of Heaven.

Raise my children to be written in the Book of Life.

Raise my children *(names)*, O Lady, to be made worthy of
the Kingdom of Heaven and make them heirs of
eternal blessings.

KONTAKION IV

HAVING within a tempest of doubting thoughts, and wanting to give
my children to drink of eternal life, I weep. Thus, having
remembered Thy most rich mercies, I sing to Thy Son with hope and with
a contrite heart: ALLELUIA!

OIKOS IV

HAVING heard Thy voice, crying to Thy Son, "Preserve in Thine
inheritance those whom Thou hast given me unto the ages," I
stretch out my hands and my heart towards Thy loving-kindness,
entreating that Thou wilt keep my children among Thy servants, and fulfil
these my petitions:

Raise my children in thy most holy inheritance.

Raise my children with all Thy Saints.

Raise my children to be Thy servants, fulfilling all
Thy commands.

Raise my children to seek help from Thee alone.

Raise my children to inherit eternal life.

Raise my children *(names)*, O Lady, to be made worthy of
the Kingdom of Heaven and make them heirs of
eternal blessings.

KONTAKION V

MAY the Morning Star, which is Thy Son, O Most Holy Virgin, shine
with unfading light in the hearts of my children, that they may cry
to God: ALLELUIA!

OIKOS V

HAVING seen my diligent supplication rising like incense to Thy glory, turn not Thy face away from my children, though they turn away from Thee, but all the more, hear the cry of my lips, singing to Thee:

Raise my children to be poor in spirit, that they May inherit
the Kingdom of Heaven.

Raise my children to weep, that they may be comforted.

Raise my children to be meek, that they may inherit
the earth.

Raise my children to hunger and thirst after righteousness,
that they may be filled.

Raise my children to be merciful, that they may
obtain mercy.

Raise my children to be pure in heart, that they may
see God.

Raise my children to be peacemakers, that they may be
called the sons of God.

Raise my children *(names)*, O Lady, to be made worthy of
the Kingdom of Heaven and make them heirs of
eternal blessings.

KONTAKION VI

All we the faithful ever proclaim Thee the defence of orphans, widows and mothers, and of all Thy children who pray and cry unto Thee: ALLELUIA!

OIKOS VI

WITH rays of grace teach my children so that enlightened by Thee on high they may see they path leading to life eternal and follow on it, nourished beneath Thine all-powerful protection in the Church of Thy Son where there is unending light. For the sake of this, hear me who dost cry to Thee thus:

> Raise my children to be the light of the world, that their light may shine before men, and that seeing their good deeds, men will glorify their Father in Heaven.

> Raise my children to be the light of the world, that their light may shine before men, and that seeing their good deeds, men will glorify their Father in Heaven.

> Raise my children to be enlightened by Thy Son, that in His light they may see light and direct their steps towards Him.

> Raise my children always to turn the eyes of their heart to the Redeemer of all.

> Raise my children to be guided to the habitation of the Righteous by the Morning Star which is Thy Son.

> Raise my children to be meek and silent and to tremble before the word of God.

> Raise my children to love Thee and Thy Son not only with their minds but also with their Hearts.

> Raise my children *(names)*, O Lady, to be made worthy of the Kingdom of Heaven and make them heirs of eternal blessings.

KONTAKION VII

DESIRING for my children eternal salvation, with tears I stand before Thy most honourable icon, O Lady, that disdaining not my supplication, thou wilt cry to Thy Son: ALLELUIA!

OIKOS VII

B Y the wondrous and incomprehensible action of Thy Son, lead my children with Thy merciful hand beneath Thy gracious protection, that with sincerity I may cry to Thee:

> Raise my children to seek first the Kingdom of God and
> His Righteousness.

> Raise my children to walk the narrow way leading to
> life eternal.

> Raise my children to do the will of Thy Son and God in
> every place.

> Raise my children to long to inherit the Kingdom of Heaven.

> Raise my children to be numbered among Thy chosen ones.

> Raise my children *(names)*, of Lady, to be made worthy of
> the Kingdom of Heaven and make them heirs of
> eternal blessings.

KONTAKION VIII

W HERE will my children, wandering in the greatly perilous and stormy valley of the world, receive joy and consolation, if not in Thee, O Most Pure One. Travel with them and teach them the true path, that they may cry to God: ALLELUIA!

OIKOS VIII

T O all art Thou a merciful Mother, O Lady, and I desire that I may become Thy child. Thus, I place my children in Thy hands and in humility, I beg of Thee:

> Raise my children to keep vigil and pray that they may not
> fall into temptation.

Raise my children to be merciful so that their Father in
Heaven will be merciful to them.

Raise my children in purity of childhood, for to children
belongs the Kingdom of God.

Raise my children to be the least of all, that they may be great
before God.

Raise my children to fulfil the Word of God, and to be
partakers of the heavenly blessedness for which they
came into being.

Raise my children to have good hope in the Kingdom
of Heaven.

Raise my children *(names)*, O Lady, to be made worthy of
the Kingdom of Heaven and make them heirs of
eternal blessings.

KONTAKION IX

FILL the souls and hearts of my children with all good, driving
away from them the spirit of evil atheism, giving to each of them
as is needed from Thy compassion toward all, that I may cry
unto God: ALLELUIA!

OIKOS IX

DELIVER my children from association with falsely-theorizing orators,
who speak lies about Thine all-powerful intercession, and look
upon me, faithfully singing:

Raise my children to love Thee with all their hearts
and minds.

Raise my children to open their lips only in the praise and
glory of Thy blessings.

Raise my children to await the coming of Thy Son with tears.

Raise my children in watchful and continual prayer.

Raise my children to stand always before Thee
with reverence.

Raise my children to bear good fruit.

Raise my children *(names)*, O Lady, to be made worthy of
the Kingdom of Heaven and make them heirs of
eternal blessings.

KONTAKION X

DESIRING to save the world, Thy Son came from heaven to call, not the righteous, but sinners to repentance. For the sake, of this, pray to Thy Son that having been saved through Thee my children may call unto God: ALLELUIA!

OIKOS X

SURROUND my children with indestructible walls, O Heavenly Queen, that under Thy blessed protection, they may accomplish a multitude of good deeds, and that with them I may cry to Thee thus:

Raise my children to be leaders in doing the will of Thy
Son and God.

Raise my children to hate sin and all transgression.

Raise my children to love good and all virtue.

Raise my children in blameless purity.

Raise my children to ascent the ladder of their lives
every day.

Raise my children to turn their eyes to Thy compassion in
the midst of sorrows.

Raise my children to serve Thee in obedience and chastity.

Raise my children *(names)*, O Lady, to be made worthy of
the Kingdom of Heaven and make them heirs of
eternal blessings.

KONTAKION XI

MAKE my children *(names)* worthy always to hymn Thine unshakable
intercession, and through Thy grace direct their lips to sing
unto God: ALLELUIA!

OIKOS XI

O SHINING lamp from on high, make the lives of my children to burn
and their hearts to melt day and night with love for Thee, and Thy
Son, and for their neighbours, and disdain me not who cry to Thee:

Raise my children to love Thee with all their hearts
and minds.

Raise my children to open their lips only in the praise and
glory of Thy blessings.

Raise my children in watchful and continual Prayer.

Raise my children to stand always before Thee
with reverence.

Raise my children to bear good fruit.

Raise my children *(names)*, O Lady, to be made worthy of
the Kingdom of Heaven and make them heirs of
eternal blessings.

KONTAKION XII

FILL the hearts of my children with the inexpressible grace of the Holy
Spirit, so that they may love only Thy Son and God, and Thee,
O Most Good One, that being inspired by Thee, I may cry to the King
of all: ALLELUIA!

OIKOS XII

SINGING of Thy loving-kindness, I pray Thee, who feeds and hast mercy on my children; cease not to intercede for them with Thy Son, for I believe that all is possible for Thee, and do Thou fulfil these, my entreaties:

Raise my children to be filled with the Holy Spirit.

Raise my children to be found on the right hand at the Judgement Seat of Thy Son.

Raise my children to live in a holy manner.

Raise my children to dwell securely on the path of faith by the grace of the Spirit of God.

Raise my children to hunger and thirst insatiably for the overshadowing of the Holy Spirit.

Raise my children to be perfect as our Father in Heaven is perfect.

Raise my children *(names)*, O Lady, to be made worthy of the Kingdom of Heaven and make them heirs of eternal blessings.

KONTAKION XIII

O ALL-HYMNED Mother of our Sweetest Jesus! Accept this small hymn of supplication for my children as a sweet fragrance and take them under Thy compassionate protection. Grant them to think, know, hear, say, and do, only that which brings them close to Thee and Thy Son, and helps them attain eternal salvation. And send them in this present life all that is profitable for the salvation of their souls, that they may cry to God: ALLELUIA. *(Thrice.)*

And again, Oikos I and Kontakion I are read.

OIKOS I

INTERCEDE with Thy Son and God, O most Holy One, that an angel from heaven be sent to my children, just as to Thee was sent a most mighty protector, the Archangel Gabriel; and vouchsafe me to cry to Thee thus:

> Raise my children to be earthly angels.

> Raise my children to be heavenly men.

> Raise my children to be Thy servants.

> Raise my children to cry out to Thee:

> "Rejoice, O Full of Grace, the Lord is with Thee!"

> Raise my children *(names)*, O Lady, to be made worthy of
> the Kingdom Of Heaven and make them heirs of
> eternal blessings.

KONTAKION I

VICTORIOUS Leader and Good Nurturer of the Christian race, we Thy servants, delivered from evil, sing out grateful thanks to Thee. But as Thou hast invincible might deliver my children from all dangers that with tears I may cry to Thee:

> Raise my children *(names)*, to be made worthy of the
> Kingdom of Heaven, and make them heirs of eternal
> blessings.

PARENTS' PRAYER FOR THEIR CHILDREN

LORD Jesus Christ, Son of God, for the sake of the prayers of Thy Most Pure Mother, hearken unto me, Thine unworthy servant *(name)*, O Lord, govern in mercy my children, Thy servants *(names)*. Have mercy on them and save them, for Thy name's sake.

O LORD, forgive them all their transgressions, voluntary and involuntary, that they may be perfected before Thee. O Lord, set them on the true path of Thy commandments and enlighten their minds with the Light of Christ unto salvation of their souls and the healing of their bodies.

B LESS them, O Lord, at home, at school, in their journeys and in every place of Thy dominion. Preserve and shelter them, O Lord, from flying bullets, arrows, the sword, poison, and fire, from mortal wounds and sudden death. Guard them, O Lord, from all visible and invisible enemies, and from all danger, evil, and misfortune.

H EAL them O Lord, from all sickness, deliver them from every impurity, and lighten their spiritual sufferings. Grant them, O Lord, the grace of Thy Holy Spirit and a long life; grant them health and chastity in all piety and love, and to live in accord with all their neighbours, near and far.

M ULTIPLY and strengthen them, O Lord, in mental ability and bodily strength, given to them by Thee. Bless them to lead a pious life and, if it is pleasing to Thee, grant them married life and honourable childbearing.

F OR Thy name's sake, O Lord, give me, Thy sinful and unworthy servant, a parental blessing for my children and Thy servants, both in this present time, morning, noon and night, and also in Thine eternal, almighty and all-powerful Kingdom.

A MEN. O God, Maker of all creation, Thou hast made me worthy to be the mother/father of a family, and through Thy goodness hast bestowed children upon me; and so I dare to say: these children are Thine, for Thou hast given them being, hast infused them with an immortal soul, and hast raised them to life through baptism.

A ND in accordance with Thy will Thou has adopted them and received them into the bosom of Thy Church. Send down to me

Thy gracious help in raising my children, for the glory of Thy name. Bestow on me patience and strength to do Thy will.

TEACH me to plant in their hearts the root of true wisdom-the fear of the Lord-that all their lives they may tremble at Thy words. Open to them the understanding of Thy law. Until the end of their days let them act with the sense that Thou art everywhere present.

PLANT in their hearts loathing for every transgression, that they may be pure in their signs. O Righteous Judge, who punishes children for their sins, but sprinkle them with the dew of Thy grace.

O HEAVENLY Father, order the fate of my children according to Thy blessings, do not deprive them in this life of their daily bread, send down to them in due time all that is necessary for the acquisition of blessings in eternity.

BE merciful to them, when they sin before Thee; look not upon the sins of their youth and ignorance; chastise them and have mercy on them, but turn not Thy face away from them. Turn not Thy face from them in the day of their tribulation, that they may not fall into temptations beyond their strength.

COVER them with Thy mercy, that Thine Angel may walk with them and preserve them. Abandon not my children, O Lord, and give them that which is profitable for salvation. AMEN.

PRAYER TO THE MOTHER OF GOD

O MOST Holy Lady Virgin Theotokos, do Thou save and preserve under Thy protection my children *(names)*, all youths and infants, baptized and unnamed, and those in their mother's wombs. Cover them with Thy maternal garment; preserve them in the fear of God and in obedience to their parents. Entreat my Lord and Thy Son that He may give them that which is profitable for their salvation. I entrust them to Thy maternal care, for Thou art a Divine protection for Thy servants.

PRAYER TO THE GUARDIAN ANGEL

O HOLY Angel, Guardian of my children (names), keep under Thy protection my children *(names)* from demonic arrows, and from the eyes of the seducer, and preserve their hearts in angelic purity. AMEN, AMEN, AMEN.

PRAYER FOR CHILDREN WHO HAVE DIFFICULTY LEARNING.

O LORD Jesus Christ our God, who didst dwell in the hearts of the Twelve Apostles, and Who, by the power of grace of Thine All Holy Spirit, didst descend in the form of fiery tongues and didst open their lips so that they began to speak in other tongues. This same Lord Jesus Christ our God: Do Thou send down Thy Holy Spirit on Thy child *(name)*, and plant in his (her) heart the Holy Scriptures which Thou, by Thy most pure hand, didst inscribe on tablets and give to the Lawgiver Moses, now and ever and unto ages of ages. AMEN.

PRAYER FOR UNBORN INFANTS

R EMEMBER, O Lord, Lover of Mankind the souls of Thy departed servants, infants who died accidentally in the wombs of Orthodox mothers from unknown cause, either from difficult birth, or from some carelessness and who therefore did not receive the Mystery of Holy Baptism. Baptize them, O Lord, in the sea of Thy compassions, and save them by Thine inexpressible grace. AMEN.

MOST HOLY MOTHER OF GOD, SAVE US!

AKATHIST OF THE FELIXSTOWE ICON OF THE MOTHER OF GOD

KONTAKION I

IN times of old Thy sacred image was honoured in Suffolk's holy land, O Most Pure Maiden Mary and Mother of our God. Then in times of darkness and impiety, Thy holy shrine was taken across the sea. But now as Thou art honoured anew in the town of Thy servant Felix, do Thou intercede for us with Thy Son, Christ our Saviour, that we may cry out to Thee with faith:

> Rejoice; O Lady, Who dost ever comfort and protect those who pray unto Thee with faith!

OIKOS I

ANGELS and men alike marvelled at the grace of the Holy Spirit which came forth from Thy shrine to comfort and protect those oppressed in dark and wicked times. Again, they marvelled as Thou wast taken across the stormy sea to a safe haven in a faraway land. And now we too marvel, for Thou art come again to our shores to comfort and protect us anew in these latter times. Wherefore, we cry out to Thee with faith:

Rejoice; Blessing and Protection of the Isles!

Rejoice; Mother of the Church and Mother of Christians!

Rejoice; Bringer of the faithful to a safe haven!

Rejoice; Consoling of the humble!

Rejoice; Warming of the hearts of the forsaken!

Rejoice; Comforting of the sick and weary!

Rejoice; Grace-bearing Lady, forgiving our foolish ways!

Rejoice; Strengthening of the weak in faith!

Rejoice; Sweetness of the broken-hearted!

Rejoice; Guide of those who have lost the way!

Rejoice; Gatherer of the faithful in the last times!

Rejoice; Thou Who dost make us ready to enter into the Heavenly Jerusalem!

Rejoice; O Lady, Who dost ever comfort and protect those who pray unto Thee with faith!

KONTAKION II

O LADY of the Isles, we have known, we have continually beheld Thy gentle grace and consolation, we confess Thy mild heartedness and know Thy tender love, wherefore we cry out to Thee with faith: ALLELUIA!

OIKOS II

WHO can understand the mind of God? Who can speak of His mysterious blessings? Who is privy to His counsel? For He raiseth up and He casteth down, He humbleth and He exalteth, He afflicteth and He healeth. Therefore, He humbled us on account of our sins and cast down our land, taking away the ancient love of the Orthodox Faith. To whom then shall we flee in our sorrow, to whom then shall we stretch out our hands, if not unto Thee, O All Pure Lady? Wherefore with repentant heart we cry out to Thee with faith:

Rejoice; Thou Who dost intercede with Thy Son for us!

Rejoice; Thou Who dost protect us from righteous wrath!

Rejoice; Thou Who dost cleanse us from our sins!

Rejoice; Thou Who dost intercede for the forgiveness of all!

Rejoice; Thou Who dost lighten the way with hope for us!

Rejoice; Thou Who through Thine Image dost comfort broken hearts!

Rejoice; Thou Who dost gather together the scattered faithful!

Rejoice; Thou Who dost cover all with Thy most Precious Veil!

Rejoice; Thou Who dost quell the divisions and tumults of those who have lost the Faith!

Rejoice; Thou Who dost set at naught the Councils of the ungodly!

Rejoice; Thou Who dost pilot those who sail through the sea of life!

Rejoice; Thou Who in Thy care dost forsake none!

Rejoice; O Lady, Who dost ever comfort and protect those
who pray unto Thee with faith!

KONTAKION III

MIGHTY works have appeared through Thee and grace hath poured
forth, O Most Blessed Virgin, moving all to cry out to Thee with
faith: ALLELUIA!

OIKOS III

AS Thou dost possess love beyond words, O Most Good Lady, Thou
dost make the light of Thy grace to shine forth in the places of
darkness and sorrow. Wherefore Thou hast not forsaken us as orphans,
but through Thine Image Thou hast come to us who glorify Thy mild-
heartedness and cry out to Thee with faith:

Rejoice; Sea of wonders!

Rejoice; Abyss of mercy!

Rejoice; Ever flowing wellspring of grace!

Rejoice; Unquenchable source of healing!

Rejoice; Warmth and comfort of the meek!

Rejoice; Thou Who hast surpassed the laws of nature!

Rejoice; Thou Who dost turn our gloom into bliss!

Rejoice; Thou Who dost change our tears and sorrow into
joy and gladness!

Rejoice; Thou Who dost turn persecution into victory to the
wonder of all!

Rejoice; Thou Who dost defend us who are oppressed!

Rejoice; Thou Who dost put to shame the hopes of
our enemies!

Rejoice; Thou Who dost gladden the hearts of those who
sing unto Thee!

Rejoice; O Lady, Who dost ever comfort and protect those
who pray unto Thee with faith!

KONTAKION IV

IN times of trouble when temptations assail us, when sorrow and pain
visit us, when patience and love fail us, we hasten to Thine Image and
pouring forth our tears before Thee, we cry out from the depths of our
hearts: Stretch out Thy God-bearing hands, speak unto us words of
wisdom, lead us up out of evil, that with thankful hearts we may cry out to
Thee with faith: ALLELUIA!

OIKOS IV

IN times of old the English people heard of Thy glory and hastened to
Thee, crying aloud: How is it that this is granted unto us, that the
Mother of the Lord is come even unto our home at the very ends of the
earth? And beholding Thine Image, O Lady, they began to sing and cry
out to Thee with faith:

Rejoice; O Eden Who gavest birth to the Tree of Life!

Rejoice; O Garden of Paradise Who gavest birth to
the Church!

Rejoice; O blossom Who makest fragrant all England!

Rejoice; O most pure Lily adorning the whole world!

Rejoice; O fruitful vine slaking the thirst of all!

Rejoice; O hallowed bough fruiting for all mankind!

Rejoice; O beloved shade of the Providence of God!

Rejoice; New Eve, giving birth to the salvation of Old Adam!

Rejoice; Thou Who dost cut off the roots of all our
passions!

Rejoice; Thou Who dost sow a garden of virtue!

Rejoice; Thou Who dost plant prayer in our hearts!

Rejoice; Thou Who dost vouchsafe us to partake
of Paradise!

Rejoice; O Lady, Who dost ever comfort and protect those
who pray unto Thee with faith!

KONTAKION V

LIKE unto a star guided by God through the night sky, Thy precious
Image hath returned unto us as of old. In times past the great
and mighty bowed down before Thee, but now it is for us Thy
humble and thankful servants to keep festival and cry out to Thee
with faith: ALLELUIA!

OIKOS V

BEHOLDING the plans of the ungodly to destroy Thine Image, Thou
didst deign to voyage across the sea. Now, coming over the great
ocean, in Orthodox wise Thou art restored to Thy sea-girt Dowry and the
mystery of our story turneth full circle. Wherefore, beholding this
blessing, with fear and love we cry out to Thee with faith:

Rejoice; Invincible fortress of mercy, peace and love!

Rejoice; Unshakeable stronghold of beauty, goodness
and truth!

Rejoice; Thou Who hast put to shame the new Herods who
have no love for Thee!

Rejoice; Thou Who hast rendered vain the schemings of the enemies of the Orthodox Faith!

Rejoice; Thou Who hast stopped the mouths of the blasphemers!

Rejoice; Thou Who hast restored Thine Image to the English land!

Rejoice; Thou Who hast preserved Thine Image undistorted!

Rejoice; Thou Who dost avert Thy gaze from the evil deeds of men!

Rejoice; Thou Who dost not turn away Thy most pure countenance from us sinners!

Rejoice; Thou Who hast escaped the wiles of wicked and foolish men!

Rejoice; Thou Who dost shine forth forgiveness to the repentant!

Rejoice; Thou Who dost open the doors of the Mercy of God to all!

Rejoice; O Lady, Who dost ever comfort and protect those who pray unto Thee with faith!

KONTAKION VI

ALL through the English land the faithful proclaim Thy tender mercy, O Heavenly Queen! For since first Thou didst come unto Thine Isles, we have been saved again and again from the righteous chastisement merited by our manifold sins. Wherefore, as by Thy mercy Thou hast saved us in times past, so do Thou now save us once more, that in thanksgiving we may cry out to Thee with faith: ALLELUIA!

OIKOS VI

SHINE forth upon us the light of hope before the end, O Most Pure Mother of God, Who in Thy birth-giving hast proclaimed the splendour of salvation to the whole universe. Forsake us not to the hands of the Enemy forever, and forgive us the times of unfaithfulness when our forebears were led into error. May the English land once more become Mary's Dowry as of old. May the love of God flower herein in these latter times. May churches and monasteries be raised up once more. May the people, delivered from cruel errors, celebrate with joy and gladness, confessing the Holy Trinity in truth, knowing the Holy Spirit according to the words of the Saviour, and cry out to Thee with faith:

Rejoice; Thou Who dost enlighten all human minds with Thy love!

Rejoice; Thou Who didst adopt mankind at the words of Thy Son!

Rejoice; Mother of God and Mother of Christians!

Rejoice; Thou Who takest away every sickness and healest every disease!

Rejoice; Unweaning comfort of those in captivity!

Rejoice; Unceasing consolation of those in bonds!

Rejoice; Unending protection of those persecuted for righteousness' sake!

Rejoice; Patience of those who suffer for the faith!

Rejoice; Crown of martyrs!

Rejoice; Retribution of tormentors!

Rejoice; Loosing of the bonds of those who are bound!

Rejoice; Freedom of those captive in body and soul!

Rejoice; O Lady, Who dost ever comfort and protect those
who pray unto Thee with faith!

KONTAKION VII

WISHING to admonish those who had forsaken Him, God
the Righteous Judge permitted the English land to fall away from
the Orthodox Faith. The nations of the West were in turmoil, error
abounded for a thousand years, but now the end is not far. All who
set their hope in Thee, O Lady of the Isles, swiftly flee unto Thee,
awaiting the Saviour, Who hath given Thee to the faithful as a sure
and steadfast hope before the end. Wherefore we cry out to Thee
with faith: ALLELUIA!

OIKOS VII

TERRIBLE signs and dread wonders have been shown forth in these
latter days, O Mother of God. The earth hath been filled with
blood, kingdoms have fallen, locusts have filled the airs, fire hath fallen
from the skies, yet the Orthodox Faith hath remained and the Church
returned to us who for long were orphaned. True worship of the Trinity,
true confession of the Spirit and the times and the seasons of the Saints
are kept, the Faith is preached unto all the ends of the earth. Gathering
together the faithful remnant from Thine Island-Dowry and conquering
our enemies, Thou art come anew to Eastern shores, O Queen of all.
Beholding this new wonder, we all pray and with hearts and minds
repenting, we cry out to Thee with faith:

Rejoice; O mighty leader Whose glorious light shineth from
the East to the West!

Rejoice; Thou in Whom all peoples set their hope!

Rejoice; Pillar and confirmation of the Church!

Rejoice; Defence and protection of every shrine!

Rejoice; Victory Who doth vanquish the world!

Rejoice; Thou Who dost save those who had lost hope!

Rejoice; Thou Who dost hearken to heartfelt prayer!

Rejoice; Help of the helpless and Hope of the hopeless!

Rejoice; Thou Who dost trample Satan beneath our feet!

Rejoice; Thou Who dost protect us from enemies!

Rejoice; Thou Who through Thy presence dost
strengthen us!

Rejoice; Thou Who dost shield us beneath Thy
Protecting Veil!

Rejoice; O Lady, Who dost ever comfort and protect those
who pray unto Thee with faith!

KONTAKION VIII

THOU hast revealed a wondrous sight, O Most Holy Virgin, for Thou
dost return to English shores from across the sea. Nigh on one
thousand years have passed and yet the memory of Thee hath not died in
the Isles. May true veneration of Thee here be restored through Thy Son
our Saviour Christ. Beholding the righting of age-old wrong, we receive
Thy mysterious blessing with fear and trembling and in awe, we cry out to
Thee with faith: ALLELUIA!

OIKOS VIII

THOU dost enfold the whole world in the arms of Thy love, O Ever-
Virgin Mary. Thy journey hath been from the East even unto the
West, that all might bow down before Thee in godliness. Wherefore, as
the Light from the East, shine down upon us, forget not Thy Dowry of
old, forsake not Thine Isles and their sinful peoples, O Lady, that from
the depths of repentant souls we may cry out to Thee with faith:

Rejoice; O joy of all joys!

Rejoice; O unending cup of tender love!

Rejoice; O consolation of the latter times!

Rejoice; O sweet delight of the age to come!

Rejoice; Thou Who dost mercifully look down from heaven
       unto earth!

Rejoice; Thou Who dost forsake the joys of heaven for
       our salvation!

Rejoice; Thou Who dost enter with grace into the hearts
       of all!

Rejoice; Bringer of blessings and secret hopes!

Rejoice; Thou Who dost hallow our hearts with
       Thine Image!

Rejoice; Thou Who dost make the homes of the poor more
       splendid than royal palaces!

Rejoice; Thou Who dost make glorious the churches of
       God with thy lowly countenance!

Rejoice; Thou Who dost dwell in the homes and hearts of all
       who honour Thee!

Rejoice; O Lady, Who dost ever comfort and protect those
       who pray unto Thee with faith!

KONTAKION IX

PEOPLE of every age and position hasten unto Thee, O Bride of God, Whose hands once held God but now hold us instead. Thou dost enlighten and console all, warming the broken-hearted in Thy God-bearing hands, O Queen of Heaven. Wherefore, making glad, we cry out to Thee with faith: ALLELUIA!

OIKOS IX

THE eloquence of men is thwarted; their flowing streams of words run dry, for they are powerless to find words to praise Thee, O Virgin Mary, for no mouth can praise Thee as is meet. Yet, should we altogether fall silent, the very stones of the earth will cry out in praise of Thee. Wherefore, unworthy though we are, our earthen lips cry out to Thee with faith:

Rejoice; Inspired sayings of the Apostles!

Rejoice; Heartfelt songs of the Martyrs!

Rejoice; Words of fire uttered by the Prophets!

Rejoice; Golden speech of the Fathers of the Church!

Rejoice; Bold confession of righteous Priests of Christ!

Rejoice; Mystic strength of unceasing prayer of the Saints!

Rejoice; Reward of those who struggle against the passions!

Rejoice; Indomitable protection of the persecuted!

Rejoice; Rest of the aged and guide of the young!

Rejoice; Glory of mothers and boast of maidens!

Rejoice; O Daughter of Adam and Mother of our God!

Rejoice; Thou Who dost shine with the glory of which
          words cannot speak!

Rejoice; O Lady, Who dost ever comfort and protect those
          who pray unto Thee with faith!

KONTAKION X

O MOST Holy Mother of God, we call upon Thee again, pray that the world may yet be saved. The plots and snares of the Evil One are spread over all the face of the earth, the nations rage and storms of worldly temptations rise up against the Church of God, though She will prevail even against the gates of Hell. Wherefore, as of old in Cana of Galilee, only say a word to Thy Son and our God, that He may change the water of temptation and human sorrow into the wine of repentance and divine gladness, that we may unceasingly cry out to Thee with faith: ALLELUIA!

OIKOS X

O MOST Holy Bearer of God, be Thou for us an invincible rampart against the legions of enemies, seen and unseen, who so sorely persecute us. Fight staunchly and unfailingly for us, who cry out to Thee with faith:

Rejoice; Thou Who dost stretch out Thy God-bearing hands to us!

Rejoice; Thou Who dost trample the spirits of malice beneath our feet!

Rejoice; Thou Who dost put to shame the plans of the demons, carried out by deluded men!

Rejoice; Thou Who dost make evil to flee away at the thought of God!

Rejoice; Thou Who dost drive the illusions of despair from us!

Rejoice; Thou Who dost still the surging sea of life!

Rejoice; Thou Who dost command the storms of temptation to cease!

Rejoice; Thou Who dost pilot the tempest-tossed!

Rejoice; Thou Who dost deliver us from the depths of sorrow!

Rejoice; Thou Who dost stretch forth Thy hands to those
who perish!

Rejoice; Thou Who dost set our feet upon the path
of salvation!

Rejoice; Thou Who dost strengthen our hearts for battle!

Rejoice; O Lady, Who dost ever comfort and protect those
who pray unto Thee with faith!

KONTAKION XI

As Thy Son accepted the widow's mite, do Thou also accept our song,
O All-Holy Lady, and grant that we may ever offer up our prayers
unto Thee, Who dost guide our life through the shadows of this world.
Grant us forgiveness of our sins, that we may enter into the Kingdom of
Heaven and cry out to Thee with faith: ALLELUIA!

OIKOS XI

STRETCH out Thy Protecting Veil over all the earth, O Most Good
Lady. Shine forth like the full moon in the dark night of ungodliness
and blasphemy. Enlighten our Isles once more with the splendour of
Thy purity, that our voices may rise up once more and cry out to
Thee with faith:

Rejoice; Thou Who art in truth clothed with the Sun!

Rejoice; Thou Who art crowned with the Stars!

Rejoice; Thou Who art adorned with raiment woven
with gold!

Rejoice; Beauty resplendent beyond all speech to tell!

Rejoice; Brightness fairer than the morning star!

Rejoice; Warmth dearer than the Sun!

Rejoice; Ray of hope from the age to come!

Rejoice; Unfading light of angels and men!

Rejoice; Sunrise driving away the demon hordes of the night!

Rejoice; Thou Who dost enlighten the darkness of unbelief!

Rejoice; Thou Who dost clothe with the armour of light!

Rejoice; Thou Who art scented with the fragrance of virtue!

Rejoice; O Lady, Who dost ever comfort and protect those
who pray unto Thee with faith!

KONTAKION XII

G RACE upon grace we have received through Thee, O Most Pure
Maiden Mary. Those who call upon Thee with faith go not empty
away, for all receive the gift of God according unto their need and are
crowned with joy. Wherefore we cry out to Thee with faith: ALLELUIA!

OIKOS XII

W E hymn Thee, we magnify Thee, we bow down before Thee,
O Most Pure Lady. Unable to praise Thee, as is meet, we
fall down before Thy precious Image, and in repentance, we cry out to
Thee with faith:

Rejoice; Sweet dawn of our souls!

Rejoice; Bright daybreak of our hearts!

Rejoice; Blessed morning of our lives!

Rejoice; Height beyond our understanding!

Rejoice; Unfading glory!

Rejoice; Unceasing bliss!

Rejoice; Unending goodness!

Rejoice; Gladness beyond words!

Rejoice; Thou Who alone art truly Blessed!

Rejoice; Thou Who art exalted above all Creation!

Rejoice; Thou Who art with the faithful at the hour of death!

Rejoice; Thou Who even at the Dread Judgement dost save
those who hope in Thee!

Rejoice; O Lady, Who dost ever comfort and protect those
who pray unto Thee with faith!

KONTAKION XIII

O LADY praised by all, Mother of the Church and all Christians, emulating Thy Son and our Saviour in Thy tender mercy, Thou dost cry unto us: Fear not, little flock! I am with you and none is against you! Wherefore, falling down before Thee with love and giving thanks with tears, we cry out to Thee with faith: Alleluia! *(Thrice.)*

And again, Oikos I and Kontakion I are read.

OIKOS I

A NGELS and men alike marvelled at the grace of the Holy Spirit which came forth from Thy shrine to comfort and protect those oppressed in dark and wicked times. Again, they marvelled as Thou wast taken across the stormy sea to a safe haven in a faraway land. And now we too marvel, for Thou art come again to our shores to comfort and protect us anew in these latter times. Wherefore, we cry out to Thee with faith:

Rejoice; Blessing and Protection of the Isles!

Rejoice; Mother of the Church and Mother of Christians!

Rejoice; Bringer of the faithful to a safe haven!

Rejoice; Consoling of the humble!

Rejoice; Warming of the hearts of the forsaken!

Rejoice; Comforting of the sick and weary!

Rejoice; Grace-bearing Lady, forgiving our foolish ways!

Rejoice; Strengthening of the weak in faith!

Rejoice; Sweetness of the broken-hearted!

Rejoice; Guide of those who have lost the way!

Rejoice; Gatherer of the faithful in the last times!

Rejoice; Thou Who dost make us ready to enter into the
Heavenly Jerusalem!

Rejoice; O Lady, Who dost ever comfort and protect those
who pray unto Thee with faith!

KONTAKION I

IN times of old Thy sacred image was honoured in Suffolk's holy land,
O Most Pure Maiden Mary and Mother of our God. Then in times of
darkness and impiety, Thy holy shrine was taken across the sea. But now
as Thou art honoured anew in the town of Thy servant Felix, do Thou
intercede for us with Thy Son, Christ our Saviour, that we may cry out to
Thee with faith:

Rejoice; O Lady, Who dost ever comfort and protect those
who pray unto Thee with faith!

PRAYER TO THE MOST HOLY MOTHER OF GOD

O MOST Holy Maiden Mary and Mother of our God, Lady of the
Isles, our sure hope and calm haven, blessing of our lives, joy of
those who grieve, healing of the sick, wisdom of the darkened, reward of
the wronged, Thou seest our misfortune, Thou seest our sorrow, help us

for we are weak, guide us for we wander, Thou knowest our sins, may they be forgiven as the Lord deigneth. Deliver our land from its errors, restore the Orthodox Faith to Thine Isles and Thy peoples, and make us once more to be Thy Dowry. Save and preserve Thy servants *(Names)* and all of us here present who pray unto Thee with tears. Comfort and protect us beneath Thy Precious Veil, for we have none other than Thee, O Bearer of God, to comfort and protect us unto the ages of ages. AMEN.

AKATHIST TO THE CHINESE MARTYR SAINTS OF THE BOXER REBELLION

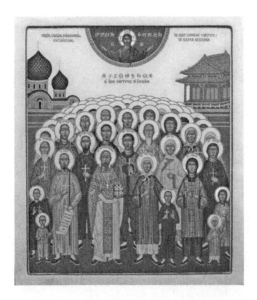

KONTAKION I

THE divine Metrophanes, the martyred shepherd, with his great and faithful flock, have hallowed China with their blood; wherefore we praise them with sacred hymns, for they were faithful to Christ even unto death.

Rejoice; O stars of the Orient!

OIKOS I

THY holy martyrs O Lord did not see earthly glory as a treasure to be held, but facing the torments of men and the wisdom of demons humbled themselves for Thy sake, even unto death. Wherefore, O

Righteous Father, as through them Thou brought the priceless pearl to an unbaptized land, grant us Thy Spirit and great mercy for our souls. Rejoice, O stars of the Orient. As a new Herod, the hand of the Boxers fell on the infants of the Church, writing on the doorpost of each soul the mark of the Lamb in the blood of the lambs, sealing them for the new Passover, that all might cry aloud:

> Rejoice; ye righteous ones, tearing down the banner of worldliness!

> Rejoice; ye abandoners of the kingdom that passeth away!

> Rejoice; ye resistors of the legions of Hades!

> Rejoice; ye swords in the Hand of the Righteous God!

> Rejoice; ye lanterns of the Holy Spirit!

> Rejoice; ye who drench the demonic flame with the waters of baptism!

> Rejoice; ye celebrants of the new Passover!

> Rejoice; ye children of the new Israel!

> Rejoice; ye pearls of greatest price!

> Rejoice; ye jade diadems in the treasury of God!

> Rejoice; ye jewelled gates of the heavenly Jerusalem!

> Rejoice; ye loyal subjects of the true Celestial court!

> Rejoice; O stars of the Orient!

KONTAKION II

HOLY Isaiah didst foretell: A shoot shall come forth from the root of Jesse, and thereby the earth shall be full of the knowledge of the

Lord. Wherefore, O Lord, do we praise Thee, for Thou hast in truth kept the fullness of Thy word, filling the earth with knowledge of Thee that we may cry: ALLELUIA!

OIKOS II

As the new Bethlehem in the land of Manchuria, not least amongst the rulers of the present world, while last in obtaining the baptism of remission of sins, art first in witness to the eastern lands, for out of you came forth a flock who would lay down their lives like their Shepherd, crying:

Rejoice; O heirs of the household of the blessed prince of Chan-Timur!

Rejoice; O blood brothers of the martyrs of K'ang Chi!

Rejoice; O spiritual descendants of Beijing's prisoners for Christ!

Rejoice; O new tribe of the New Israel!

Rejoice; O least of all nations and last baptized!

Rejoice; O great star of the eastern sky!

Rejoice; O children of the land of silken majesty robed in Majesty!

Rejoice; O new Damascus road, illumination of the silk roads!

Rejoice; O light in the darkness which darkness cannot consume!

Rejoice; O witnesses of the Light!

Rejoice; O voices of the eastern wilderness!

Rejoice; O voices crying, "Prepare ye the way of the Lord!"

Rejoice; O stars of the Orient!

KONTAKION III

O UR Lord Christ warned that the impious shall cast out the faithful, speaking of these things that we should not stumble; calling the faithful to the knowledge that the infidel shall think in his butchery he offers service to God. Wherefore, O Father, hearken to us in our struggle, and enlighten us with Thy Truth as we sing to Thee: ALLELUIA!

OIKOS III

T HE prophets declared Thy suffering, O Christ, and Thou camest being incarnate of the Theotokos, reflecting the Image of God fully in the image of man, that we may grow to the fullness of Thy Likeness, wherefore as Thy martyrs do share in Thy sufferings, they too share in Thy Likeness that we may proclaim:

Rejoice; ye whom human might couldst not persuade!

Rejoice; ye for whom the might of Christ was thy defence!

Rejoice; ye who overturned the censer of idolatry!

Rejoice; ye who yearned for the incense of the Heavenly Realm!

Rejoice; ye who are trod underfoot by the legions of men!

Rejoice; ye who lay down life for the sake of your
      Brother, Christ!

Rejoice; ye who scatter the lots of the idols of fortune!

Rejoice; ye heirs of the Heavenly Fortune!

Rejoice; O ye merciful and meek of soul!

Rejoice; O ye righteous and pure of heart!

Rejoice; ye who are persecuted for righteousness' sake!

Rejoice; and be exceedingly glad, for great is your reward in
the heavens!

Rejoice; O stars of the Orient!

KONTAKION IV

THE Lord saith unto the scornful Jews: Destroy this temple and in
three days I will raise it up. And so hath the Lord done unto the
temples of the bodies of His martyrs as He saith, that we might cry unto
Him: ALLELUIA!

OIKOS IV

TOGETHER in an unbaptized land, you built a temple to God with
holy hands, but when faced with the flames of the demon's host, you
chose Life in the temple not made with hands, putting to death the things
of the body, putting on life according to the Spirit that we may say:

Rejoice; O lambs of the eastern Zion!

Rejoice; oblations of Christ's shrine in the east!

Rejoice; ye who preached the Word in a new tongue!

Rejoice; ye whose holy books hallowed the pagans' fire!

Rejoice; ye who raised a Temple to Christ as new children
of Solomon!

Rejoice; ye sanctifiers of the pagan temple shrine!

Rejoice; thrice-blessed children of the holy fire!

Rejoice; confessors who walk in the flame of death with the
Flame of Life!

Rejoice; ye who repent in burning sackcloth and ashes!

Rejoice; ye who are mingled with the ashes of Christ's
holy temple!

Rejoice; O sacrifices who scorned sacrifice to the new Baal!

Rejoice; O carriers of the Holy Flame!

Rejoice; O stars of the Orient!

KONTAKION V

THE priests of Baal doth conspire against the Lord's anointed, revelling in the strength of their throng, but doused in the waters of the Redeeming God, the wood of the sacrifice dost burst forth with holy flame, scattering the wicked hosts that we might praise the Lord our God, and sing unto Him: ALLELUIA!

OIKOS V

TEACHER and shepherd, our holy father Mitrophan, alone amongst his people as a priest of the Lord, called by the enemy to exceed the fire of their hate with the fire of faith, O thou who hallowest thy name Tsz Chung, unto thee do we cry:

Rejoice; ye of poor talent and little virtue whom God hath
made great!

Rejoice; ye disciple of Nicholas the Enlightener!

Rejoice; ye witness of Christ's crowning of thy native land!

Rejoice; ye witness of the crowning in glory of thy wife
and sons!

Rejoice; O pillar of faith amidst the blows of the faithless!

Rejoice; O last-standing pillar of Christ's temple in Harbin!

Rejoice; O hallowed martyr of Christ who fell beneath the
date tree!

Rejoice; O hallowed martyr hung faithfully on the Tree
of Life!

Rejoice; O lonely priest of God who sat beneath the broom
tree, yet without despair!

Rejoice; O Mitrophan, arise and eat the Bread of Life!

Rejoice; O wind, storm, and fire that touchest not God's
holy one!

Rejoice; O still small voice of the Spirit of God!

Rejoice; O star of the Orient!

KONTAKION VI

IN the abasement of themselves with fasting, sackcloth, and ashes, the
race of Ninevites didst turn back the wrath of God; and like unto them
didst the kinsmen of Esther repent, trusting not in their own righteousness,
but rather in the mercies of God towards those who honour Him,
therefore let us sing to Him: ALLELUIA!

OIKOS VI

ESTHER beheld the plotting of the unrighteous Haman, and although
his wicked schemes were set to destroy the sons of Israel, the
children of the Lord humbled themselves before Him, granting them
deliverance from certain death. Wherefore do we praise Tatiana, the
Esther of the east, who by humility of martyrdom stole Life from the hand
of death, that her soul might be saved and that we might cry:

Rejoice; O Li, who by meekness were exalted!

Rejoice; O Tatiana, name-bearer of her sister martyr
in Christ!

Rejoice; O Eastern Esther, loyal friend of thy people!

Rejoice; O Tatiana, loyal wife of Mitrophan, and true
daughter of Christ!

Rejoice; Precious mother of the flock at Harbin!

Rejoice; Precious name in the prayers of the Mother
of God!

Rejoice; Loving-kindness written in the red of thy blood!

Rejoice; Christian witness written in the stripes of thy pain!

Rejoice; Blossom of strength, boast of womanhood!

Rejoice; One in flesh with thy husband, one in witness with
thy cross!

Rejoice; O mother-martyr of thy people!

Rejoice; O daughter of Christ our God!

Rejoice; O star of the Orient!

KONTAKION VII

RIGHTEOUS Gideon wondered at the word of the Lord, trusting with Israel in his own hand; but lessening their strength with the judgement of the water, the Lord made greater His victory in judgement over Midian. Let us now as the servants of God place all our hopes, in the Strength beyond strength and cry: ALLELUIA!

OIKOS VII

AS a new-born Theodore, fresh from the waters of baptism as a gift of God, standing before thine emperor, called by thy rank to sacrifice, thou disdained the incense and instead washed clean thy land with the baptism of thy blood. Unto thee O soldier of Christ do we cry:

Rejoice; O brother of George, Demetrius, and Theodore!

Rejoice; O soldier in the army of the righteous!

Rejoice; O defender of the maiden Mother of God!

Rejoice; O victor of martyrdom!

Rejoice; O vanquisher of the wicked serpent of Death!

Rejoice; O husbandman of the phoenix of Eternal Life!

Rejoice; O son of the proud and holy father!

Rejoice; O child of the Joyful and All-Holy Spirit!

Rejoice; O champion of the Eternal Son!

Rejoice; O pride of the land of the eastern sun!

Rejoice; O Isaiah, who hath borne grief and sorrows!

Rejoice; O thou who by Christ's stripes hath been healed!

Rejoice; O star of the Orient!

KONTAKION VIII

DECLARING with courage her willingness to suffer all the abasement of her Saviour Christ, holy Maria was wounded thus on hand and foot, bearing the marks of Christ on her very body. So as she found true birth in baptism in the place named for the Mother of God, in a like fashion was she born unto Life by the prayers of the Theotokos, crying: ALLELUIA!

OIKOS VIII

AS the blessed Maria hurried to enter the house of her Lord, the very temple named for the Mother of her God, her heart leapt within her, and filled with the Spirit, she declared Christ with a loud cry, that we all might declare:

Rejoice; thou namesake of the Mother of God!

Rejoice; thou whose heart leapt at the sound of the Name of thy Lord!

Rejoice; thou chrysanthemum of the new Eden!

Rejoice; thou lotus blossom that blossomed unto Life!

Rejoice; thou who camest early to declare the Risen Lord!

Rejoice; thou who will share His empty tomb at the
Last Day!

Rejoice; thou who seeketh Life in death!

Rejoice; thou who declarest the Truth to those who would
not believe!

Rejoice; thou who at once denied the idols of thy people!

Rejoice; thou who thrice denied liberty from Eternal Liberty!

Rejoice; thou newly freeborn of an enslaved land!

Rejoice; thou Maria of the eastern Egypt!

Rejoice; O star of the Orient!

KONTAKION IX

THE LORD bestowed His Strength to Israel through the child David, and called Israel to humility through the mouth of the shepherd of Tekoa. As it was as a babe that Our Lord vanquished the legions of Death, let us recall with awe the mystery of the Lord's mightiness in Harbin, for here too doth the Lord manifest His strength in weakness, wherefore let us be instructed by the life of John as we sing: ALLELUIA!

OIKOS IX

THE LORD called the Twelve together and declared: He who desirest to be first must be last of all. Then taking in His arms a faithful child, He called those assembled to receive one as this, for he who receiveth such receives not simply the Son, but the Father in Heaven Who sent Him. Wherefore we recall John, a child, like unto this, who wast received unto the Lord with manly strength, that we who honour him should cry:

Rejoice; O child of God, the least of all!

Rejoice; O innocent one, first in God's sight!

Rejoice; O meek one, reviled by demons as a demon!

Rejoice; O small one, glorified by God as a champion
of Christ!

Rejoice; O lamb, dishonoured by a thousand cuts!

Rejoice; O lion, honoured by thousands in the heavenly
throng!

Rejoice; O thirsting one, denied refreshment by thy
neighbours!

Rejoice; O little one, refreshed by the Water springing up
unto salvation!

Rejoice; O young one, youngest of the martyrs of Harbin!

Rejoice; O faithful one, who by grace feelest not pain!

Rejoice; O bold one, holy confessor of Christ!

Rejoice; O victorious one, vanquisher of a thousand
demons!

Rejoice; O star of the Orient!

KONTAKION X

B Y GOD'S grace Sarah begot many nations by Abraham, and Elizabeth
and Zachariah bore the Forerunner of Christ. Let us also praise the
Lord for righteous Ia and holy Paul, who begot eternal life by their
martyrdom and prayers and let us sing: ALLELUIA!

OIKOS X

ANANIAS and Sapphira testified their love for Mammon, wherefore they tasted the singular sting of death; but Christ was the testimony of holy Paul and righteous Ia, for he didst die with the Lord's name on his lips, and she didst suffer martyrdom a second time. So holy Peter declares to them, "How dost the Spirit of the Lord test you?"; and we the faithful do sing in solemn reply:

Rejoice; O blessed Paul, faithful martyr of Christ!

Rejoice; twice-blessed Ia, faithful teacher of the flock!

Rejoice; goodly servant, ever-faithful unto death!

Rejoice; noble sharer in the Passion of the Lord!

Rejoice; holy Paul, boast of all the Seraphim!

Rejoice; righteous Ia, bright companion of the Cherubim!

Rejoice; humble servant, archetype of piety!

Rejoice; noble teacher, instructor in the ways of purity!

Rejoice; friend of Stephen, O lamb led unto slaughter!

Rejoice; friend of Catherine, out-witter of philosophers!

Rejoice; holy servant of the house of sacred martyrs!

Rejoice; holy bride, exemplar of steadfastness!

Rejoice; O stars of the Orient!

KONTAKION XI

THRICE-HOLY is the cry of the multitude, the heavenly host around the Heavenly Throne, let us in hope therefore join the angels' song, and chant the thrice-holy: ALLELUIA!

OIKOS XI

THE righteous Maccabees withstood with godly strength the threats of the pagan legions, and foresaw the Holy Cross as a balance testing the righteous, weighing the righteousness of God with the boasts of the world, offering the choice to all between life and Eternal Life. Wherefore do we sing to the martyrs of the east, who wisely chose the eternal prize:

Rejoice; O Kui-Kin, new Clement of Asia!

Rejoice; O Hai Chuan, baptized in blood Matthew!

Rejoice; Holy Sergius, blessed son of Tsz Chung!

Rejoice; Holy servant of the priesthood of Christ!

Rejoice; Holy Anna, friend of mothers and widows!

Rejoice; Holy children, inheritors of a heavenly birthright!

Rejoice; Holy nameless one, known only unto God!

Rejoice; ye unburied, buried with Christ that ye may rise!

Rejoice; ye defiled of pagans, washed clean in the Blood of the Lamb!

Rejoice; ye suffering witnesses of numberless sufferings!

Rejoice; ye blessed, who escaping death held firm in faith!

Rejoice; O ye martyrs of Christ in the east!

Rejoice; O stars of the Orient!

KONTAKION XII

THE holy Apostle saw a great wonder: for it was in a vision, as if in a dream. Behold, here stands a new heaven, and a new earth, for the first heaven and earth are passing away. Wherefore, the Lord saith He shall make all things new. Let us therefore cry unto Him: ALLELUIA!

OIKOS XII

THE LORD foresaw the tribulation of the martyrs, whom He said would be hated by all nations for His own sake, and exhorted that those who endured to the end that they would be saved. Wherefore let us preach unto all nations the gospel of the kingdom at the end of the age, that we the faithful might shout with joy with God's holy elect:

Rejoice; O dawn of the final days!

Rejoice; O first fruits of the great age of martyrs!

Rejoice; O witnesses of Christ against idolatry!

Rejoice; O confessors of the God-man in the age of godlessness!

Rejoice; O citizens of the Kingdom to come!

Rejoice; O strangers in a strange land!

Rejoice; O confessors of Christ crucified!

Rejoice; O declarers of foolishness to the Greeks!

Rejoice; O advocates who are stumbling blocks to Jews!

Rejoice; O out-witters of the philosophers of the east!

Rejoice; O righteous company of saints!

Rejoice; O blessed host of new martyrs of China!

Rejoice; O stars of the Orient!

KONTAKION XIII

THE LORD saith: A little while and you will weep and mourn, yet the impious world shall rejoice. You the faithful will all be sorrowful, yet your sorrow shall be turned to rejoicing. Wherefore, O Righteous Father, let us rejoice in Thee as we cry: ALLELUIA!

This Kontakion is said thrice;
then the first Oikos is recited once again:

As a new Herod the hand of the Boxers fell on the infants of the Church, writing on the doorpost of each soul the mark of the Lamb in the blood of the lambs, sealing them for the new Passover, that all might cry aloud:

Rejoice; ye righteous ones, tearing down the banner of worldliness!

Rejoice; ye abandoners of the kingdom that passeth away!

Rejoice; ye resistors of the legions of Hades!

Rejoice; ye swords in the Hand of the Righteous God!

Rejoice; ye lanterns of the Holy Spirit!

Rejoice; ye who drench the demonic flame with the waters of baptism!

Rejoice; ye celebrants of the new Passover!

Rejoice; ye children of the new Israel!

Rejoice; ye pearls of greatest price!

Rejoice; ye jade diadems in the treasury of God!

Rejoice; ye jewelled gates of the heavenly Jerusalem!

Rejoice; ye loyal subjects of the true Celestial court!

Rejoice; O stars of the Orient!

AKATHIST TO THE HOLY MARTYRED NUN ELIZABETH AND THE OTHER NEW MARTYRS OF ALAPAYEVSK

KONTAKION I

Come, all ye who love Christ, and let us offer up a hymn of praise unto the martyred nun Elizabeth, who was chosen by the Lord of hosts to serve as an example of Christian piety and love for those who desire to follow in His steps. For, spurning the vanity of worldly possessions, rank and cares, she dedicated her whole life to the aid of those in need. Wherefore, it hath pleased Christ our God to crown her ascetic labours with the diadem of martyrdom; and, dwelling now in His heavenly kingdom, she maketh supplication unto God, that He deliver from misfortunes and perils all who chant unto her with joy:

Rejoice; O venerable martyr Elizabeth, true model of
Christian sacrifice!

OIKOS I

THE Creator of the angels and Lord of mankind led thee from the
delusion of heresy to the divine knowledge of the Truth, O blessed
Elizabeth, that thy loving heart and soul might renew Christian love, which
had grown cold in the land of Russia: for through thine efforts the hearts
of men again warmed to the word of God, and the Master of all
vouchsafed thee to live a life exalted above thy peers, in love, humility and
fervent prayer. Wherefore, we ever chant unto thee, as is meet:

Rejoice; lamb burning with the love of God!

Rejoice; handmaid of Christ the Lord!

Rejoice; scroll whereon the Holy Spirit inscribed the
Christian virtues!

Rejoice; divinely wise princess and new martyr!

Rejoice; daughter who forsook thy father's house and turned to
Holy Orthodoxy!

Rejoice; vessel wherein the wine of gladness and the oil of
healing are mingled together!

Rejoice; upholder of the traditions of piety!

Rejoice; treasure-house of compassion!

Rejoice; radiant star resplendent with heavenly glory!

Rejoice; O venerable martyr Elizabeth, true model of
Christian sacrifice!

KONTAKION II

CHRIST found thee a lily among thorns and chose thee to adorn His garden of Holy Orthodoxy, O venerable one: for he Who alone knoweth the hearts of men perceived from on high thy great love for thy neighbour, and bestowed upon thee a wealth of spiritual gifts, that we might come to understand the mystery of God's great mercy, enabling us to take part with thee therein and to join chorus with thee in chanting unto Him: Alleluia!

OIKOS II

KNOWING in thy heart that God's will ruleth over all creation, and seeking to obey His will alone, thou was well pleased to shoulder the great cross which He prepared for thee, O holy one: for when thou didst witness the cruel and pitiless slaughter of thy husband, thy heart was pierced with grief and sorrow, as with a two-edged sword; yet thou didst take courage, and uttered the Saviour's own words: "Father, forgive them, for they know not what they do." And seeking to turn this vile deed to goodness, thou didst beseech him who committed the murder to repent. And we too beg thine intercession before the Lord, that He avert His righteous anger from us who chant to thee such praises as these:

Rejoice; thou who didst deem mercy greater than sacrifice!

Rejoice; thou who prayest for sinners and penitents!

Rejoice; thou who didst bear thy cross to a new Golgotha!

Rejoice; thou who didst not reject the crown of thorns
offered thee!

Rejoice; thou didst put jealously to flight!

Rejoice; thou who reprovest those who fall away from truth
and grace!

Rejoice; thou who didst not set the love of family above the
love of God!

Rejoice; thou who didst fulfil the words of Christ!

Rejoice; thou who didst seek out the good in every man!

Rejoice; thou who was sent unto Russia, to turn her away
from evil to the good!

Rejoice; thou who dost ever cry out to Christ: Lord, have
mercy!

Rejoice; thou who standest invisible in our midst as we pray!

Rejoice; O venerable martyr Elizabeth, true model of
Christian sacrifice!

KONTAKION III

THE power of the Most High overshadowed thy sorrow and pain, O
royal passion-bearer, and finding sweet consolation therein thou
didst die to this world, that thou mightest live in Christ: thou didst shun the
fleeting pleasures and vanities of this life, didst clothe thyself in garments
of joy and salvation, and didst abide in palaces, praying and chanting to
God therein: ALLELUIA!

OIKOS III

WITH a fervent desire to serve thy fellow man, thou didst gather a
multitude of souls to labour for God; and, raising up a house of
mercy, which thou didst dedicate to the Protection of the all-holy
Theotokos, O holy Elizabeth, thou didst choose our holy mothers Martha
and Mary as the heavenly patrons, emulating them as paragons of piety
and good works. And mindful of the magnitude of thy charitable deeds
and Christian virtues, we praise thy memory, chanting thus:

Rejoice; thou who didst open thy heart to good deeds!

Rejoice; thou who didst gather the virtues into a spiritual
sheaf!

Rejoice; thou who hast been reckoned among the friends
of Christ!

Rejoice; thou who didst hearken to His words!

Rejoice; thou who dost ever rejoice in thy Lord!

Rejoice; thou who fillest our hearts with joy when we call
upon thy name!

Rejoice; thou who rewardest those who seek thy
heavenly aid!

Rejoice; thou who dost speedily fulfil the requests of those
who have recourse to thee with faith!

Rejoice; thou who has adorned the city of Moscow!

Rejoice; obedient handmaid of the holy Mary and Martha!

Rejoice; thou who didst hide thy good works from the eyes
of the haughty!

Rejoice; thou who dost call all of us to perform deeds
of mercy!

Rejoice; O venerable martyr Elizabeth, true model of
Christian sacrifice!

KONTAKION IV

THOSE who were tempest-tossed amid the tumults of life and
foundered upon the floods of the passions didst thou guide to
the calm haven of salvation which thou didst establish in the royal
city of Moscow, O holy Elizabeth; for having opened thy heart unto
God, thou didst open its doors to the children of God, showing them
the mercy of their heavenly Father.   Wherefore, thou hast now

been shown to be the patroness of the forgotten and oppressed. Cover us all with thy holy protection, that we may be moved to cry aloud to our good God: ALLELUIA!

OIKOS IV

ACCEPTING the counsel of the elders of the Hermitage of Saint Zosimas, thou didst prove thyself to be an obedient daughter of the Orthodox Faith, O venerable martyr, so that thine own words brought profit and consolation to all who hearkened unto thee. Thou wast a most wise abbess and a loving mother, who tended well the flock entrusted to thee, teaching them how to care for the afflicted as a sister of mercy by thine own example, O holy princess. Wherefore, tend thou also the ailments of our souls, that we may cry aloud unto thee:

Rejoice; thou who anointest all with the oil of mercy!

Rejoice; thou who stillest the tempest of sorrows!

Rejoice; instruction of those who turn to Orthodoxy!

Rejoice; pillar of truth set firmly upon the rock of the Faith!

Rejoice; thou who dost rescue us from the mire
of despondency!

Rejoice; thou who feedest the orphan and the widow!

Rejoice; thou who didst embrace charity with thy
whole heart!

Rejoice; thou who didst exchange a palace for a poor and
humble cell!

Rejoice; thou who didst put aside thy royal robes to don the
hair shirt of asceticism!

Rejoice; thou who didst lay thy princely coronet at the feet
of the Saviour!

Rejoice; thou who didst take up the Cross as a kingly
sceptre!

Rejoice; thou who didst love God more than earthly honour
and glory!

Rejoice; O venerable martyr Elizabeth, true model of
Christian sacrifice!

KONTAKION V

THOU hast been revealed to us as a most radiant star adorning the
vault of the firmament of the Church, O martyr of Christ. And
ever illumined by the effulgence of thy sufferings, unto Christ, the Judge
of the contest, do we offer hymnody of thanksgiving for thee, and we
chant unto Him: ALLELUIA!

OIKOS V

THROUGH the guidance of the heavenly intercessors who shone forth
in Russia — the venerable Sergius of Radonezh, and Peter, the
divinely eloquent Metropolitan of Moscow, in company with Martha and
Mary, the sisters beloved of Christ — the narrow and royal path which
alone leadeth to salvation was disclosed to thee, and travelling it thou
becamest a model for all Orthodox Christians dwelling in the Russian
Empire, showing them how to unite the ideals of ascetic endeavour and
charitable acts. Wherefore, for thee grace was added unto grace, and
whilst thou wast yet alive, the report of thy holiness spread far and wide.
The pious cried out in wonder to God Who is wondrous in His saints:
"Glory be to Thee, O Lord!" and to thee they uttered such praises as
these:

Rejoice; scion of a royal house who tended the sores of
paupers with thine own hands!

Rejoice; paragon of monastic virtue and rule of faith!

Rejoice; thou who didst reject worldly praise and hast
received heavenly rewards!

Rejoice; thou who dost partake of everlasting splendour
on high!

Rejoice; thou who didst expose spiritual deception!

Rejoice; thou who didst strengthen the common folk in the
true Faith!

Rejoice; thou who dost ever summon the faithful to prayer
and vigilance!

Rejoice; thou who didst adopt the Russian nation as
thy homeland!

Rejoice; thou who didst spurn the praises of men!

Rejoice; beacon guiding all to the safe harbour of heaven!

Rejoice; thou who didst labour for Christ in the midst of
the world!

Rejoice; O venerable martyr Elizabeth, true model of
Christian sacrifice!

KONTAKION VI

HOW can angels and men refrain from wonderment when they
ponder the depths of they love and compassion? For thy convent
was not only a spiritual haven for those seeking salvation, but also a well-
spring gushing forth torrents of consolation upon those parched by the
burning heat of the passions. By thine own examples where thy sisters,
the handmaidens of Christ, taught how to comfort the sorrowing, tend
the sick, teach the ignorant, correct the erring, and prepare the dying for
the life which is to come. Wherefore, thy nuns joined chorus with thee
to praise the Lord continually, chanting unto Him: ALLELUIA!

OIKOS VI

AS a true image of piety thou didst venerate the wonder-icons and holy relics enshrined throughout the Russian land. Her monasteries and countless churches witnessed thine ascetic feats and fervent prayers. Thy tears, shed in such profusion, adorned thy person like lustrous pearls and moved to wonder those who beheld thee. And we who cherish thy holy memory exalt in spirit, crying out to thee:

Rejoice; image of piety who delighted to venerate the sacred
icons of the Mother of God!

Rejoice; thou who dost ever bless those who have recourse
unto thy precious relics!

Rejoice; wise pilgrim whose destiny was the kingdom of
heaven!

Rejoice; adornment of Holy Russia!

Rejoice; thou who art ever magnified by the Holy Church!

Rejoice; thou who didst not forsake Russia in her time of
tribulation!

Rejoice; thou who didst perceive the providence of God in
all that befell thee!

Rejoice; thou who didst teach others to set their hope on
Christ alone!

Rejoice; thou who wast present when the venerable
Seraphim was glorified!

Rejoice; thou who didst venerate his grace-bearing relics!

Rejoice; thou who didst hear the prophecy of that
Holy Father!

Rejoice; thou who didst prophesy the down-fall of the
Orthodox monarchy!

Rejoice; O venerable martyr Elizabeth, true model of
Christian sacrifice!

KONTAKION VII

WHEN those who been told slanderous tales about thee were
brought before thee, O royal martyr, they perceived thine
innocence and blamelessness and the holiness of thy life, for thou didst
sacrifice thyself for the good of others, and thy heart was ever intent
upon their needs, so that thou didst ever move them to chant unto
God: ALLELUIA!

OIKOS VII

"THIS is no new creation or concept, neither do I depart from the
Church traditions," thou didst declare unto those who sought to
discredit thy convent and labours; "I only repeat what the Church
teacheth; for it is Christ Who saith: 'Love thy neighbour', and the divine
Theologian doth manifestly thunder: 'If ye do not love your neighbour
whom ye see, ye cannot love God Whom ye see not.'" Thou didst but
renew that which had grown old, and hast revealed to us the essence of
true love in the miracle of thy life. Wherefore, we chant to thee thus:

Rejoice; thou who dost ever care for our souls!

Rejoice; holy princess, worthy of all praise!

Rejoice; thou who didst unite love and mercy, as a bridge
joineth land to land!

Rejoice; thou who didst know well saving words of grace!

Rejoice; thou who wast persecuted for righteousness' sake!

Rejoice; for truly great is thy reward in the heavens!

Rejoice; thou who didst silence blasphemy and impiety by
thy faith in Christ!

Rejoice; thou who didst most humbly endure the calumny
and slander hurled at thee by thine own countrymen!

Rejoice; thou who didst love righteousness and hate
falsehood!

Rejoice; thou who didst not seek to avoid the reproaches of
men, that thou mightest receive praise from the Lord!

Rejoice; thou who didst love the Gospel above all else!

Rejoice; thou who didst ever delight in the words thereof!

Rejoice; O venerable martyr Elizabeth, true model of
Christian sacrifice!

KONTAKION VIII

HAVING beheld a sight strange to all – the fall of an empire once
dedicated to God, the desecration of all that is holy, and the public
ridicule of the martyred Emperor Nicholas, – thou didst shed endless
streams of tears for all the tribulations which had befallen thine adopted
homeland. Yet trusting in God, and believing this to be His holy will, thou
didst never cease to cry out to Him: ALLELUIA!

OIKOS VIII

IN a moment, in the twinkling of an eye, the nation was overtaken by
chaos, thy family was taken away, and all thy friends stood afar off.
Only a few fearless hierarchs came to comfort thee and thy sisters, O royal
martyr. Thy convent was as a sheep-fold beset by ravening wolves; yet
thou didst remain undaunted by their depredations during those violent
days, ever preserving thy flock from harm by thy supplications.
Wherefore, receive from us these praises:

Rejoice; royal servant of the omnipotent King!

Rejoice; handmaid of the Queen of heaven!

Rejoice; thou who with the royal martyrs wast prey to
grievous slanders!

Rejoice; thou who didst find consolation in service of God!

Rejoice; thou who didst not judge the sinful lies of men!

Rejoice; thou who didst refuse to condone their misdeeds!

Rejoice; thou who didst uproot the tares of evil growing in
the royal garden!

Rejoice; thou who didst not approve of vile and wicked
deeds!

Rejoice; thou who ever helpest us to see the will of God in
all things!

Rejoice; thou who didst rebuke the riotous multitude with
thy courage!

Rejoice; for thou didst not turn away from the hapless Tsar
when he was mocked and abused!

Rejoice; thou who with him and his family dost ever rejoice
in heaven!

Rejoice; O venerable martyr Elizabeth, true model of
Christian sacrifice!

KONTAKION IX

THE angelic armies on high were stricken with awe, beholding Holy
Russia bound and led to bloody slaughter by those who wage war
against God; for, bleeding and dying in the arena of martyrdom, the land is
dyed red with the blood of the countless new martyrs, who cry out
continually to the Lord of hosts: ALLELUIA!

OIKOS IX

THE vile minions of Satan, sinful men with hands reeking of the blood of the innocent, openly reviled God, and mockingly asked thee how thou who art of royal blood couldst minister to the poor and lowly, O royal passion-bearer. But we marvel at thy patience and humility, and cry out unto thee:

Rejoice; thou who didst quench the flames of discontent
with thy tears!

Rejoice; thou who didst lament the woes of Russia, as
Martha and Mary wept over Lazarus!

Rejoice; thou who didst submit to the will of God!

Rejoice; thou who didst behold the Saviour enthroned
on high!

Rejoice; venerable martyr of royal birth!

Rejoice; thou who didst put to shame those who
mistreated thee!

Rejoice; thou who dost bless those who bless thee!

Rejoice; thou who wipest the tears away from those
who grieve!

Rejoice; thou who dost calm our troubled hearts!

Rejoice; thou who bowest down before the throne of God,
offering Him our entreaties!

Rejoice; thou who art ever attentive to His decrees!

Rejoice; thou who dost continually preserve us from
all harm!

Rejoice; O venerable martyr Elizabeth, true model of
Christian sacrifice!

KONTAKION X

WISHING to make thee captive, O martyr, evil-minded men arrived
at thy convent on the third day of Pascha, to separate thee from
thy flock; for after the holy Patriarch Tikhon the Confessor blessed thee
and thy nuns, the wicked fell upon thee and took thee away into exile. Yet
knowing what was to follow, thou didst take with thee thy faithful
companion, the venerable Barbara, and with thee chanted the hymn of
victory unto the risen Christ: ALLELUIA!

OIKOS X

BANISHED to the heart of Russia, hidden away from the eyes of the
world, with prayer and fasting thou didst prepare for thy departure
from this life, O Elizabeth, when Companion Barbara, and with the holy
Princes Sergius, John, Igor, Constantine and Vladimir, who were all to
share in thy sufferings and receive incorruptible crowns from the hands
of the Saviour. And sharing together in the delights of heaven, attend ye
unto our praises:

Rejoice; ye who ever pray for the salvation of Russia!

Rejoice; ye who, though cast down by the ungodly into the
depths, have been raised on high by Christ!

Rejoice; ye who shed the scarlet robe of royalty and put
on the purple robe of martyrdom!

Rejoice; ye who were not deceived by the deceit of the
evil one!

Rejoice; ye who lift up your hands to God in supplication!

Rejoice; ye who cast away earthly riches to receive treasure
in heaven!

Rejoice; patient sufferers who endured all for the Lord!

Rejoice; ye who put to shame those who took your lives,
but could not slay your souls!

Rejoice; ye who received wreaths of victory fashioned by the
hand of the Creator!

Rejoice; bright constellation of holy stars shining in the
firmament of the Church!

Rejoice; O venerable martyr Elizabeth, true model of
Christian sacrifice!

KONTAKION XI

O THE glorious wonder! A mine depleted of its ore is shown to be
full of the lustrous gold of grace and piety! A shaft sunk deep into
the bowels of the earth is shown to be a ladder extending up to heaven,
whereby Elizabeth and her companions ascend from the depths unto the
heights of paradise! O holy martyrs, ye blessed ones, as ye delight in
celestial joys forget not us who celebrate the memory of your godly
struggles, that with you we also may chant the angelic hymn: ALLELUIA!

OIKOS XI

T HE minds of men, darkened by their fallen state, are unable to devise
for you hymns worthy of the pangs and sufferings ye endured, O
holy passion-bearers of Christ; for ye were like unto the youths of Ephesus
who fell asleep of death in a shaft sunk into the earth, only to awaken in
the splendid mansions of heaven, where ye now receive from us our poor
praises:

Rejoice; ye seven-branched lampstand burning before the
throne of God!

Rejoice; glory of Alapayevsk!

Rejoice; ye who planted the tree of life amid the barren
mountains and watered it with your blood!

Rejoice; royal passion-bearers, adorned with kindly diadems
more precious than gold and costly jewels!

Rejoice; O Barbara, devoted daughter of thy spiritual
mother!

Rejoice; ye who intercede for your compatriots who find
themselves amid suffering and exile!

Rejoice; O Sergius, valiant confessor of the true Faith!

Rejoice; O brethren, equal in number to the Trinity!

Rejoice; O Princes John, Igor, and Constantine, who were
like unto the holy youths in the fiery furnace!

Rejoice; O Vladimir, prince and martyr, who foresaw
thine own suffering and death!

Rejoice; ye who have washed your souls clean in the streams
of your blood!

Rejoice; ye who stand before the Saviour in the ranks of
the new martyrs and confessors!

Rejoice; O venerable martyr Elizabeth, true model of
Christian sacrifice!

KONTAKION XII

WITH the words of praise shall we weave a wreath of victory to
adorn the new passion-bearers of Alapayevsk? For even if we try
to recount their manifold labours, our own weakness, and hardness of
heart puts us to shame. For while they ever sought after the Lord, we ever
stray father away from Him. Wherefore, come ye speedily to our aid, and
drive our enemies, visible and invisible, far away from us, that unvexed
and at peace, we may chant aloud unto God: ALLELUIA!

OIKOS XII

WE chant your praises, O holy new martyrs of Alapayevsk, for when faced with death, ye manifestly confessed Christ as God in the presence of the ungodly. Wherefore, the martyred nun Barbara received from the hand of God a wreath fashioned of truth and obedience, and her royal companions were endowed with two-fold crowns of majesty and martyrdom for their struggles. And thus hath Christ the Lord, the Judge of the contest, shown us all that it is meet to glorify them with such praises as these:

Rejoice; boast of the Urals!

Rejoice; ye who shone forth like rays out of a dark pit!

Rejoice; ye who sanctified a lowly mine-shaft!

Rejoice; ye who were like unto Joseph, who was likewise cast into a pit by envious brethren!

Rejoice; ye who were like unto Daniel, who was thrown into a lion's den!

Rejoice; ye who have summoned countless other new martyrs to the banquet of the Bridegroom!

Rejoice; ye who were welcomed to the mansions of heaven by your kin, the martyred Tsar and his holy family!

Rejoice; ye who were slaughtered by the godless and unbelieving!

Rejoice; O Elizabeth, who didst bind thy companions' wounds and tend to their hurts!

Rejoice; thou who didst encourage and strengthen them until the moment of their soul's departure!

Rejoice; for thou didst chant fitting hymns as their life ebbed away!

Rejoice; thou who before an icon of the Saviour didst
surrender thine own soul into His hands!

Rejoice; O venerable martyr Elizabeth, true model of
Christian sacrifice!

KONTAKION XIII

O ALL-PRAISED and venerable martyr Elizabeth, with the other
passions-bearers of Alapayevsk – the martyrs Barbara, John, Igor,
Constantine, Vladimir, and Sergius, accept this, our meagre hymnody of
praise, which we offer to you in honour of the sufferings and violent death
ye endured for Christ; and beseech the all-holy Trinity our God, that we
be delivered from the perils and evil circumstances which beset us
throughout our life: that with you and all the new martyrs and confessors
of Russia we may ever chant unto the omnipotent Lord of heaven and
earth: ALLELUIA! *(Thrice.)*

And again, Oikos I and Kontakion I are read.

OIKOS I

THE Creator of the angels and Lord of mankind led thee from the
delusion of heresy to the divine knowledge of the Truth, O blessed
Elizabeth, that thy loving heart and soul might renew Christian love, which
had grown cold in the land of Russia: for through thine efforts the hearts
of men again warmed to the word of God, and the Master of all
vouchsafed thee to live a life exalted above thy peers, in love, humility and
fervent prayer. Wherefore, we ever chant unto thee, as is meet:

Rejoice; lamb burning with the love of God!

Rejoice; handmaid of Christ the Lord!

Rejoice; scroll whereon the Holy Spirit inscribed the
Christian virtues!

Rejoice; divinely wise princess and new martyr!

Rejoice; daughter who forsook thy father's house and turned
to Holy Orthodoxy!

Rejoice; vessel wherein the wine of gladness and the oil of
healing are mingled together!

Rejoice; upholder of the traditions of piety!

Rejoice; treasure-house of compassion!

Rejoice; radiant star resplendent with heavenly glory!

Rejoice; O venerable martyr Elizabeth, true model of
Christian sacrifice!

KONTAKION I

COME, all ye who love Christ, and let us offer up a hymn of praise
unto the martyred nun Elizabeth, who was chosen by the Lord of
hosts to serve as an example of Christian piety and love for those who
desire to follow in His steps. For, spurning the vanity of worldly
possessions, rank and cares, she dedicated her whole life to the aid of
those in need. Wherefore, it hath pleased Christ our God to crown
her ascetic labours with the diadem of martyrdom; and, dwelling now
in His heavenly kingdom, she maketh supplication unto God, that He
deliver from misfortunes and perils all who chant unto her with joy:

Rejoice; O venerable martyr Elizabeth, true model of
Christian sacrifice!

Holy Royal Martyr Grand Duchess Elizabeth, Pray Unto
God For Us!

Holy New Martyr Barbara and All New Martyrs of Russia, Pray
Unto God For Us!

Glory Be To God for All Things!

AKATHIST TO SAINT HERMAN OF ALASKA

KONTAKION I

O CHOSEN Doer of Wonders, most glorious favourite of Christ, our God bearing Father Herman, Alaska's adornment, the joy of all Orthodox in America. We sing to thee, our heavenly protector and powerful intercessor before God, these songs of praise. Cease not to pray for thy children, who cry fervently unto thee:

> Rejoice; our Venerable Father Herman of Alaska, America's most glorious doer of wonders!

OIKOS I

FATHER Herman, the Creator of the angelic hosts called upon thee to proclaim the Orthodox faith in a new land and to be the founder of the monastic way in the remote lands of the north. Thou wast sent, as wast the Apostle Paul, to those sitting in darkness so that the light of Orthodoxy might illumine all the ends of the earth. We, the inhabitants of the American continents, bring thee, our heavenly protector, this thanksgiving and sing thee this song of praise:

Rejoice; our Father Herman, our glory, our adornment!

Rejoice; bearer of the light of the true faith to our lands!

Rejoice; ascetic glorified by God!

Rejoice; most honoured branch of Valaam Monastery!

Rejoice; praise and joy of the Church in America!

Rejoice; comforter and protector of all of us!

Rejoice; our Venerable Father Herman of Alaska, America's most glorious doer of wonders!

KONTAKION II

IN thine early youth, O Venerable One, enkindled by the flame of love for the Lord, thou desired to serve God and Him alone. As an offering, thou dedicated thy youth to God, beginning thy journey from the hermitage of Valaam, where choirs of monastics sing ceaselessly unto God: ALLELUIA!

OIKOS II

THE Most High granted thee spiritual wisdom in thy youth that thou might know the beauty and sweetness of heaven. For this reason, the wise Igumen Nazarius, teacher of the venerable Seraphim of Sarov, taught thee God's wisdom and the Lord's way. Therefore, the Holy Church praises thee:

Rejoice; glorious Herman dedicator of thy youth to Christ!

Rejoice; disciple together with Seraphim of Sarov!

Rejoice; performer of spiritual labours in glorious Valaam!

Rejoice; honoured by all the brethren of Valaam Monastery!

Rejoice; student of spiritual wisdom in Valaam!

Rejoice; glorified now by the Orthodox Church!

Rejoice; our Venerable Father Herman of Alaska,
    America's most glorious doer of wonders!

KONTAKION III

THE Most High directed the divinely-wise primate of the Church in Russia, Gabriel, to send missionaries of the Orthodox Faith to Alaska. The apostolic choice fell upon thee, O Venerable Herman, therefore, all the people enlightened by the Light of Christ through thy labours and the personal example of thy life, sing unto the Lord: ALLELUIA!

OIKOS III

SHOWING great zeal not only in thy spiritual labours as a novice, but also in thine Apostolic fervour as thou preached to a people sitting in darkness, thee, O Venerable Herman, revealed the light of Christ to them with great power. Remembering thine apostolic labours and thy efforts to preach, with love we praise thee:

Rejoice; uncomplaining giver of obedience to thy
    spiritual father!

Rejoice; preacher who brought the Good News from afar!

Rejoice; faithful son of Holy Russia!

Rejoice; adopted son of North America!

Rejoice; initiator of the monastic way in our land!

Rejoice; zealous preacher of the Orthodox Faith!

Rejoice; our Venerable Father Herman of Alaska,
    America's most glorious doer of wonders!

KONTAKION IV

O VENERABLE Father Herman, thou endured storms of evil attacks and sorrows, by thine efforts thou persevered in this new land. Therefore, Christ glorified thee with the gift of foresight, enriching thee with miracles, granting thee the Kingdom of Heaven where, together with the angels, thou praise God in song: ALLELUIA!

OIKOS IV

H EARING of the miracles revealed to thy people when a forest fire and tidal wave were made to cease by thy prayers, we implore thee from the depths of our hearts and entreat you to aid us who call to thee:

Rejoice; ascetic and prophet glorified by God!

Rejoice; holy favourite of God!

Rejoice; our intercessor and healer!

Rejoice; helper of many who called out to thee!

Rejoice; healer of many afflicted and suffering!

Rejoice; our merciful and humble father!

Rejoice; our Venerable Father Herman of Alaska,
America's most glorious doer of wonders!

KONTAKION V

O VENERABLE One, thou shone like the North Star on Spruce Island, the New Valaam, illuminating all of America with the brightness of thy love and prayer, full of God's power, so that from every corner of it the Orthodox people will sing fervently to God: ALLELUIA!

OIKOS V

OBSERVING thy humility, all are in awe of thee, O Father Herman, for thy rigorous asceticism and perseverance in monastic struggles. In this thou followed the example of Anthony of the Caves, the founder of monasticism in Russia, even as he that of Anthony the Great, the first monk of the world. Thou, the founder of monasticism in our land, chose in thy great humility, the way of a simple monk. Therefore, the holy choir of hierarchs and hieromonks sings these songs of praise to thee:

Rejoice; founder of monasticism in our land!

Rejoice; imitator of Anthony the Great and Anthony
of the Caves!

Rejoice; crowned, as they were, with heavenly glory!

Rejoice; founder of a glorious hermitage!

Rejoice; source of holy relics for the faithful!

Rejoice; fountain of miracles for the whole world!

Rejoice; our Venerable Father Herman of Alaska,
America's most glorious doer of wonders!

KONTAKION VI

THE wilderness of the north proclaims thy works and miracles, revealing thee to be a new branch of the vineyard of the Church of Russia in America. The forests and wilderness are permeated with thy prayers. Following the example of the ancient hermits, thou cried out in the silence of the night to God: ALLELUIA!

OIKOS VI

THOU enlightened a people who were living in darkness; thou showed them an example of the monastic way of life. O our God-bearing Father Herman, pray that we all, giving thanks to the Lord, may ceaselessly sing you these words of praise:

Rejoice; first saint of our land!

Rejoice; founder of the monastic way in our land!

Rejoice; faithful servant of the Holy Trinity!

Rejoice; humble founder of the church of the Resurrection!

Rejoice; glorious hermit of the hermitage of Spruce Island!

Rejoice; loving father of the children who came to him!

Rejoice; our Venerable Father Herman of Alaska,
      America's most glorious doer of wonders!

KONTAKION VII

THE LORD chose thee, O Venerable One, to bring the light of the knowledge of God to the land of the Aleuts and there to sow the seeds of the Orthodox faith. Thou taught all to embrace the true faith and to call out to God: ALLELUIA!

OIKOS VII

HAVING reached the heights through prayer, O Venerable One, thou didst not forget the needs of others. Thou manifested great concern for homeless orphans, building an orphanage and a school for them and taught them the commandments of the Lord. In gratitude to God for thy labours, accept from us these praises:

Rejoice; defender of the poor and orphaned!

Rejoice; their good protector!

Rejoice; builder of a home for the orphaned!

Rejoice; servant to God with thy labours!

Rejoice; provider of earthly bread to the orphaned!

Rejoice; nourisher of orphans with words of eternal life!

Rejoice; our Venerable Father Herman of Alaska,
America's most glorious doer of wonders!

KONTAKION VIII

THE LORD who loves mankind, O Venerable One, gave thee the gifts of foresight and healing in His desire to manifest through thee a source of compassion for his people. Thou showed them the love of God through thy works and many words of instruction. Illumined by the light of thy spiritual labours, the people called to the Lord: ALLELUIA!

OIKOS VIII

THE people transformed by the light of the Christian Faith, came to thee in times of illness and sorrow. As a father who loved his children, thou interceded for all, bringing forth healing and comfort to all who came to thee for help. Thy glory hast gone forth into all the earth and we, thy spiritual children, glorify thee with these words:

Rejoice; our merciful father!

Rejoice; our unmercenary and gracious physician!

Rejoice; merciful healer of our infirmities!

Rejoice; our speedy helper in time of trouble and need!

Rejoice; foreseer of coming events as of the present!

Rejoice; perceptive reprover of hidden transgressions!

Rejoice; our Venerable Father Herman of Alaska,
America's most glorious doer of wonders!

KONTAKION IX

THOU spokest with the angels, O Venerable One, and revealed how angels came to thee in thy hermitage and thou hadst sweet conversation with them. Now thou art in the Kingdom of Heaven where with hosts of angels thou prayest ceaselessly to the Creator: ALLELUIA!

OIKOS IX

WHO can enumerate the miracles witnessed by thy people? The waves of the sea and a fire in the forest were calmed by thy prayers. When there was a great tidal wave, thou caused the stormy seas to cease by thy prayers before the icon of the Mother of God, saying: "The water shall not go beyond this line." Therefore, we sing unto thee thus:

Rejoice; wondrous pacifier of the waters!

Rejoice; deliverer from the threat of fire!

Rejoice; safe harbour for the hierarch Innocent who called
    to thee from the sea!

Rejoice; for through thy prayers the wind at sea wast calmed!

Rejoice; source of many miracles during thy life!

Rejoice; fount of many miracles even after thy death!

Rejoice; our Venerable Father Herman of Alaska,
    America's most glorious doer of wonders!

KONTAKION X

WE bring to thee a song of praise, O Venerable Father, concerning thy righteous life. We sing praises of thy honoured death. Thou foreknew the day and hour of thy blessed end. Most glorious also wast thy burial. For forty days, a great storm raged at sea and thy prophecy concerning thy burial wast fulfilled. Thy disciple Gerasim, sensing a wondrous fragrance at the time of thy death, sang unto God: ALLELUIA!

OIKOS X

THOU were a most glorious doer of wonders during thy life, O Father. At thy death, thou manifested this wondrous miracle: thy body remained incorrupt in the chapel for many days after thy death. The Aleut people who saw a flaming pillar ascending to Heaven at the hour of thy death, sang to you thus:

Rejoice; for thy righteous end has assured us of thy holiness!

Rejoice; for thy ascension to Heaven was like a pillar of fire!

Rejoice; for thy relics, exuding a fragrance of sanctity, remain as our inheritance!

Rejoice; for many miracles are made manifest at thy reliquary!

Rejoice; for thou hast provided us with a source of holy water and healing!

Rejoice; for from this water many who are afflicted receive healing!

Rejoice; our Venerable Father Herman of Alaska, America's most glorious doer of wonders!

KONTAKION XI

O HOLY Father, from thy hermitage in the north, in the midst of the wilds of nature, thou sang ceaseless praises to the Holy Trinity. Moved by the Spirit, thou foresaw the great flowering of this vineyard planted in the soil of America and thou called out with the angels of Heaven: ALLELUIA!

OIKOS XI

TO all future members of the monastic order, thou art a source of light and inspiration. For thou foretold, O Venerable One, the founding of a monastery and of an Archbishop's throne in this land. Today a choir of hierarchs and of monastics glorifies thee in these words:

Rejoice; instructor of monastics and converser with angels!

Rejoice; most glorious founder of the ascetic way in our land!

Rejoice; foreseer of the growth of this great vineyard of Christ!

Rejoice; fulfilment of this prophecy to the coming generations!

Rejoice; giver of a true image of the monastic way!

Rejoice; for thy love is made manifest to all!

Rejoice; our Venerable Father Herman of Alaska, America's most glorious doer of wonders!

KONTAKION XII

SEEING thy grace and thy great boldness before God, we entreat thee, O Venerable Father Herman, to pray fervently to the Lord, that He will protect His Holy Church from faithlessness and schism, from false teaching and wilfulness, that we may sing to God Who has dealt bountifully with us: ALLELUIA!

OIKOS XII

WE praise thy glorification, O Venerable One, we bless thee, O most powerful intercessor and protector of our Church, and with love we sing unto thee:

Rejoice; protector of all who honour thee!

Rejoice; speedy intercessor and helper to all!

Rejoice; founder of Orthodoxy in our land!

Rejoice; confirmation of those who come to the
Orthodox Faith!

Rejoice; most glorious protector of the Church in America!

Rejoice; her first saint and her wondrous Father!

Rejoice; our Venerable Father Herman of Alaska,
America's most glorious doer of wonders!

KONTAKION XIII

O MOST glorious favourite of God, Our Venerable Father Herman, accept this humble prayer we offer up in praise to thee. Standing now before the Throne of the Almighty Lord, ceaselessly pray for us. In joy, we sing to God: ALLELUIA! *(Thrice.)*

And again, Oikos I and Kontakion I are read.

OIKOS I

FATHER Herman, the Creator of the angelic hosts called upon thee to proclaim the Orthodox faith in a new land and to be the founder of the monastic way in the remote lands of the north. Thou wast sent, as wast the Apostle Paul, to those sitting in darkness so that the light of Orthodoxy might illumine all the ends of the earth. We, the inhabitants of the American continents, bring thee, our heavenly protector, this thanksgiving and sing thee this song of praise:

Rejoice; our Father Herman, our glory, our adornment!

Rejoice; bearer of the light of the true faith to our lands!

Rejoice; ascetic glorified by God!

Rejoice; most honoured branch of Valaam Monastery!

Rejoice; praise and joy of the Church in America!

Rejoice; comforter and protector of all of us!

Rejoice; our Venerable Father Herman of Alaska, America's
most glorious doer of wonders!

KONTAKION I

O CHOSEN Doer of Wonders, most glorious favourite of Christ, our
God bearing Father Herman, Alaska's adornment, the joy of all
Orthodox in America. We sing to thee, our heavenly protector and
powerful intercessor before God, these songs of praise. Cease not to pray
for thy children, who cry fervently unto thee:

Rejoice; our Venerable Father Herman of Alaska, America's
most glorious doer of wonders!

PRAYER

O MOST wondrous, favourite of God, our venerable Father Herman,
as a good labourer thou didst your great spiritual work in a harsh
climate in this land. In thy service to God, thou were faithful in the little
things. And, as the Lord said: "thou hast been faithful over a few things, I
will make thee ruler over many things." Now, when this word hast been
fulfilled in thee, the Lord hath set thee over our whole Church, as her
heavenly protector. We call upon thee in fervent prayer: Entreat the Lord
to keep our Holy Church steadfast in Orthodoxy and to reveal her to be
an adornment of our land. May He protect her from all the dark powers
of the enemy and drive out all adversaries. May He grant us purity of faith
and beauty of soul. Pray He will grant us all the spirit of peace and love,
the spirit of humility and meekness and drive out the sin of pride. Save us
from self-praise. Be our guard against false teachings. Give healing to the
sick; to the sorrowful be a comfort. To those who hunger for spiritual
truth, give the heavenly food; that we may attain our true desire, and
receive the reward of faithful servants at the final Judgment. With all the
saints, we will praise with song: the Life creating Trinity, the Ineffable
Father, the True and Only-Begotten Son, the Comforter, Holy Spirit,
for ever. AMEN.

PRAYER TO THE VENERABLE HERMAN OF ALASKA

This Prayer is said before his holy relics, or before his holy icon on the day of his glorification August 9/July 27.

O VENERABLE Father Herman, we praise and glorify our God and Creator. All the earth, and everything within it, acknowledges Him as Creator and Eternal father. Heaven and earth, angels and men, together, praise and glorify Him: the most glorious company of the Apostles, the praiseworthy fellowship of the prophets, the great and noble gathering of the Martyrs, and the whole community of the saints, all praise Him. On this day, the Holy Catholic and Apostolic Church gives thanks to God for thee, O Venerable Elder of Spruce Island. We thy heirs and children gather at thy holy reliquary and gaze with awe at thy sacred relics in the knowledge that thy soul joins together with the Apostles, Prophets, Martyrs, Saints, and the Heavenly Hosts before the throne of the Most Merciful God in praise of the Holy Trinity. O Venerable Hermit of Spruce Island, instructor in the faith of the Holy Trinity, our spiritual father and intercessor before the throne of Almighty God, pray for peace within the Church and dispel all disunity, faithlessness, and discord. Come to the aid of our spiritual leaders that they may always be true and effective instruments of the Holy Spirit, enable them to proclaim the truth of the Gospel with power, give them the wisdom to enlighten the unenlightened and the spirit to inspire all to love the knowledge of God; fortify them with the perseverance to defend the Church, even unto death, from all enemies both within and without and at all times. May the hearts of thy spiritual children be filled with that faith and love of the Holy Church which thou manifested in thy holy life; pray Him to deliver us from the temptations which cause us to fall; renew in us a child-like faith in our Heavenly Father; teach us to place our trust in God, and in Him alone; satisfy our thirst for the true knowledge of God; show us how to serve God faithfully; transfigure our life that it may truly reflect the image and likeness of God within us. O Holy Father and Patron of the Church in America: be a physician to the weak in faith; be a support to the fallen; be a defender to the defenceless; be a bulwark of strength to the weary in spirit; be a guide to the travellers by sea, by land and by air; be our heavenly intercessor. O Venerable Father Herman of Alaska, together with all the saints and the heavenly hosts, pray to God that on each of us He will bestow wisdom for our mind, strength for our will, light for our spirit, enabling us to attain to the true peace of life which is from God alone. We praise with joyous and grateful hearts, the Life-Creating Trinity: Father Almighty, Only-Begotten Son, Comforter, Holy Spirit, now and ever, and unto ages of ages. AMEN.

AKATHIST TO SAINT IGNATY BRIANCHANINOV

KONTAKION I

HAVING been chosen by the Heavenly King and glorified by Him, O holy hierarch, Father Ignaty, now celebrating thine all-honourable memory, we zealously pray to thee: guide us on the path of salvation; from enemies visible and invisible, from sorrows and sickness, rescue us who lovingly call to thee:

Rejoice; O holy hierarch Ignaty, thou model and teacher of repentance and prayer!

OIKOS I

ARCHANGELS and Angels marvel at thy life, O holy hierarch Ignaty, how from a young age thou didst have great zeal for God, and how thou didst conduct thy life according to His commandments without wavering. Startled by thy prudence, with compunction we call out to thee:

Rejoice; having comforted thy sorrowful childless parents
   with thine own birth!

Rejoice; fine branch of an honourable family!

Rejoice; unceasing joy of thy guardian Angel!

Rejoice; having surprised thy parents and teachers by thy
   meekness and submissiveness!

Rejoice; having prepared thyself for monastic obedience
   from childhood!

Rejoice; having compelled thy youthful soul toward God!

Rejoice; having spent thine adolescence in prayer and Godly
   contemplation!

Rejoice; having been an example of prayer and obedience
   for thy younger brothers and sisters!

Rejoice; O holy hierarch Ignaty, thou model and teacher
   of repentance and prayer!

KONTAKION II

THY parents, observing thy great gifts, directed thee to the royal city to be trained for the future acceptance of a military commission. And thou, O chosen one of God, being young in years, yet old in understanding, whilst honouring all of these corruptible and transitory things, didst strive with heart and mind toward the Single Beauty and Indescribable Sweetness — the Lord Jesus Christ, singing to Him: ALLELUIA!

OIKOS II

THOU didst receive divine reason from thy beloved Saviour Christ, O marvellous Ignaty, when, being yet a child, thou didst comprehend the hand of the Heavenly Creator and Fashioner in all the visible forms of this world. Wherefore, glorifying thee, we extol thee thus:

Rejoice; having contemplated the Invisible God in the visible appearances of nature!

Rejoice; having loved the quiet and solitude of the forest!

Rejoice; having had great zeal for God from thy childhood years!

Rejoice; having scorned everything beautiful and sweet of this world!

Rejoice; having received a heavenly reward from the Master!

Rejoice; having retained the Jesus prayer unceasingly on thy lips and in thy mind!

Rejoice; having shown perfect love for the Lord!

Rejoice; having borne thy beloved Jesus constantly within thy heart!

Rejoice; O holy hierarch Ignaty, thou model and teacher of repentance and prayer!

KONTAKION III

THOU wast overshadowed by the power of the Highest, O most blessed father, when thou didst reject all that is considered good in this world, and according to the commandments of Christ the Saviour, didst take up the cross, and follow Him without turning back, unceasingly singing in thy heart: ALLELUIA!

OIKOS III

HAVING had in thy soul the ardent desire to renounce the world and follow Christ, thou didst fear neither the anger of the Tsar, nor the interdictions of thine elders, and while still living in the world, thou didst adorn thyself with the monastic life. Wherefore, honouring thy manhood and love for the Sweetest Lord Jesus, we bless thee thus:

Rejoice; having shown adamantine hardness of soul in
> thy youth!

Rejoice; having desired the great treasure of weekly
> communion of the Holy Mysteries of Christ!

Rejoice; having now joined Christ in the heavens, for whom
> thou didst yearn while still on earth!

Rejoice; having irrigated the Godly seed, strewn on the good
> earth of thy heart, with thine abundant tears!

Rejoice; for although in the midst of worldly tares, thou
> didst bring forth the hundredfold fruit of virtues
> for the Lord!

Rejoice; zealous keeper of purity of soul and body!

Rejoice; wonderful adornment of chastity!

Rejoice; for thy handsome countenance bore witness to the
> beauty of thy soul!

Rejoice; O holy hierarch Ignaty, thou model and teacher of
> repentance and prayer!

KONTAKION IV

THE storm of doubting thoughts did not sway thee, O blessed Ignaty, when, not being afraid of the anger of the Tsar, thou didst refuse a military commission, and taking upon thyself the yoke of Christ and scorning the world with its temptations, thou didst settle in the desert, and there, having acquired the desired peace of thy soul, thou didst sing aloud to God: ALLELUIA!

OIKOS IV

WHEN it was announced in thy homeland, all thy relatives were surprised, that thou, a youth adorned with beauty and gifts, didst withdraw to the desert, having despised the glory of this world and its sweetness. And an Angel in the heavens rejoiced exceedingly and glorified God, having snatched thee from the vain path of the world and having set thee on the narrow path of monastic life, leading to the Heavenly Kingdom. We, too, praising thy holy zeal for God, call to thee:

Rejoice; having preferred the calling of a soldier of the Heavenly King to that of an earthly king!

Rejoice; having fiercely taken up arms against temptations approaching from the world, the flesh, and the devil!

Rejoice; having defeated all the machinations of the enemy with the weapon of God, the Cross of Christ!

Rejoice; having been vested with the armour of righteousness!

Rejoice; having donned the helmet of salvation!

Rejoice; having loved the spiritual sword, the word of God, more than any weaponry of mankind!

Rejoice; having guarded thyself from the arrows of the evil one with the shield of faith!

Rejoice; having received the angelic rank of ineffable blessedness in the heavens!

Rejoice; O holy hierarch Ignaty, thou model and teacher of repentance and prayer!

KONTAKION V

THOU wast like unto a star, moved by the providence of God, O most reverend Ignaty, when thou didst present thyself to the abbot of a poor and remote monastery, requesting to be received into the ranks of the brethren. And the Abbot, having examined thee, saying nothing in opposition, blessed thee at the outset of thy monastic path. And thou, having attained the realization of thy life-long hopes, and having given thanks, in compunction didst glorify God thy Benefactor: ALLELUIA!

OIKOS V

ALL the brothers of the monastery were surprised, witnessing thy great zeal in the fulfilment of obedience, by which thy spiritual father tested thy humility. And, we, honouring thy podvigs and labours, which thou didst take up in thy youth voluntarily for Christ's sake, cry to thee with compunction:

Rejoice; having lifted thy cross upon thy shoulders and
having followed Christ!

Rejoice; having voluntarily selected the narrow and
sorrowful path of monastic life!

Rejoice; having never turned back!

Rejoice; having overcome the spirit of pride with
thy humility!

Rejoice; not having buried thy talent in the earth!

Rejoice; having used it for the glory of God and for the
salvation of the souls of men!

Rejoice; having revived many souls, soiled in sins, with thy
divinely wise writings!

Rejoice; having heard the sweet voice of the Heavenly
Husbandman: "Good and faithful servant,
enter into the joy of thy Lord"!

Rejoice; O holy hierarch Ignaty, thou model and teacher of
repentance and prayer!

KONTAKION VI

B Y humility, fasting, and, most of all, unceasing prayer, thou didst
fiercely take up arms against the fleshly passions, O holy hierarch,
until thou didst subjugate the flesh to thy spirit, wherefore thou dost now
appear with the choirs of Angels before the Throne of the Most Holy
Trinity, continually praising God: ALLELUIA!

OIKOS VI

T HE Grace of God within thee shone abundantly, when, having
accepted the angelic rank, thou wast soon honoured with the dignity
of the priesthood. And thy spirit, having been accepted into the embrace
of the Father that was opened to thee, tasted unutterable blessings. And
when the Lord selected thee to be the abbot of the monastery
of Pelshemsk, day and night thou didst weep over thy spiritual sheep,
entrusted to thee by God, so that not a single one of them would perish
for the sake of thy negligence. Rejoicing over this Divine providence,
we call to thee:

> Rejoice; having beheld the consummation of thy hopes in
> the acceptance of the angelic rank!

> Rejoice; having imitated Hieromartyr Ignatius the God-
> bearer, thy heavenly protector!

> Rejoice; having borne the Lord Jesus Christ in thy heart
> constantly, as he did!

> Rejoice; having received the dignity of the priesthood as a
> great gift of God!

> Rejoice; having been the namesake of fire, and having
> enflamed others with the fire of faith and love
> toward God and neighbour!

Rejoice; having offered the Bloodless Sacrifice with great
reverence and fear!

Rejoice; having reverently honoured the Most Undefiled
Mother of Christ our God as the Most Pure, Holy
Dwelling-Place and Treasury of God's Glory!

Rejoice; having raised the well-adorned temple named for
her, the Merciful Gatekeeper, in the habitation!

Rejoice; O holy hierarch Ignaty, thou model and teacher
of repentance and prayer!

KONTAKION VII

THE LORD Who loves mankind, not wanting to cover a holy lamp of
thy virtues, but rather to illumine all, that all men should glorify the
Heavenly Father, seeing thee, led thee out from the desert dwelling for
laborious obedience. Marvelling at this providence by God, with
compunction, we call out: ALLELUIA!

OIKOS VII

THE LORD gave thee to the new monastery of the venerable Sergius
near the royal city, as the superior and good shepherd, tirelessly
caring for thy spiritual flock and being an ardent advocate for the beauty of
the habitation. Wherefore thy brotherhood glorifies thee, calling out:

Rejoice; having imitated the Heavenly Protector of thy
habitation, the venerable Sergius, abbot
of Radonezh!

Rejoice; having beautified it with marvellous churches
and buildings!

Rejoice; having led thy children as a loving father along the
path of salvation to the Heavenly Kingdom!

Rejoice; having accepted those thirsting to start the monastic
path into the habitation with love!

Rejoice; having led guilty monks to tearful repentance with
thine admonitions!

Rejoice; having given to all brothers an example of monastic
podvigs by thy disposition and life as a good pastor!

Rejoice; having been prepared to sacrifice thine own soul for
their salvation!

Rejoice; glory and praise of monastics!

Rejoice; O holy hierarch Ignaty, thou model and teacher
of repentance and prayer!

KONTAKION VIII

THOU wast a newcomer and wanderer on earth, O holy hierarch, as
other men. However, from thy youth, the Lord chose thee, as His
God-pleaser; for with thy life and God-inspired writings thou didst serve
the Lord diligently. And we send up praise to God thy Benefactor, crying
out to Him: ALLELUIA!

OIKOS VIII

HAVING perfected all of the virtues, thou wast truly an angel in the
flesh, O holy hierarch Ignaty, receiving with love all who fled to
thee, consoling their sorrows, directing them to the path of repentance,
and teaching them constant prayer and heartfelt tears. Wherefore both
the rich and poor, the noble and common people, thy spiritual offspring,
call to thee:

Rejoice; O new Chrysostom, having led many lost souls on
the path of repentance to God with thy many
fiery words!

Rejoice; having enlightened the souls and hearts of all those
who honour thee, with thy writings!

Rejoice; having directed to pray for one's enemies!

Rejoice; having prayed for thine own enemies with
  warm love!

Rejoice; having taught us to recognize the scourge of God
  toward our correction in those who attack!

Rejoice; having presented the tears of Ezekiel and
  purification of Manasseh to the spiritual
  eyes of the repentant!

Rejoice; having depicted the podvigs and labours of the
  ancient ascetics in thy divinely wise works!

Rejoice; having imitated them in thy life completely!

Rejoice; O holy hierarch Ignaty, thou model and teacher
  of repentance and prayer!

KONTAKION IX

THE entire angelic army and choir of holy hierarchs marvelled, beholding thee, the new God-pleaser, beaming with great labours and podvigs. And we, blessing thee, cry out to God who glorified thee: ALLELUIA!

OIKOS IX

THOU didst depart unto a new laborious obedience at a remote region of our fatherland, O holy hierarch Ignaty, when the archiepiscopal staff from the Pre-eternal Archbishop, our Lord Jesus Christ, was entrusted to thee by the Archpastor of the royal city in the Kazan cathedral of the Heavenly Queen. Understanding in this the will of God- that the Gospel of His Kingdom should be preached in a foreign country, we humbly call to thee:

Rejoice; having received the grace of God abundantly
  in ordination!

Rejoice; having fulfilled the Apostolic teachings and having
  given all of the faithful to drink of its saving streams!

Rejoice; faithful labourer in the vineyard of Christ!

Rejoice; spiritual lute, perfected by the Holy Spirit!

Rejoice; divinely inspired adornment of hierarchs!

Rejoice; for thy beloved Lord spoke by thy mouth!

Rejoice; for although having left thy spiritual flock in the
monastery of venerable Sergius, thou didst not forget
any in thy prayers!

Rejoice; merciful intercessor for all of the faithful and
unfaithful who call on thee for help!

Rejoice; O holy hierarch Ignaty, thou model and teacher
of repentance and prayer!

KONTAKION X

O VERBURDENED by the bodily infirmities and podvigs of life, thou
didst retire to the monastery of holy Nicholas on the river Volga, O
holy hierarch Ignaty, desiring to prepare thy soul for departure from this
world, where finishing thy days in unceasing prayer and divine
contemplation, thou didst sing aloud to God: ALLELUIA!

OIKOS X

T HOU wast a quick helper and comforter, O holy hierarch Ignaty,
not only for those who came to thee, but also for those living
far away, comforting them with thy letters, cheering and enlightening
their souls. Wherefore, all those who honour thy divinely wise works
proclaim to thee:

Rejoice; our good shepherd!

Rejoice; having never turned away those who came to thee!

Rejoice; having embraced those requesting thy help, near
and far, with thy love!

Rejoice; having reverently admitted those who honour thy
writings into intimate unity with thy soul!

Rejoice; having taught thy spiritual offspring Christian
patience!

Rejoice; having directed us to look for God's Providence in
our sufferings!

Rejoice; having taught thy children to give way to Providence
completely!

Rejoice; having preached that we should request of God, the
perfection of His will in us, as great mercy!

Rejoice; O Holy hierarch Ignaty, thou model and teacher
of repentance and prayer!

KONTAKION XI

THOU didst offer the all-compunctious song to the Most Holy Trinity
each day of thine earthly life, O all-praised Ignaty. And now
standing before the Throne of the King of Glory, pray for us, who honour
thy holy memory, that purified by prayers and repentance, together with
thee, we may praise God unto the ages of ages: ALLELUIA!

OIKOS XI

IN thy life, thou wast a great luminary of the Holy Orthodox Church, O
holy hierarch Ignaty, wherefore the Lord, the Ruler of All, gave thee a
blessed end and glorified thee in the Heavens. We beseech thee, O
merciful holy hierarch, to request, on behalf of us sinners, too, who pray
for thy help and intercession, a peaceful and painless end to our lives, a
good answer at the Terrible Judgment of Christ and the inheritance of the
Heavenly Kingdom, that we might joyfully call to thee:

Rejoice; having marked the righteousness of thy life with a
righteous end!

Rejoice; having foreseen thine imminent departure!

Rejoice; having met the Heavenly Bridegroom with the lamp
of thy soul burning!

Rejoice; having beheld the resurrection of the Saviour with
the myrrh-bearing women at thine end!

Rejoice; having withdrawn none of thine intercession for
those who honour thy repose!

Rejoice; having covered all those who zealously pray to
thee with thy grace and care!

Rejoice; having taught thy children to hold firm to the one
true holy Orthodox faith!

Rejoice; having strictly forbidden to accept any heretical
delusion or attend crafty persuasion!

Rejoice; O holy hierarch Ignaty, thou model and teacher
of repentance and prayer!

KONTAKION XII

GRACE was given to thee from God, O holy hierarch of Christ Ignaty, to pray for us and guide us on the path of salvation, that purified by repentance, we might be admitted to the most well-adorned bridal chamber of the Saviour, and there, with thee and with all those sanctified by God, joyfully praise Him: ALLELUIA!

OIKOS XII

CHANTING hymns unto God, Who is wondrous in His saints, we praise thee, O blessed Ignaty, as a friend of Christ, having acquired the heavenly blessedness by the unwavering working of the Lord's commandments. Pray for us sinners, that we may be fellow partakers of the Lord's banquet, who compunctiously call to thee:

Rejoice; having acquired the Heavenly Kingdom with thy
deep humility, with poverty of spirit!

Rejoice; having preached that we should lay this virtue as the foundation of all monastic podvigs!

Rejoice; having been consoled by the Lord Himself in crying over thy sins!

Rejoice; having received the inheritance of eternal life for thy meekness of soul!

Rejoice; having searched not for perishable food on earth, but rather the truth of Christ, which now completely fills thee in the heavens!

Rejoice; having been pardoned by God the Giver of Mercy, for thy mercy toward thy neighbours!

Rejoice; having beheld God by thine angelic purity of heart!

Rejoice; having forgiven thy slanderers for the Lord's sake, and as a peacemaker, having been awarded the great treasure of adoption by God!

Rejoice; O holy hierarch Ignaty, thou model and teacher of repentance and prayer!

Kontakion XIII

O WONDERFUL saint of Christ, O holy hierarch Father Ignaty! Accept this service which, although small, is nonetheless, brought to thee from the hearts of those who love and honour thee, and deliver us by thine all-powerful intercession from every grievance, illness and sorrow; warm our souls which have been cooled, with the fire of faith and love towards God; grant us repentance before the end; be a guide for us to the Heavenly Kingdom, that there with thee and all those who have pleased God, we may sing to Him unto the ages of ages: ALLELUIA! *(Thrice.)*

And again, Oikos I and Kontakion I are read.

OIKOS I

ARCHANGELS and Angels marvel at thy life, O holy hierarch Ignaty, how from a young age thou didst have great zeal for God, and how thou didst conduct thy life according to His commandments without wavering. Startled by thy prudence, with compunction we call out to thee:

Rejoice; having comforted thy sorrowful childless parents
with thine own birth!

Rejoice; fine branch of an honourable family!

Rejoice; unceasing joy of thy guardian Angel!

Rejoice; having surprised thy parents and teachers by thy
meekness and submissiveness!

Rejoice; having prepared thyself for monastic obedience
from childhood!

Rejoice; having compelled thy youthful soul toward God!

Rejoice; having spent thine adolescence in prayer and Godly
contemplation!

Rejoice; having been an example of prayer and obedience
for thy younger brothers and sisters!

Rejoice; O holy hierarch Ignaty, thou model and teacher
of repentance and prayer!

KONTAKION I

HAVING been chosen by the Heavenly King and glorified by Him, O holy hierarch, Father Ignaty, now celebrating thine all-honourable memory, we zealously pray to thee: guide us on the path of salvation; from enemies visible and invisible, from sorrows and sickness, rescue us who lovingly call to thee:

Rejoice; O holy hierarch Ignaty, thou model and teacher
of repentance and prayer!

PRAYER TO HOLY HIERARCH IGNATY

O GREAT and wonderful saint of Christ, O holy hierarch Father Ignaty! Mercifully accept our prayers brought to thee with love and thanksgiving! Hear us orphaned and helpless ones, who bow down before thee with faith and love and request thy warm intercession for us before the Throne of the God of Glory. We know that the prayer of a righteous man availeth much, to win the Master's favour. Thou didst have an ardent love for the Lord from thy youth and having desired to serve Him alone, thou didst consider all the beautiful things of this world as nothing. Denying thyself and having taken up thy cross, thou didst follow Christ. Thou didst voluntarily take upon thyself the narrow and most-sorrowful path of monastic life, and on this path thou didst acquire great virtues. With thy writings, thou hast filled the hearts of men with deep reverence and submissiveness before the Almighty Creator, and fallen sinners with thy wise counsels in consciousness of thy nothingness and sinfulness, and taught them to flee unto God in repentance and humility, while reassuring them with hope in His mercy. Thou didst never turn away those who came to thee, but thou wast a kind and loving father and pastor to all. And now, do not abandon us, who earnestly pray to thee and entreat thy help and intercession. Obtain for us, from our Lord Who loveth mankind, spiritual and physical health, establish our faith, strengthen our power, utterly exhausted in the temptations and grievances of this age; warm with the fire of prayer our hearts which have been cooled, help us, who are being cleansed by repentance, to receive a Christian end to this life and to enter the most well-adorned bridal chamber of the Saviour with all of the elect, and there, together with thee, to bow down to the Father, and to the Son, and to the Holy Spirit, unto the ages of ages. AMEN.

AKATHIST TO SAINT INNOCENT OF MOSCOW EQUAL TO THE APOSTLES AND ENLIGHTENER OF ALASKA

KONTAKION I

(Tone VIII)

O HOLY Father, Good Shepherd of the Flock entrusted to thee by the Lord! Thou dedicated all thy strength and heart, all thy mind and soul to Christ! In the remotest regions, thou laboured tirelessly without thought of earthly reward for the sake of His Holy Church and the salvation of all. We, the recipients of thy great spiritual legacy, offer to thee this hymn of praise. As thou standest before the Throne of the Lord of Glory, intercede for our land and its people! That united in One, Holy Orthodox Church we may gratefully sing unto thee:

Rejoice; O Holy Father, Metropolitan Innocent, Equal to
the Apostles and Enlightener of Alaska!

OIKOS I

O HOLY Father Innocent! Thy glory hast shone from the Far Eastern lands to the Western World. From humble origins in a Siberian village, thou rose to world renown as a modern Apostle. The Lord chose thee to bring the Orthodox Faith to the ancient Peoples of Alaska and Asia, who together with us honour thee with these songs of praise:

Rejoice; Imitator of the Apostles and their Successor!

Rejoice; Evangelizer of the Arctic Peoples!

Rejoice; Scholar and Teacher of the Aleuts!

Rejoice; Illuminator of the Eskimos and Indians!

Rejoice; Humble genius whose footsteps were guided
by the Lord!

Rejoice; Visionary Architect of the Orthodox Church
in America!

Rejoice; O Holy Father Innocent, Equal to the Apostles and
Enlightener of Alaska!

KONTAKION II

T HOU distinguished thyself as a young student, displaying thy many interests and talents by excelling in thy studies at home and in school. Thy greatest joy wast the service of God and His Holy Church. Thy uncle instructed thee in the ways of piety and faith so that from an early age thou sang unto the Lord: ALLELUIA!

OIKOS II

IN thy youth, the Lord prepared thee for thy lifetime of service by enabling thee to study various disciplines. Remembering thy dedication, we thankfully celebrate thy memory:

Rejoice; Thy talents were employed in the service of Christ!

Rejoice; Thy achievements inspire all who are familiar
with them!

Rejoice; Skilled craftsman, imitator of the Carpenter of
Nazareth!

Rejoice; Clock-maker who proclaimed the Timeless One!

Rejoice; Thy teachers marvelled at thy intelligence!

Rejoice; Thy spiritual children praise thy humility!

Rejoice; O Holy Father Innocent, Equal to the Apostles and
Enlightener of Alaska!

KONTAKION III

COMPLETING thy preparation at the seminary at Irkutsk, thou accepted the Divine Call to the missionary frontier of Alaska. Together with thy wife, the beloved Katherine, thou set out on thy Apostolic journey to Russian America, as thou sang unto the Lord: ALLELUIA!

OIKOS III

AS a newly ordained priest thou showed great determination in reaching thy destination, 1,000 miles away, in the Bering Sea. Thou willingly forsook all, for the sake of the Gospel of Christ, traveling for many months over frozen tundra and treacherous seas. Inspired by thy dedication, we sing unto thee:

Rejoice; Apostle to America!

Rejoice; Heroic Founder of Orthodoxy in the Western World!

Rejoice; Imitator of the Holy Apostle Paul!

Rejoice; Courageous voyager on the northern seas!

Rejoice; Thy dedication equalled that of the Apostles!

Rejoice; Thy perseverance was a Gift of the Holy Spirit!

Rejoice; O Holy Father Innocent, Equal to the Apostles and Enlightener of Alaska!

KONTAKION IV

ARRIVING at Unalaska, you rendered thanks to the Lord for your safe passage. Kneeling on the beach together with all those in your company, thou praised God with the hymn: ALLELUIA!

OIKOS IV

TOGETHER with thy tutor, the Aleut chieftain Ivan, thou studied the Native language and devised a writing system for it. Thou laboured for many years, preparing the Word of God for publication in the Aleut tongue. Thou astounded the indigenous peoples with thine ability to preach to them in their own language, thus enlightening them with the Light of Christian Truth. We glorify God for bringing thee to our shores and honour thine evangelical accomplishments:

Rejoice; Ennoblement of Ancient Peoples!

Rejoice; Father of Learning in Alaska!

Rejoice; Teacher of Virtue and Divine Truth!

Rejoice; Catechist of those seeking Righteousness!

Rejoice; Thy vision inspires all future missionaries!

Rejoice; Thy brilliance illumines the arctic night!

Rejoice; O Holy Father Innocent, Equal to the Apostles and
Enlightener of Alaska!

KONTAKION V

THOU travelled throughout the Aleutian region, braving storms and hostile seas in thine efforts to evangelize thy scattered flock. Warmed by thy love for the Lord, thou journeyed in thy bidarka on the icy waves, softly singing to the Creator of all: ALLELUIA!

OIKOS V

DURING the ten years thou remained in the Aleutian Islands, thou devoted much time and energy to the study of the land, people, and wildlife of the area. Thou kept careful records of thy experiences and observations so that this heritage could be preserved for future generations. Thou opened schools for the Native children so that they could advance in the knowledge of God and His Creation. Praising the Lord for His bounties, we offer a hymn to thee:

Rejoice; Patient instructor of the simple and the wise!

Rejoice; Scholar and Teacher of the Aleutian languages!

Rejoice; Preserver of Alaska's ancient heritage!

Rejoice; Dispeller of the darkness of ignorance!

Rejoice; Perceptive observer of the wonders of Creation!

Rejoice; Messenger of the Good News of Salvation!

Rejoice; O Holy Father Innocent, Equal to the Apostles and
Enlightener of Alaska!

KONTAKION VI

H AVING created a written language for the Native people, thou developed textbooks for them so that they could become literate. Reading the Word of God in their own tongue, and giving thanks to God, the Aleuts sang with joy: ALLELUIA!

OIKOS VI

O HOLY Father, thou travelled beyond the limits of thine own extensive district into the land of the Eskimo people. Thou brought to the natives of Bristol Bay the sanctifying Grace of Holy Baptism. Thou made the Nushagak River a new Jordan for them, bringing Christianity to the northern shores of the Bering Sea, where thou art remembered today with these words of praise:

Rejoice; Enlightener of the Eskimo Nation!

Rejoice; Sanctification of the Nushagak!

Rejoice; Husbandman sent to the plentiful harvest!

Rejoice; Labourer in the Vineyard of Christ!

Rejoice; Warrior clothed in the armour of Truth!

Rejoice; Soldier armed with the Gospel of Peace and the sword of Prayer!

Rejoice; O Holy Father Innocent, Equal to the Apostles and Enlightener of Alaska!

KONTAKION VII

U SING thy talents, thou erected the first Orthodox Cathedral in the New World, designing the Temple and supervising its construction thyself. The faithful celebrated the consecration of the new church, singing the hymn of Thanksgiving: ALLELUIA!

OIKOS VII

TRANSFERRING the centre of thy missionary activity to the city of New
Archangel, thou began anew the evangelization of the Tlingit People.
Thou became proficient in their language and preached the Gospel in
their villages winning converts to Christ by thy knowledge of medicine as
well as theology. Thou admired the nobility of these proud warriors, who
together with us offer these praises to thee:

Rejoice; Teacher of the Tlingit Indians!

Rejoice; Physician of souls and bodies!

Rejoice; Fearless apostle, protected by God!

Rejoice; Illuminator of the Northern Peoples!

Rejoice; Mountain rising above the clouds of error!

Rejoice; Harbour sheltering from treacherous seas!

Rejoice; O Holy Father Innocent, Equal to the Apostles and
Enlightener of Alaska!

KONTAKION VIII

THOU wast summoned to appear before the Holy Synod to present
thy many translations for ecclesiastical approval. Thou returned to
thy homeland by circumnavigating the globe; arriving at St. Petersburg,
thou praised God in song: Alleluia!

OIKOS VIII

LEARNING of the repose of thy wife, Katherine, during thine absence,
thou prayerfully visited the Holy monasteries at Kiev and Zagorsk
in order to discern the Lord's Will. The Emperor himself, impressed
with thine apostolic fervour and achievements, approved thine elevation
to the rank of bishop. Returning to Alaska, thou wast welcomed with
these words:

Rejoice; Thou took up the Cross and followed Christ!

Rejoice; Thou first brought the Joy of the Resurrection
to Alaska!

Rejoice; Thou were inspired by the heroic example of St.
Innocent of Irkutsk!

Rejoice; Thou promoted the apostolic labours of St.
Nicholas of Japan!

Rejoice; Thou wast among the first to ask the Elder Herman
to intercede for thee!

Rejoice; By his prayers, thou arrived safely in Kodiak!

Rejoice; O Holy Father Innocent, Equal to the Apostles and
Enlightener of Alaska!

KONTAKION IX

A S bishop of the Russian colony, thou renewed thine efforts to
bring the Gospel to all Alaska. Thou opened a seminary in Sitka
for the training of indigenous clergy and designed a new cathedral for
the capital city. Thou also constructed the clock for the church bell
tower. When the Holy Temple was completed, thou sang out in
gratitude unto the Lord: ALLELUIA!

OIKOS IX

A S overseer of the huge diocese which included Eastern Siberia as
well as Alaska, thou dispatched priests to areas where no
missionaries had ever gone. Thine own son-in-law was assigned to the
Nushagak, while thy former student, Father Jacob, set out for the Yukon
delta. Because of thy great vision for the future of Orthodoxy in this land,
we honour thee with these hymns:

Rejoice; Good Shepherd of the Arctic!

Rejoice; First Hierarch of America!

Rejoice; Our guide to the Kingdom of God!

Rejoice; Benefactor of the needy and oppressed!

Rejoice; Thy foresight determined the growth of the Church
in Alaska!

Rejoice; Thy boundless energy established the True Faith in
the North!

Rejoice; O Holy Father Innocent, Equal to the Apostles and
Enlightener of Alaska!

Kontakion X

WITH characteristic enthusiasm thou visited the peoples of the Amur Valley in Siberia and began yet again to study their languages and traditions. Together with the Aleuts and Tlingits, they learned to praise the Almighty Creator with the song of Thanksgiving: ALLELUIA!

Oikos X

TRANSFERRING thy headquarters to the Far East, thou bid farewell to the New World and returned to the Old. Following the example thou hadst set for them, the Native clergy of Alaska continued your work in America. Through them, we have become thy spiritual children and venerate thy memory in these words:

Rejoice; Student of Alaskan languages and Teacher of the
True Word!

Rejoice; Preacher 'in tongues' like the Apostles on
Pentecost!

Rejoice; Thou published the Gospel in the Aleut language!

Rejoice; Thou founded schools for the enlightenment of the
Native Peoples!

Rejoice; Thou directed the evangelization of Alaska and
Siberia!

Rejoice; Thou planted the seeds of the Orthodox Faith on
American soil!

Rejoice; O Holy Father Innocent, Equal to the Apostles and
Enlightener of Alaska!

KONTAKION XI

THOU spent thine entire life labouring in remote regions for the
propagation of the Holy Faith. In thy later years, thou wast called
to yet another great task. Thou wast elected Metropolitan of Moscow to
succeed the venerable Philaret. As thou journeyed across the frozen
steppes of Asia en route to thine enthronement, thou sang in amazement
unto God: ALLELUIA!

OIKOS XI

THOU revitalized the missionary spirit of thy homeland by
organizing societies for the support of evangelical enterprises.
Thou assisted thy former flocks with thy holy prayers and material aid.
We who have benefited from these labours sing to thee in gratitude:

Rejoice; Thou wast faithful in little things!

Rejoice; Thou hast been set over much!

Rejoice; Rushing Wind dispelling the fog of ignorance
and fear!

Rejoice; Mighty River watering the spiritual wilderness!

Rejoice; Precious Vessel filled with the Holy Spirit!

Rejoice; Adornment of the Church in the Old World and
the New!

Rejoice; O Holy Father Innocent, Equal to the Apostles and
Enlightener of Alaska!

KONTAKION XII

WITH the same humility thou exhibited throughout thine earthly
life, thou asked that no eulogies be delivered at thy burial.
Instead, thou requested an edifying sermon be preached for the benefit of
all. Learning of thy falling asleep, thy spiritual children commended thy
soul unto the Lord, singing: ALLELUIA!

OIKOS XII

THE heirs of thy spiritual legacy throughout the New World rejoice
today at thy glorification, O Holy Father. Asking for thy prayers for
the Church in America, we gather to celebrate thy remarkable
achievements with these words:

Rejoice; Inspiration of Orthodox pastors and teachers!

Rejoice; Indicator of the Way to the Kingdom of Heaven!

Rejoice; Faithful steward in the Household of Faith!

Rejoice; Farsighted Champion of Orthodoxy!

Rejoice; Loving Father of your spiritual Children!

Rejoice; Intercessor for all who come to the Orthodox Faith!

Rejoice; O Holy Father Innocent, Equal to the Apostles and
Enlightener of Alaska!

KONTAKION XIII

O HOLY Father, Bishop Innocent! As we remember all the glorious deeds thee so humbly accomplished, we are inspired by thy vision, courage, and perseverance. Pray therefore that we may be accounted worthy to continue thy work in the New World, and to sing gratefully unto the Lord: ALLELUIA! *(Thrice.)*

And again, Oikos I and Kontakion I are read.

OIKOS I

O HOLY Father Innocent! Thy glory hast shone from the Far Eastern lands to the Western World. From humble origins in a Siberian village, thou rose to world renown as a modern Apostle. The Lord chose thee to bring the Orthodox Faith to the ancient Peoples of Alaska and Asia, who together with us honour thee with these songs of praise:

Rejoice; Imitator of the Apostles and their Successor!

Rejoice; Evangelizer of the Arctic Peoples!

Rejoice; Scholar and Teacher of the Aleuts!

Rejoice; Illuminator of the Eskimos and Indians!

Rejoice; Humble genius whose footsteps were guided
by the Lord!

Rejoice; Visionary Architect of the Orthodox Church
in America!

Rejoice; O Holy Father Innocent, Equal to the Apostles and
Enlightener of Alaska!

KONTAKION I

(Tone VIII)

O HOLY Father, Good Shepherd of the Flock entrusted to thee by the Lord! Thou dedicated all thy strength and heart, all thy mind and soul to Christ! In the remotest regions, thou laboured tirelessly without thought of earthly reward for the sake of His Holy Church and the salvation of all. We, the recipients of thy great spiritual legacy, offer to thee this hymn of praise. As thou standest before the Throne of the Lord of Glory, intercede for our land and its people! That united in One, Holy Orthodox Church we may gratefully sing unto thee:

Rejoice; O Holy Father, Metropolitan Innocent, Equal to
the Apostles and Enlightener of Alaska!

PRAYER TO SAINT INNOCENT

O HOLY Hierarch and Father Innocent! The Lord chose thee and ordained thee to go and bring forth much fruit in His new vineyard on the frontiers of Russia and America. Thou dedicated thy life to building up the Body of Christ in the New World and the Old, and brought the treasures of the Holy Apostolic Faith to Alaska and Siberia. We, thy spiritual children, kneel before thy holy icon and ask thee to intercede for the Holy Orthodox Church in thine adopted and native lands. As thou wast humble and kind, help us by thy prayers to be patient and generous. As thou persevered under difficult circumstances in a remote and lonely region, strengthen us in our dedication to Christ and His Gospel. As thou loved God and thy flock and devoted thy life in service to them, pray to Our Lord that our hearts may be filled with love for Him and our neighbour. Thou planted the seeds of the Orthodox Faith in Alaskan soil: implore the Lord that we may be accounted worthy to continue the work thou so gloriously began, to bring the Light of Christ to every corner of America. Thou indicated the Way into the Kingdom of Heaven by thy words and example: intercede for the salvation of all of us who venerate thy holy memory. By thy holy prayers may we become worthy of the precious spiritual heritage which God hath entrusted unto us through thee, and sing eternally the praises of the Holy, Consubstantial, and Life-Creating Trinity; the Father and Creator who is without Beginning; the Son, Our Lord and Saviour who became Man in order to sanctify and save us; and the Comforter, the Holy Spirit who enlightens and enlivens all, now and ever, and unto ages of ages. AMEN.

AKATHIST TO SAINT JOHN OF SHANGHAI AND SAN FRANCISCO

KONTAKION I

Tone VIII

CHOSEN wonderworker and superb servant of Christ, who pourest out in the latter times inexhaustible streams of inspiration and multitude of miracles. We praise thee with love and call out to thee:

> Rejoice; O holy Hierarch John, wonderworker of the latter
> times!

OIKOS I

AN angel in the flesh wast thou manifested in the latter times by the grace of God Who ever careth for men. Seeing the beauty of thy virtues, we thy children now cry out to thee:

> Rejoice; thou who didst live in virtue from earliest childhood!

> Rejoice; thou who didst ever live in fear of God and do His holy will!

> Rejoice; thou who didst manifest the grace of God in numberless virtues!

> Rejoice; thou who didst mystically hear the distant prayers of those in distress!

> Rejoice; thou who wast filled with love for thy fellow men and didst do all possible for their salvation!

> Rejoice; thou who dost bring joy to all who pray to thee in faith and love!

> Rejoice; O holy Hierarch John, wonderworker of the latter times!

KONTAKION II

SEEING the abundance and variety of thy virtues. O holy Hierarch, we see in thee a living source of God's wonders in our time. Thou dost refresh with thy love and miracles all who cry in faith to God: ALLELUIA.

OIKOS II

BEING filled with love, thou wast also filled with theology. O holy Father. And in thee the knowledge of God flowed forth again in love for suffering men. Do thou teach us also to know the true God in love as we call out to thee in admiration.

> Rejoice; firm stronghold of Orthodox truth!

> Rejoice; precious vessel of the gifts of the Holy Spirit!

> Rejoice; righteous accuser of impiety and false doctrine!

Rejoice; ardent doer of the commandments of God!

Rejoice; severe ascetic who gavest thyself no repose!

Rejoice; loving shepherd of the flock of Christ!

Rejoice; O holy Hierarch John, wonderworker of the
      latter times!

KONTAKION III

B Y GOD'S mercy thou wast manifest as a father to orphans and
instructor of the young, raising them in the fear of God and
preparing them for the service of God. Therefore, all thy children
look to thee with love and cry out with gratitude to God: ALLELUIA.

OIKOS III

D WELLERS in heaven should be praising thee and not we on earth,
for our words are feeble beside thy deeds. Yet offering to God
what we have we cry out to thee thus:

Rejoice; thou who didst protect thy children by thy constant
      prayer!

Rejoice; thou who didst ever guard thy flock by the sign of
      the Cross!

Rejoice; thou whose love knew no bounds of country or race!

Rejoice; bright luminary beloved by all!

Rejoice; model of spiritual meekness!

Rejoice; giver of spiritual consolation to those in need!

Rejoice; O holy Hierarch John, wonderworker of the
      latter times!

KONTAKION IV

B EWILDERED by thy deeds of piety and love, we know not how to praise thee worthily, O Hierarch John. Thou didst travel to the ends of the earth to save thy people and preach the gospel to those in darkness. Thanking God for thine apostolic labours, we cry out to Him: ALLELUIA!

OIKOS IV

T HE people of many lands beheld thy life and marvelled at God's mercies even in these latter times. And so we also, marvelling, cry out in awe:

Rejoice; enlightener of those in the darkness of unbelief!

Rejoice; thou who didst follow Thy people to the farthest East and West!

Rejoice; fountain of miracles poured out by God!

Rejoice; loving chastiser of those who have gone astray!

Rejoice; speedy comfort to those who repent of their sins!

Rejoice; support of those who go on the right path!

Rejoice; O holy Hierarch John, wonderworker of the latter times!

KONTAKION V

T HOU wast manifest as a vehicle of God's power to stop the destructive forces of fallen nature, O holy Hierarch, preserving Thy people on the island from the deadly wind and storm by Thy prayer and the sign of the Cross. So preserve us also who cry out in wonder unto God: ALLELUIA!

OIKOS V

A LL who have trusted in Thy help in desperate circumstances and adversities have found deliverance, O bold intercessor before the Throne of God. Therefore, we too do place our hope in Thee to protect us in dangers by Thy prayers before God as we call out to Thee:

Rejoice; thou who didst stop the powers of nature from doing harm to thy flock!

Rejoice; thou who providest by Thy prayer for all in need!

Rejoice; inexhaustible bread for the hungry!

Rejoice; abundant wealth for those who live in poverty!

Rejoice; consolation for those in sorrow!

Rejoice; quick uplifting for those who have fallen!

Rejoice; O holy Hierarch John, wonderworker of the latter times!

KONTAKION VI

T HOU wast manifest as a new Moses, leading his flock out of slavery, O Hierarch John. Deliver us also from slavery to sins and the enemies of God as we cry out to God: ALLELUIA!

OIKOS VI

T HOU didst the impossible and persuade the authorities of this world to have pity on thy flock, O good shepherd. Pray for us now that we may live in peace and quiet, saving our souls as we gratefully cry to thee:

Rejoice; helper of all who call upon thee in faith!

Rejoice; thou who deliverest from death and disaster!

Rejoice; thou who preservest from lies and slander!

Rejoice; preserver of the innocent from bonds!

Rejoice; thou who foilest the attacks of the unrighteous!

Rejoice; destroyer of lies and exalter of truth!

Rejoice; O holy Hierarch John, wonderworker of the
    latter times!

KONTAKION VII

O LOVER of the saints of East and West, thou didst restore to the Orthodox Church the saints of the West, of lands which had fallen away from the truth. Now with these saints thou dost pray for us to God as we on earth cry out to God: ALLELUIA!

OIKOS VII

O FERVENT venerator of the holy Hierarchs of Gaul, thou wast manifest in the latter times as one of them, exhorting thy flock to preserve the same Orthodox faith that they confessed, and astonishing the peoples of the West by thy holy life. Now preserve us in that same faith as we cry out to thee:

Rejoice; new Martin by thy miracles and ascetic feats!

Rejoice; new Germanus by thy confession of the
    Orthodox faith!

Rejoice; new Hilary by thy divine theology!

Rejoice; new Gregory by thy love for God's saints!

Rejoice; new Faustus by thy gentle love and monastic
    fervour!

Rejoice; new Caesarius by thy firm yet loving rule of the
    Church of God!

Rejoice; O holy Hierarch John, wonderworker of the
    latter times!

KONTAKION VIII

AT the end of thy life, O holy Hierarch, thou wast called to the New World, to offer there thy witness of ancient Christianity and to suffer persecution for thy righteousness, thus perfecting thy soul for heaven. Now marvelling at thy patience and long-suffering, we all cry out to God: ALLELUIA!

OIKOS VIII

O LABOURER of Christ's vineyard who knew no rest even at the end of thy much-toiling life, help us now in our labours as we strive to be faithful to Christ, crying out in praise to thee:

Rejoice; thou who didst endure to the end and so attain salvation!

Rejoice; thou who wast deemed worthy to die before the icon of the Mother of God!

Rejoice; thou who didst keep thy faith and courage in the midst of unjust persecution!

Rejoice; thou who didst labour to the end for thy flock and meet death sitting as a hierarch!

Rejoice; thou who didst return through the air to be buried amidst the flock!

Rejoice; thou who workest wonders for those who come to thy sepulchre with faith and love!

Rejoice; O holy Hierarch John wonderworker of the latter times!

KONTAKION IX

ALL angel-kind rejoiced at thy soul's ascent to their celestial home marvelling at the wonders thou didst perform on earth through the action of the Holy Spirit, to whom we sing: ALLELUIA!

OIKOS IX

O RATORS find it impossible to describe thy life of sanctity with their many and eloquent words, O righteous John, for thou didst become a living house for the power of the ineffable God. Yet, unable to fall silent at the wonder shown to our age of feeble faith, we glorify thee:

Rejoice; divine palace where from the counsel of the Good
King is given!

Rejoice; small and humble abode containing the spacious
beauty of angels' mansions!

Rejoice; thou who didst gain a house not made with hands,
eternal in the heavens!

Rejoice; infirmary wherein all manner of diseases are
divinely healed!

Rejoice; closet wherein thy holy labour of prayer was hidden!

Rejoice; blessed temple of the Holy Spirit!

Rejoice; O holy Hierarch John, wonderworker of the
latter times!

KONTAKION X

W ISHING to save the world, the Saviour of all hath sent a new saint among us and through him hath called us out of the dark recesses of sin. Hearing this call to repentance, the unworthy ones in turn cry out to God: ALLELUIA!

OIKOS X

T HOU art a wall sheltering us from adversity, O Hierarch John, for through thy heavenly intercessions we are delivered from the attacks of demonic passions and from afflictions which beset us on earth. Before thy firm support of prayer, we cry with faith:

Rejoice; sight to the blinded!

Rejoice; strength and life to those on the bed of death!

Rejoice; God-revealed advice to those in doubt and
confusion!

Rejoice; refreshing water to those perishing in the heat of
sorrow!

Rejoice; loving father to the lonely and abandoned!

Rejoice; holy teacher of those who seek the Truth!

Rejoice; O holy Hierarch John, wonderworker of the
latter times!

KONTAKION XI

THY life was a hymn to the Most Holy Trinity, surpassing others in thought, word and deed, O most blessed John. For with much wisdom thou didst explain the precepts of the true Faith, reaching us to sing with faith, hope and love to the one God in Trinity: ALLELUIA!

OIKOS XI

WE see thee as a radiant lamp of Orthodoxy amidst the darkness of ignorance, O God-chosen pastor of Christ's flock, our Father John. For even after thy repose thou dost speak the truth to the ignorant and give instruction to those who seek guidance and to all who cry to thee:

Rejoice; radiance of divine wisdom to those in ignorance!

Rejoice; rainbow of quiet joys for the meek!

Rejoice; thunder to stubborn sinners!

Rejoice; lightning of the zeal of God!

Rejoice; rain of God's dogmas!

Rejoice; shower of theological thoughts!

Rejoice; O holy Hierarch John, wonderworker of the
     latter times!

KONTAKION XII

G RACE hath been poured out in the last days upon us all. Beholding
    this grace come forth from a holy hierarch who once did
walk among us, let us receive it with reverence and thanksgiving, crying
to God: ALLELUIA!

OIKOS XII

S INGING in praise to God, the heavenly choir of saints rejoiceth that He
    hath not forsaken the fallen and unbelieving world, but hath
manifested His almighty power in Thee, his meek and humble servant. O
blessed John, with all the saints we greet Thee and give honour to Thee:

Rejoice; new star of righteousness shining in heaven's
     firmament!

Rejoice; new prophet who wast sent before the final
     unleashing of evil!

Rejoice; new Jonah warning all of the wages of sin!

Rejoice; new Baptist drawing all to a life of prayer
     and repentance!

Rejoice; new Paul suffering to preach the gospel in the spirit
     of truth!

Rejoice; new apostle whose miracles instil in us faith and awe!

Rejoice; O holy Hierarch John, wonderworker of the
     latter times!

KONTAKION XIII

O HOLY and most wondrous Hierarch John, consolation for all the sorrowing, accept now our prayerful offering that through thy prayers to our Lord we may be spared Gehenna and by Thy God-pleasing intercession, we may cry eternally: ALLELUIA! *(Thrice.)*

And again, Oikos I and Kontakion I are read.

OIKOS I

A N angel in the flesh wast thou manifested in the latter times by the grace of God Who ever careth for men. Seeing the beauty of thy virtues, we thy children now cry out to thee.

Rejoice; thou who didst live in virtue from earliest childhood!

Rejoice; thou who didst ever live in fear of God and do His holy will!

Rejoice; thou who didst manifest the grace of God in numberless virtues!

Rejoice; thou who didst mystically hear the distant prayers of those in distress!

Rejoice; thou who wast filled with love for thy fellow men and didst do all possible for their salvation!

Rejoice; thou who dost bring joy to all who pray to thee in faith and love!

Rejoice; O holy Hierarch John, wonderworker of the latter times!

KONTAKION I

C HOSEN wonderworker and superb servant of Christ, who pourest out in the latter times inexhaustible streams of inspiration and a multitude of miracles. We praise thee with love, and call out to thee:

Rejoice; O holy Hierarch John, wonderworker of the
    latter times!

PRAYER I

O wondrous Hierarch John, thou didst stretch thy heart to encompass within it a multitude of people from among diverse nations and peoples who honour thee. Look down at the humility of our words, which we offer out of love for thee, and help us, O saint of God, to cleanse ourselves from all defilement of flesh and spirit, so that we may labour for the Lord with fear and rejoice in Him with trembling. What shall we render unto thee for that joy which we have felt, beholding thy sacred relics in the holy church, and glorifying thy memory? Truly, we have nothing to offer thee, except if we begin to correct our lives, becoming new men instead of old. Be an intercessor for us of this grace of renewal, O holy John; help us in our weaknesses; heal our sicknesses; cure our passions by thy prayers. O thou who didst depart this temporal life unto life eternal, to which the all-pure Mistress, the Directress of the Russian diaspora, guided thee by her wonder-working Kursk-Root Icon, whose companion thou wast on the day of thy repose, thou dost now rejoice in the choir of the saints who glorify the one God, Who is worshipped in Trinity, the Father, the Son and the Holy Spirit, now and ever, and unto the ages of ages. AMEN.

PRAYER II

O beloved Hierarch John, good shepherd and beholder of the hearts and minds of men! Thou prayest for us now at the throne of God, as thou thyself didst say after thy death: "Even though I have died, yet am I alive." Beseech the most compassionate God, that He grant us forgiveness of sins, that we may come wakefully to our senses, and cry out to God, asking that we be given the spirit of humility, the fear of God and piety in all the ways of our life. As thou wast a merciful nurturer of orphans and a skilled instructor on earth, be thou now a guide and Christian understanding for us amid the turmoil of the Church; hearken to the groaning of the troubled youth of our corrupt times, who are tempest-tossed by most wicked demonic possession, and mercifully regard the despondency of our weak pastors, caused by the inroads of the corrupting spirit of this world, and who languish in idle indifference. Hasten thou to make supplication, we cry to thee with tears, O fervent advocate; visit us, who are orphaned, scattered over the face of all the world and in our homeland, astray in the darkness of the passions, yet who by our feeble love are drawn to the light of Christ and await thy fatherly instruction; that, having acquired piety, we may be shown to be heirs of the kingdom of heaven, where thou abidest with all the saints, glorifying our Lord Jesus Christ, to Whom be honour and dominion, now and ever, and unto the ages of ages. AMEN.

AKATHIST TO SAINT JULIANA OF LAZAREVO

KONTAKION I

O RIGHTEOUS and merciful Juliana, who wast chosen by God, and amidst worldly cares didst in thy soul live in Christ, as in heaven; and who didst abide in great stillness, loving silence within thy heart! Glorifying the Lord Who hath glorified thee; with compunction, we sing to thee a hymn of praise. Do thou, who endured grievous sorrows in thy life, pray for us, who are tempest-tossed by perils and sins, and entreat the merciful Saviour to grant us salvation of soul and deliverance from misfortunes, that, giving thanks unto God, we may glorify thee, saying:

Rejoice; O merciful Juliana, boast of Murom and
adornment of women!

OIKOS I

A PURE angel, from earliest childhood thou didst love the angelic monastic life; but the Creator of all, Who arrangeth all things in the depths of His wisdom, ordained a different path of salvation for thee-that thou please Him with a holy life within honourable matrimony. Wherefore, from childhood He led thee to the kingdom of God through many trials: for when thou wast a maiden six years of age, thou hadst already become a grieving orphan; and as a young bride, thou didst soon take up the cross of motherhood. And we, though stricken with awe at this wondrous providence, yet compunctiously praise thee with faith:

Rejoice; thou who wast born into wealth, to parents who
loved the poor – Justin and Stephanida!

Rejoice; thou who, deprived of thy mother, wast raised an
orphan outside thy father's house!

Rejoice; right fragrant lily who blossomed within the
tranquillity of the forests of Murom!

Rejoice; radiant star set alight by God in the village of
Lazarevo!

Rejoice; thou who in thy heart acquired love for Christ and
His all-pure Mother!

Rejoice; pure ewe-lamb who from childhood sought the
monastic order!

Rejoice; meek and obedient one, who by the will of God
wast entrusted to a husband!

Rejoice; righteous mother who, having lived in the world,
hast been numbered among the saints!

Rejoice; O merciful Juliana, boast of Murom and
adornment of women!

KONTAKION II

SEEING thee standing in vigil all night, the enemy of the Christian race assailed thee with vile terrors. But thou, O blessed heifer, didst cry out with tearful entreaty to thy guide, the all-wondrous Nicholas; and the wonder-worker straightway appeared to thee, and the demons vanished like smoke. Then the holy hierarch blessed thee, saying: "O my daughter, be thou of steadfast good cheer, for Christ the Lord hath commanded me to preserve thee from all evil. And do thou chant to Him without fear, ever crying aloud like the angels: ALLELUIA!"

OIKOS II

THE human mind is at a loss how, whilst living in this vain world, O blessed mother, thou didst in soul abide untroubled in the mansions of heaven; how, living amid abundant wealth, thou didst regard it dispassionately as something belonging to others and entrusted to orphans; how, bearing thy cross in honourable matrimony, though thou wast like a nun amid the world, thou didst raise many holy children. And we, knowing what is impossible for men, and praising God Who can accomplish all things, with undoubting faith honour thee thus:

Rejoice; quiet dove who unceasingly conversed with God
    in prayer!

Rejoice; obedient disciple who knewest how to live in both
    abundance and in want!

Rejoice; faithful spouse who saved thy husband by being a
    model of meekness!

Rejoice; much suffering mother who entrusted thy pure
    children to the Lord!

Rejoice; chaste woman who pleased God by childbearing
    and holiness!

Rejoice; merciful lady who, following the Gospel, didst
    meekly minister to thine own servants!

Rejoice; handmaid of Christ, who kept His commandments
throughout thy life!

Rejoice; thou who wast obedient to Paul, doing all things for
the glory of God!

Rejoice; O merciful Juliana, boast of Murom and
adornment of women!

KONTAKION III

THE power of the Most High gave thee the strength to bear thy heavy
cross without complaint, when the pure souls of four of thy sons and
two of thy daughters flew aloft in blessedness like quick-winged birds,
departing this life while yet in childhood. And thou thyself, O divinely
wise mother, like a turtledove soaring up in soul to the mansions of
paradise, gavest thanks unto God for all things, and wast comforted by thy
remaining children. And concerning the departed, with the righteous Job
thou didst say with compunction: "The Lord gave, and the Lord hath
taken away. And now my little children glorify God with the angels most
sweetly, and fervently entreat Him on behalf of their parents, offering up,
with their pure mouths, the seraphic hymn: ALLELUIA!"

OIKOS III

POSSESSED of a heart which hath pity for all, and which is overflowing
with grace-filled love, O Juliana, thou didst truly show thyself to be a
merciful mother when God visited thy land with a terrible famine; for,
though thou didst thyself experience want, thou wast sustenance for those
who hungered and thirsted, a guide for the blind and the halt, protection
and vesture for the unsheltered, and comfort for all. And thy least,
hungering brethren, rending praise unto God, earnestly blessed thee thus:

Rejoice; thou who illumined the dark time of famine with
the light of love!

Rejoice; thou who rendered mercy unto Christ in the guise
of thy least brethren!

Rejoice; thou who like the warm sun shinest forth earthly
 good things!

Rejoice; thou whose left hand knew not what thy right hand
 was doing!

Rejoice; thou who, feeding the starving with bread, didst
 deliver them from death and torment!

Rejoice; thou who, warming the desperate with a word of
 welcome, didst greatly console them!

Rejoice; thou who, seeking the kingdom of God, didst
 distribute things good for the body!

Rejoice; thou who having acquired friends through riches,
 didst find the dwellings of heaven!

Rejoice; O merciful Juliana, boast of Murom and
 adornment of women!

KONTAKION IV

AMID the tempest of misfortune which beset the whole land, when for
their sins the people were punished with a deadly plague, with great
diligence, O loving soul, thou didst fulfil the word of Christ concerning the
sick, secretly helping them without the knowledge of thy household; and
offering up fervent prayers for them, thou didst receive from God the gift
of healings, and requesting services for the departed in church, thou didst
accompany them to their everlasting rest. And now thou hast received
from God the blessed kingdom, where sickness and grief are unknown;
and joining chorus there, thou chantest unto God: ALLELUIA!

OIKOS IV

HEARING on one of those bitter days that thine eldest son had been
cruelly slain by a servant, thou wast wounded in thy maternal heart,
O cross-bearing woman. Yet thou wast not so much saddened by his
death as thou wast grieved by the suddenness of the end of his life; and

thou wast all the more distraught over the criminal murderer. But remembering the Lord Himself, Who shed drops of blood in Gethsemane, thou didst strengthen thyself in prayers to Him, immersing thy maternal sorrow in His will. And we, marvelling at thy humble faith, chant these praises as is meet:

Rejoice; thou who didst look upon this earthly life as a
    sorrowful sojourn!

Rejoice; thou who didst regard the repose of thy family as a
    brief separation!

Rejoice; thou who allayed worldly griefs with trust in the will
    of God!

Rejoice; thou who, unlike the wife of Job, strengthened thy
    despondent husband in the faith!

Rejoice; thou who forgave the senseless murderer as Christ
    forgave those who crucified Him!

Rejoice; thou who asked the Redeemer of the world that He
    give the kingdom of heaven to thy son!

Rejoice; thou who by sorrows didst detach thy heart from
    the earthly world!

Rejoice; thou who by suffering thy cross didst warm thy love
    even more greatly for God!

Rejoice; O merciful Juliana, boast of Murom and
    adornment of women!

KONTAKION V

BY the will of God thy second beloved son also met an untimely death on the field of battle; yet accepting this cross also without complaint, thou didst splendidly honour thy younger offspring with many prayers, forty memorial liturgies, and generous alms. And having consoled thy husband with good words, that he not again lose hope in God, with tears of compunctions, like a wounded dove, thou didst thyself spend many nights quietly in prayer, considering a departure from the world, and transforming funeral lamentations into the hymn of praise to the Almighty: ALLELUIA!

OIKOS V

SEEING thee yearning to hide thyself from the world in a convent, thy spouse besought thee not to leave him bereft with five children. And thou, O meek ewe-lamb, having learned humbly to cut off thine own will for the sake of others, obediently said: "Let the will of the Lord be done!" And again taking upon thy shoulder, which had been wounded by cruel sorrows, the cross given thee by God, of struggle in this world's life, thou didst increase all the more thy vigils, fasting and prayers, living in matrimony like an unmarried desert-dweller. And we, marvelling at thine obedience and ascetic feats, humbly offer thee these praises:

Rejoice; thou who didst enter into the mystery of
matrimony, which thou didst solemnly preserve!

Rejoice; spouse faithful to thy husband, whom thou didst
serve with humility!

Rejoice; ascetic mighty in this world, who didst bear thy
cross with patience!

Rejoice; victor over the carnal passions, who vanquished the
enemy in battle!

Rejoice; thou who kept thy vesture of thy soul white in this
benighted world!

Rejoice; star of quiet brilliance, shining amid the tumult
of life!

Rejoice; thou who didst pray fervently in the married state, a
model of ardour for monks!

Rejoice; sufferer, meek mother, who emulated the saints in
the torments thou didst endure!

Rejoice; O merciful Juliana, boast of Murom and
adornment of women!

KONTAKION VI

THY son Callistratus showed himself to be the proclaimer of thy life
of suffering, for he recounted to the world thy secret and wondrous
struggle: thy prayers continued throughout the night; thou didst set
sharp-edged planks as a bed for thy body; thy hands became calloused
through thy many prostrations; thy flesh became desiccated by intense
fasting; thine eyes were bathed with rivers of tears; and thy pure tongue
continually chanted the hymn: ALLELUIA!

OIKOS VI

GRACE shone forth in thy heart, O holy mother, and gave thy prayer
wings to soar far above all things. Ablaze with divine fire, and drawn
to God like a bird of paradise, thou didst desire to visit the temple of God;
for thy spirit was borne thither, casting off all the grief of life; and thou wast
sweetly consoled amid thy sorrows, receiving the gift of grace from the
Father. And we, the slothful, beholding the zeal for God which was in thy
soul, are able only to glorify thee with our tongue, crying out thus:

Rejoice; thou who, receiving the fire of grace, didst soar aloft
from earth to heaven!

Rejoice; thou who, having tasted the sweetness of paradise,
didst make thine abode in Christ Jesus!

Rejoice; thou who, burning with love for God, didst receive
from Him the gift of tears!

Rejoice; thou who, though praying in secret, didst love
church more than thy home!

Rejoice; thou who, contemplating the redemption wrought by the Lord, didst spend Fridays alone and without food!

Rejoice; thou who, emulating the incorporeal angels, didst refuse to sleep, that thou mightest pray!

Rejoice; thou who, having acquired grace in thy heart, created a temple of God within thyself!

Rejoice; thou who, receiving the Holy Mysteries, didst provide an abode for the Holy Trinity in thy soul!

Rejoice; O merciful Juliana, boast of Murom and adornment of women!

KONTAKION VII

D ESIRING, after the repose of thy friend, to cleave unto heaven with all thy soul, thou didst add struggles unto struggles, O righteous one; and emulating Christ above all, thou didst struggle ascetically in humility and love. Wherefore, thou didst receive from Him the gift of tears of compunction and a heart full of mercy for all; and living while yet on earth as though in heaven, thou didst offer praise unto God, chanting: ALLELUIA!

OIKOS VII

A NEW sign did the Lord reveal in thee: for, distributing warm garments unto all, it then being a cruel winter, thou didst cease to go to the church of God. Yet one morning, when the priest of God went to the Church of the Righteous Lazarus, he heard a voice issue forth from the icon of the all-pure Mother of God, saying: "Go and say to the merciful widow Juliana: Wherefore dost thou not come to the church of God to pray? Prayer at home is pleasing unto God, but not as is prayer in church!" And then the voice spake further, saying: "And do thou honour her, for she is not less than sixty years of age, and the Holy Spirit resteth in her!" And when thou didst with fear learn of this wondrous miracle, thou didst beseech all who heard of it to keep silence, and didst make all haste to the all-pure Mistress at the church of God, and kissing her icon with fervent tears, didst humbly offer up hymns of supplication. And the faithful people, rejoicing radiantly that the Queen of heaven, the joy of all joys, loved thee so, thus glorified thee with gladness:

Rejoice; thou who loved Christ with all thy heart!

Rejoice; thou who offered him fervent tears!

Rejoice; thou who considered love to be greater than
    prayer and fasting!

Rejoice; thou who ever attended all the services of
    the Church!

Rejoice; thou who wast called merciful by the Mother
    of God!

Rejoice; thou who within thyself wast wholly overshadowed
    by the Holy Spirit!

Rejoice; thou who received glory, not from men, but from
    the holy Theotokos!

Rejoice; tranquil radiance illumining the region of Murom!

Rejoice; O merciful Juliana, boast of Murom and
    adornment of women!

KONTAKION VIII

S TRANGE and wondrous is it to see how on earth God giveth the greatest sorrows to His beloved children, as a surety of His love for them. Wherefore, unto thee, O blessed one, who received great mercy from the Mother of God in His church, it was also fitting to receive a greater measure of griefs, that thou mightest show forth grateful love for God and thyself be glorified, and that thou mightest teach sorrowing people to have patience, that all may sing the praise: ALLELUIA!

OIKOS VIII

WHEN by God's incomprehensible providence a great famine again befell thy land, all experienced want, and even thou, the merciful widow, didst fall into dire poverty. Yet entrusting thyself and thy children to the oversight of God, thou didst command them to endure all things unto death; and thus also didst thou earnestly beseech thy servants, that they dare not to touch anything belonging to anyone else. And obedient, though they were afraid, they kept this commandment and said to thee:

Rejoice; thou only consolation in that grievous time of great famine!

Rejoice; thou who suffered in the flesh, seeking all the more the heavenly city!

Rejoice; thou who amid dread manifestations didst consider the precepts and wrath of God!

Rejoice; thou who as a mother didst have compassion for children who were tormented with hunger!

Rejoice; thou who by the power of faith didst endure sorrows without measure!

Rejoice; thou who didst instruct thy children and thy servants, who were of one mind with thee, to be obedient to the Cross!

Rejoice; thou who prayed to God, shedding tears with those who wept, and suffering with the people!

Rejoice; thou who with ardent heart didst grieve in soul for sinful Russia!

Rejoice; O merciful Juliana, boast of Murom and adornment of women!

KONTAKION IX

E VERY living creature, receiving food for itself in due season, praiseth Thee, the good God, who openest Thine all-generous hand unto all, even before Thou art asked. But Thy mighty favourite, seeking the kingdom of heaven even when deprived of the good things of Thine earth, never ceased to cry out to Thee in praise: ALLELUIA!

OIKOS IX

E ARTHLY rhetors are at a loss to describe with their tongues the pangs of mothers' souls when they are crushed by the sufferings of their beloved children; and thou, O steadfast sufferer, while pouring forth thy mercy upon all, yet unable to find bread for thine own children, didst feed them pig-weed, comforting them by saying repeatedly: "Glory to God for all things!" And we, learning the power of patience from thee, honour thee fervently with voices of praise:

Rejoice; sojourner strange to the earthly world, who didst
  bitterly wander throughout the world!

Rejoice; thou who, seeking the heavenly city, didst remain in
  this world a homeless orphan!

Rejoice; thou who, having been possessed of great wealth,
  wast shown to be a pauper, hungry and poorly clad!

Rejoice; thou who before gavest alms, but later wast among
  the children bereft of bread!

Rejoice; thou who, looking to the joy which is to come, didst
  take up thy present cross with hope!

Rejoice; thou who, having surrendered thyself to the will
  of the Lord, didst accept the path of poverty
  and wandering!

Rejoice; thou who looking to the sufferings of Christ, didst
  without murmuring endure thy cross in this life!

Rejoice; thou who, strengthened in weakness by the Spirit,
    didst in the midst of sorrows sing, "Glory to God
    for all things!"

Rejoice; O merciful Juliana, boast of Murom and
    adornment of women!

KONTAKION X

DESIRING from childhood to save thy soul, thou didst think upon God in silence with all thy heart; and diligently caring for thy kinfolk like Martha, thou didst in spirit love the portion of Mary. And ever desiring the blessed life, thou didst keep the memory of death continually in the mind, praying the Jesus Prayer in thy heart, thereby sweetening thy bitter life, until thou didst reach the vault of heaven, the uttermost desire, O venerable one, crying unto God: ALLELUIA!

OIKOS X

THOU didst show forth the power of courage in thy weak body to be a rampart which the waves of life could not demolish; and submitting to the law of nature and subjected to many sorrows, thou didst reach the end of thy life at a goodly old age. And the good God, Who alone is holy, desiring to see thee as a pure pearl, sent thee sickness on the second day of His Nativity, that when beholding the Saviour of the world, like Symeon thou mightest say to Him in parting: "Let thy handmaid depart this life in peace, O Master, that I may behold Thee, mine only Glory and the Saviour of my sinful soul." And thy kinfolk compassionately comforted thee well, saying:

Rejoice; thou who traversed the sea, reaching the calm
    haven!

Rejoice; thou who didst leave this world, awaiting the heavenly
    bridal-chamber!

Rejoice; thou who never condemned anyone, and art thyself
    not condemned by the Judge!

Rejoice; thou who, having wrought deeds of mercy, dost
enter the ranks of the all wise virgins!

Rejoice; thou who hast flown aloft to the mansions on high,
on wings of dove-like meekness!

Rejoice; thou who before didst contemplate Christ, the
gentle Light of life everlasting!

Rejoice; thou who like an all-radiant beam didst flow into the
bridal-chamber of the Father!

Rejoice; thou who hast thine abode with the choir of the
saints in the Holy Spirit!

Rejoice; O merciful Juliana, boast of Murom and
adornment of women!

KONTAKION XI

YEARNING to hear the chanting of the angels in the mansions on
high, thou didst not cease to utter tearful prayers even on thy death
bed; for, though suffering greatly in body and lying abed during the day,
at night thou didst secretly rise up to pray, and like a guttering candle
didst give off thy last flame. And when others learned of thy nocturnal
struggle, O dove of God, thou didst meekly say to them: "God
examineth the spiritual prayers even of one who is sick." For even the
angels praise Him unceasingly, crying ever: ALLELUIA!

OIKOS XI

THOUGH greatly sanctified by the holy light, the grace of the Spirit,
thou didst ever consider thyself to be a wretched sinner. Wherefore,
trusting only in the mercy of the Saviour, thou didst tearfully receive the
most Holy Mysteries after a fervent confession, O honoured one. And
thus, united in heart with thy Redeemer, and receiving the surety of the
eternal kingdom without doubting, thou didst leave unto thy children and
to all a testament of love, prayer, and almsgiving. And then, lying down,
taking up thy prayer-rope, and making the sign of the Cross, thou didst

utter thy last words: "Glory to God for all things! Into Thy hands do I commit my spirit. Amen." And thus, like a lamp guttering out, thou didst quietly fly away from the earth to the dwellings of incorruption, in a dream commanding that thy body be buried next to thy husband and friend. And we, compunctiously rejoicing with thy close kinfolk at thine unashamed and peaceful repose, following thine ascent, sing glorious praise with the angels, chanting:

Rejoice; thou who at thy final and grievous hour didst
    provide a model of humility!

Rejoice; thou who wast for us an image of prayer until thy
    reflection disappeared!

Rejoice; bride of Christ, whose head the Bridegroom
    adorned with a crown!

Rejoice; pure and holy temple who before thine end wast
    covered by God with a white kerchief!

Rejoice; thou whose holy body was more fragrant than the
    lilies of the field even after death!

Rejoice; thou who wast illumined at night by candles lighted
    by an invisible power!

Rejoice; thou who easily passed through the aerial way-
    stations because of thy mercy toward the poor!

Rejoice; thou who endured many crosses and hast reached
    the kingdom of God!

Rejoice; O merciful Juliana, boast of Murom and
    adornment of women!

KONTAKION XII

HAVING received the grace to offer up prayers for the world from which thou hast departed, in thy love thou hast not forsaken those who love thee and are beloved of thee on earth; and having splendidly attained unto the mansions of heaven, thou hast been vouchsafed blessed joy with those who passed on before thee. And thy sons, guided by thy spirit, led a pious life, teaching one another to preserve Holy Orthodoxy. And thy one daughter, Theodosia, receiving the monastic rank in thy stead, reposed in holiness in the great schema, soaring aloft unto thee, like a chick under thy wings. And we today, composing heartfelt hymns to thee with love, do earnestly pray: Entreat Christ God in our behalf, that with thee we may all ever offer up to Him, unto the ages of ages, the hymn: ALLELUIA!

OIKOS XII

O HOLY woman, the all-glorious Church of Christ singeth funeral hymns of gladness unto thee, having wondrous and beautifully found thy relics to be fragrant; and having reckoned among the choir of the saints thee who before wast blessed exceedingly by the Mother of God herself, it now rejoiceth all-radiantly: for it is meet to glorify those whom God hath glorified; for the honour rendered the saints redoundeth divinely unto God Who resteth in the saints. Wherefore, leaping up in heart and joining chorus in the Spirit, o ye Orthodox people, with the angels let us today all chant together:

Rejoice; adornment of the land of Murom!

Rejoice; ornament of the nation of Russia!

Rejoice; beauty of Christian women!

Rejoice; summit of holy mothers!

Rejoice; thou who wast upborne to paradise by the angels!

Rejoice; thou who hast been blessed by the Lord!

Rejoice; boast of thy kinsmen!

Rejoice; consolation of all who honour thee!

Rejoice; O merciful Juliana, boast of Murom and
adornment of women!

KONTAKION XIII

O MERCIFUL and pure turtledove, blessed and righteous Juliana! With thy wonted love accept these fervent praises, and as a mother full of pity, who carest for thy children, beseech the all-merciful Saviour, that He grant us a single boon-the divine grace of the Holy Spirit, wherein all the good things of earth and of heaven are hid; that having been enriched thereby, we may pass through this sorrowful life untroubled, and with thee may receive the blessed kingdom of the all-holy Trinity, gloriously crying out thereto: ALLELUIA! ALLELUIA! ALLELUIA! *(Thrice)*

And again, Oikos I and Kontakion I are read.

OIKOS I

A PURE angel, from earliest childhood thou didst love the angelic monastic life; but the Creator of all, Who arrangeth all things in the depths of His wisdom, ordained a different path of salvation for thee-that thou please Him with a holy life within honourable matrimony. Wherefore, from childhood He led thee to the kingdom of God through many trials: for when thou wast a maiden six years of age, thou hadst already become a grieving orphan; and as a young bride, thou didst soon take up the cross of motherhood. And we, though stricken with awe at this wondrous providence, yet compunctiously praise thee with faith:

Rejoice; thou who wast born into wealth, to parents who
loved the poor – Justin and Stephanida!

Rejoice; thou who, deprived of thy mother, wast raised an
orphan outside thy father's house!

Rejoice; right fragrant lily who blossomed within the
tranquillity of the forests of Murom!

Rejoice; radiant star set alight by God in the village
of Lazarevo!

Rejoice; thou who in thy heart acquired love for Christ and
His all-pure Mother!

Rejoice; pure ewe-lamb who from childhood sought the
monastic order!

Rejoice; meek and obedient one, who by the will of God
wast entrusted to a husband!

Rejoice; righteous mother who, having lived in the world,
hast been numbered among the saints!

Rejoice; O merciful Juliana, boast of Murom and
adornment of women!

KONTAKION I

O RIGHTEOUS and merciful Juliana, who wast chosen by God, and
amidst worldly cares didst in thy soul live in Christ, as in heaven;
and who didst abide in great stillness, loving silence within thy heart!
Glorifying the Lord Who hath glorified thee; with compunction, we sing
to thee a hymn of praise. Do thou, who endured grievous sorrows in thy
life, pray for us, who are tempest-tossed by perils and sins, and entreat the
merciful Saviour to grant us salvation of soul and deliverance from
misfortunes, that, giving thanks unto God, we may glorify thee, saying:

Rejoice; O merciful Juliana, boast of Murom and
adornment of women!

PRAYERS TO SAINT JULIANA OF LAZAREVO

PRAYER I

O BLESSED and righteous Juliana, who wast wondrously called the
merciful widow by the all-holy Theotokos! Unto thee, a mother
full of pity, do we earnestly have recourse, praying that we also may be
granted mercy. For, having endured many crosses in thy life, and been
thyself tried by all things, in thy supplications thou art able to help us in
our bitter trials; for, beset by many sins and weighed down by great
sorrows, we are assailed by cruel enemies. Wherefore, O mother who

bore thy crosses, ask for us the spirit of meekness and patience, sincere repentance of our sins, the power to oppose the invisible foe and to defeat them, and firm trust in the will of God amid all misfortunes and perils, that we may take up our cross without murmuring, unto the salvation of our souls, and may proceed with faith for Christ our Saviour. Moreover, beseech the all-merciful Lord, O merciful favourite of God, that He cause to dwell in us, as it did in thee, the grace of a heart which hath mercy upon all, which blesseth even one's enemies, which accuseth itself only of sins, as thou didst: for love hath grown exceeding scarce because of our iniquities; and in name only can we show ourselves to be disciples of Christ, while in heart and deed were are as pagans, caring only for ourselves with love of self. O blessed one, intercede also for the Russian land, and for all who are in dispersion, that they may receive peace and prosperity, and all the more a return to thine ancient piety, a quenching of malice and envy, and increase in brotherly love and reconciliation, repentance for our passions, and cleansing and sanctification through grace. That with one mouth and one heart we may all again confess the consubstantial and indivisible Trinity unto the ages of ages. AMEN.

PRAYER II

O MERCIFUL Juliana, helper of orphans, mother who bore thy cross! With thy generous right hand, make bestowal upon us who now pray to thee, and ask the all-merciful God, Whose very name is love, that He grant us rich mercies. Be thou a good helper unto mothers who have given birth unto children; a holy preserver of purity and love within marriage; a wise nurturer of little children and youths; a compassionate comforter of the orphaned and sorrowful; a sympathetic healer of those who are tempest-tossed by sins; a mighty defender of those subjected to trials by their enemies; and a merciful mediator before God and the all-pure Theotokos for all who ask thine aid. And pray thou all the more, O holy favourite of God, that we be given the grace of the all-holy Spirit, that preserved thereby and saved unceasingly in this life, with thee we may glorify the all-merciful Redeemer, our Lord and Saviour Jesus Christ, to Whom is due glory, with His all-good Father, and His holy and all-compassionate Spirit, unto the ages of ages. AMEN.

AKATHIST TO THE
HOLY ARCHANGEL MICHAEL

KONTAKION I

CHOSEN captain of the heavenly hosts and defender of mankind, we —
delivered by thee from afflictions — offer this hymn of thanksgiving,
and do thou, standing before the throne of the King of Glory, set us free
from all distress that we may cry unto thee with faith and love:

Hail; Michael great captain, with the hosts of heaven!

OIKOS I

AS leader of the fiery choirs of angels, it is right to praise thee with
angelic tongue, O Michael, but until — taught by thee — we have

become used to the speech of the bodiless powers, hear the praises from thankful lips though they be those of mortal beings:

> Hail; first-formed star of the world!

> Hail; candle of truth and justice, shining like gold!

> Hail; first receiver, in the choir of angels of the rays of the uncreated light!

> Hail; head of angels and archangels!

> Hail; thou in whom the creative glory of the Right Hand shines!

> Hail; thou by whom the assembly of all bodiless creatures is made beautiful!

> Hail; Michael, great chief captain with all the hosts of heaven!

KONTAKION II

BEHOLDING the splendour of thy spiritual beauty and the strength of thy right hand that is like a flash of lightning, we — wrapped as we are in the mortal flesh of this earth — but, filled with joy and thankfulness toward the Creator, cry aloud: O Archangel of God, with all the hosts of heaven: ALLELUIA!

OIKOS II

O MOST wonderful Michael, leader of the heavenly hosts, ask for us a clear understanding, free from passions, that, lifted in thought from earthly to heavenly things, we may sing a hymn of praise to thee:

> Hail; nearest beholder of the ineffable beauty and goodness of God!

> Hail; close participator in the mysteries of the all-good counsels of the most Holy Trinity!

Hail; faithful fulfiller of the pre-eternal judgments of
the Trinity!

Hail; thou at whom the heavenly hosts, with love, stand
amazed!

Hail; thou to whom those born on earth give glory!

Hail; thou before whom the hosts of heaven tremble!

Hail; Michael, great chief captain with all the hosts of heaven!

KONTAKION III

ARCHANGEL Michael, thou showeth in thyself the strength of an
unconquerable zeal for the glory of God. At the head of the choirs
of angels, thou hast withstood the arrogant daystar Satan, exceedingly
proud and breathing out evil when he and his dark fellow-servants had
been cast down into the nethermost parts of the world, while the
heavenly hosts led by you in thy glory shouted as with one voice for joy
before the throne of God: ALLELUIA!

OIKOS III

ALL Christian people have thee, O Archangel Michael, as a mighty
defender and helper in battle against the adversary. Therefore, we,
wishing to be granted thy marvellous protection, call upon thee on the day
of thy solemn feast in this way:

Hail; thee by whom Satan wast cast down like lightning
from heaven!

Hail; thee by whom humanity preserved goes up to heaven!

Hail; splendid adornment of the most radiant world on high!

Hail; most glorious defender of the fallen world here below!

Hail; never-defeated by the forces of evil!

Hail; thee, established forever by divine grace in truth and righteousness with all God's angels!

Hail; Michael, great chief captain with all the hosts of heaven!

KONTAKION IV

O CHIEF ruler of the angels, deliver us who keep thy radiant feast with joy from the storm of temptations and troubles, for thou art a mighty helper in afflictions and the preserver and defender in the hour of death of all those crying aloud to Our Lord and Our Lady: ALLELUIA!

OIKOS IV

S EEING thy boldness against the regiments of Satan, all the ranks of angels followed after thee with joy into the fight for the name and the glory of their Master, crying aloud: "Who is like unto God!" And we, seeing Satan cast down beneath thy feet cry to thee as victor:

Hail; thee by whom peace and quiet returned to heaven!

Hail; thou whom the spirit of evil was laid low even unto hell!

Hail; thou who direct the angelic armies and the hosts of the invisible world to the destruction of evil!

Hail; thou who, unseen, calm the agitation and fighting of the elements of the unseen world!

Hail; wonderful defender of those waging war with the spirits of evil!

Hail; strong helper of those on earth grown weak through the temptations and assaults of the world!

Hail; Michael, great chief captain with all the hosts of heaven!

KONTAKION V

THOU hast appeared in the Church of Khony as a divinely flowing fountain of great miracles. For, not only was a large and fearful serpent dwelling there destroyed by your strength, but a stream of water was revealed there healing all bodily ailments, that all might glorify thee, O Lord God of the angels, and all might cry out to Thee with Faith: ALLELUIA!

OIKOS V

HEARING thee and knowing thee as a great light shining amongst the choirs of angels, after God and His Holy Mother, we run to thee, wonderful Michael. With the rays of thy light, illuminate all of us who sing to thee in the following manner:

Hail; mediator of the law given by the hand of Moses on Mount Sinai!

Hail; thou by whom the judges and leaders of Israel found strength and protection!

Hail; thou, through whom the prophets and high priests of the Jews received the gift of knowledge from the all-knowing God!

Hail; thou who providest with secret wisdom the God-fearing givers of the law!

Hail; thou who put kindness and mercy into the hearts of those who administer justice and truth!

Hail; Michael, great chief captain with all the hosts of heaven!

KONTAKION VI

THOU hast announced beforehand the judgments of God when, in former times — at the sight of you — Mannah was filled with fear and perplexity, thinking that he would no longer live, but taught by his wife of the goodness of the vision, and the gentleness of thy words, from joy at having a son, Samson, who was about to be born, he cried out to God in thanksgiving: ALLELUIA!

OIKOS VI

THOU hast shone forth wonderfully, O Michael, when in the form of a man thou hast stood before Joshua, son of Nun, saying: "Take off your shoes, for I am the chief captain of the hosts of the Lord." And we, marvelling, sing to thee:

Hail; untiring guardian of leaders, rulers, and governments!

Hail; thou, swift to overthrow those withstanding authority as they oppose the command of God!

Hail; thou who appease the mighty wave of popular tumult!

Hail; invisible destroyer of vile customs!

Hail; thou who enlighten those in doubt in the hour of great perplexity!

Hail; thou who save all those tried by soul-destroying and false attacks!

Hail; Michael, great chief captain with all the hosts of heaven!

KONTAKION VII

WANTING to show that the fortunes of men are not dependent on themselves, but are always held in His Divine Hand, the Maker of all has given thee to the kingdoms of the earth as a defender and keeper, that thou mayest prepare all the tribes and peoples for the Kingdom of God that is eternal. Therefore, all of us knowing thy great service for the salvation of mankind, cry to God in thanksgiving: ALLELUIA!

OIKOS VII

The Creator and Master of all miracles has shown us a new miracle on earth through thee, chief angel, when thou miraculously saved the church built in honour of thy name from being flooded with the waters of the river. Thou commanded the rising stream to turn back into the bosom of the earth, at the sight of which the blessed Archipus together with his spiritual children cried to thee in thanksgiving:

Hail; indestructible rampart of the holy Church of God!

Hail; thou at whose behest the elements are subdued!

Hail; thou by whom all evil intents are brought to naught!

Hail; thou who bringest joy to all the faithful from the throne of the Almighty God!

Hail; thou who lead unbelievers on the path of justice and truth!

Hail; Michael, great chief captain with all the hosts of heaven!

KONTAKION VIII

HABAKKUK, the prophet, saw in his very self a strange wonder of thy power, O chief captain of God's armies, when carried off at the Divine Command, he was quickly taken from Judah to Babylon to give food to Daniel, a prisoner in the den of the lions. Therefore, amazed at the mighty effect of your strength, he cried out with faith: ALLELUIA!

OIKOS VIII

STANDING before the throne of God, Michael, thou art entirely in the heights yet thou art not far from men and women below upon the earth. Thou ever fight against the enemies of mankind's salvation. Therefore, all who wish to reach the long-desired homeland of heaven call to you with one accord:

Hail; leader of the thrice-holy hymn of the angels!

Hail; ever-ready advocate and guardian of those on earth!

Hail; who, in strange fashion, struck down Pharaoh with his faithless Egyptians in their ponderous pride!

Hail; who gloriously led the Jews in their wandering through the wilderness!

Hail; thou who quenched the flame of the fiery furnace of Babylon for the three youths!

Hail; Michael, great chief captain with all the hosts of heaven!

KONTAKION IX

JOYFUL trembling seized the monks of the Holy Mount of Athos when they saw how thou saved the God-fearing child who was thrown into the depths of the sea with a stone around his neck by money-grubbing men. The monastery that received him was adorned by thy name, O Michael, and cries to God in thanksgiving: ALLELUIA!

OIKOS IX

SPEAKERS, eloquent in words and who love clever thoughts, have not sufficient strength to declare thy might, O Michael, and how in one night thou destroyed the one hundred and eighty-five thousand warriors of Sennacherih, the king of Assyria, as a warning to him not to blaspheme the Name of the Lord in the future. We, honouring thy zeal for the glory of the truth of God, cry out to thee with gladness:

Hail; unconquerable leader of the armies of Orthodoxy!

Hail: very fear, and defeat of armies whose beliefs are evil!

Hail: planter of the Orthodox faith and worship!

Hail: uprooter of heresies and schisms that harm the soul!

Hail: thou who strengthened the pious Maccabees on the
field of battle!

Hail: thou who struck down in the temple itself Heliodorus,
the captain of the evil king, Antiochus!

Hail: Michael, great chief captain with all the hosts of heaven!

KONTAKION X

O CHIEF captain of God, be for us who wish to be saved, a firm
helper, to deliver and preserve us from distress and mishap, and
even more so from our own evil habits and sins so that, progressing in
faith, hope and love of Christ, we may thankfully cry out with joy to the
Master of angels and mankind for your strong defence: ALLELUIA!

OIKOS X

O CHIEF Captain of God, thou art a wall for all who believe and a
strong pillar in the struggles with visible and invisible enemies. With
thankful hearts and voices, we cry:

Hail; unconquerable opponent of the enemies of the Faith
and the adversaries of the Holy Church!

Hail; untiring helper of those who humbly announce the
Good News!

Hail; thou who enlighten with the light of faith those sitting in
the land of darkness!

Hail; thou who direct along the path of truth and repentance
those made foolish through false wisdom!

Hail; terrible avenger of those who call in vain upon the
Name of the Lord!

Hail; chastiser-bearing lightning for those who foolishly
mock the Mysteries of the Holy Faith!

Hail; Michael, great chief captain with all the hosts of heaven!

KONTAKION XI

O ANGEL of God, every song of praise falls short because of the multitude of miracles performed by thee not only in heaven and on earth, but also in the dark shades of the depths of the netherworld, where thou hast chained the serpent with the bonds of power of the Lord, that those delivered from the evil one's wickedness might bless the Master of heaven and earth, crying: ALLELUIA!

OIKOS XI

O CHIEF captain, thou appeared as a light-bearing servant of truth and the purity of divine worship when, foreseeing the snares of the spirit of darkness, thou hast forbidden him in the Name of the Lord, that he dare not show the hidden body of the prophet Moses, leader of the Jews, to the children of Israel lest they deify him. Therefore, while we now honour thy divinely bright feast, we cry to thee:

Hail; thou who kept the purity of knowledge of God among the Jews in the days of the Old Testament!

Hail; who by grace have many times uprooted the weeds of error in the days of the New Testament!

Hail; destroyer of heathen prophets and idols!

Hail; fortifier of Christians who struggle and suffer!

Hail; thou who fill the weak in spirit with the strength of the grace of God!

Hail; thou who clothest in the armour of faith those who fail in the flesh!

Hail; Michael, great chief captain with all the hosts of heaven!

KONTAKION XII

B EG grace for us from God in heaven as we sing to the glory of thy honourable name, O Michael, that in the shadow of thy protection we may live in all piety and purity until, set loose from the bonds of flesh and death, we may be granted to stand before the flaming throne of the King of Glory and sing with all the choirs of angels: ALLELUIA!

OIKOS XII

S INGING the praises of thy many different miracles performed for our salvation, we pray the Lord and Master of all, O Michael, that the spirit of zeal for the glory of God that is within you fail not in us who sing to thee with these hymns of praise:

Hail; thou who divinely set up in the heights of power the servants of God in time of need!

Hail; thou who invisibly bring down from the heights of strength and glory those who are unworthy and insolent!

Hail; thou, who on the last day, shall gather the chosen from the four ends of the earth!

Hail; thou by whom at the voice of God sinners shall be committed like bears to the eternal fire!

Hail; thou by whom Satan and his angels shall be cast into the lake of fire!

Hail; thou by whom the righteous shall gloriously be made to settle in the mansion of our heavenly Father!

Hail; Michael, great chief captain with all the hosts of heaven!

KONTAKION XIII

O MOST wonderful leader of archangels and angels, because of thy most marvellous service for the salvation of mankind, accept from us the sound of praise and thanksgiving now offered to thee, and as thou art filled with the strength of God, protect us with thine immaterial wings from all visible and invisible enemies, that we may cry without ceasing to the Lord glorified by thee and who glorified thee: Alleluia!

PRAYER

O GREAT and holy Michael, Archangel of God, standing at the head of the angels before the everlasting Trinity, O advocate and preserver of mankind, who — with thy hosts — hast broken in heaven the head of the daystar, Satan, the exceedingly proud one, and who always puts to shame his evil and cunning servants on earth, we run to thee with faith and pray to thee with love: be an unbreakable shield and firm bastion for the Holy Church and for our nation, protecting them with thy lightning sword. Be for us a guardian angel, a wise counsellor, and helper of our land bringing to it from the throne of the Eternal Ruling King and Lord our God enlightenment and strength, joy, peace and comfort. Be for us the chief captain and fellow-fighter of our honourable country, crowning it with glory and victory over unjust adversaries, that all who oppose us may know that God and His holy angels stand ready to defend us. Be the physician and healer of those wounded. Be the pillar and defender of those children of the Church of God that are in captivity. And forsake not, O Archangel of God, with thy help and protection, those of us who today glorify thy holy name. For, behold, though we are great sinners, yet we desire not to perish in our iniquities but to turn to the Lord and be made by Him to live for good works. Illuminate our minds with the light of the Countenance of God that shines without ceasing on the lightning-like forehead, that we may understand that the will of God concerning us is good and perfect and knows all that is right for us to do, and even that which is right to omit and overlook. Strengthen by the grace of the Lord, our weak and feeble purpose, that made firm in the commandments of the Lord we may cease to wallow in earthly thoughts drawn by the lusts of the flesh as senseless children through the perishable beauties of the world. Above all these things, ask from on high for us the true spirit of repentance, true sorrow and contrition for our sins before God, that we may spend the remaining number of our days in this temporal life, not in the satisfying of our feelings and in the bondage to our passions, but in the blotting out of the evil we have done by tears of faith and heartfelt compunction, by works of charity, chastity, and holy acts of loving mercy.

WHEN the hour of our end and of our liberation from the earthly bonds of our own bodies draws near, O Archangel of God, leave us not without defence against the earthly spirits of evil who try to hinder the entry of man into the heavenly places. Preserved by thee, may we, without hindrance, reach those all-glorious dwelling-places of Paradise where there is neither sorrow nor sighing but only life without end. May we be made worthy to behold the Face of our all-gracious Lord and Master, and falling at His feet with tears may we cry out in joy and tender feeling: Glory to Thee, our most tender, dear Redeemer, who, because of Thy great love for us, thy unworthy servants and handmaidens, have been pleased to send Thine angels in the service of our salvation! For all the powers of heaven praise Thee, and we give glory, honour, and thanksgiving to Thee: Father, Son, and Holy Spirit, now and ever, and unto the ages of ages. AMEN.

O CHOSEN captain of the heavenly hosts and defender of mankind, we, delivered by thee from all afflictions, offer this hymn of thanksgiving, and do thou, standing before the throne of the King of Glory, set us free from all distress that we may cry unto thee with faith and love:

Hail; Michael, great captain, with all the hosts of heaven!
(Thrice)

AKATHIST TO SAINT NECTARIOS OF PENTAPOLIS

KONTAKION I

IN joy of heart let us hymn with songs the newly revealed star of Orthodoxy, the newly erected bulwark of the Church; for, glorified by the activity of the Spirit, he pours forth the abundant grace of healings upon those who cry:

> Rejoice; O Father Nektarios, model of patience and
>   lover of virtue!

OIKOS I

IN the world thou were shown to be a man of heavenly mind, O Nektarios, hierarch of Christ; for having passed through life in holiness, thou were shown to be blameless, venerable, and God-pleasing in all things. Wherefore, thou hear from us such praises as these:

Rejoice; thou by whom the faithful are edified!

Rejoice; thou of whom the enemy is afraid!

Rejoice; emulator of the venerable fathers!

Rejoice; divine teacher of the Orthodox!

Rejoice; thou for whom the Church joins chorus!

Rejoice; thou in whom Aegina rejoices!

Rejoice; O Father Nektarios, model of patience and
lover of virtue!

KONTAKION II

HAVING adorned thyself with meekness of soul from thy youth, O holy father, one fervent desire consumed your heart: to become a preacher of the Holy Gospel. From childhood, thou knew the Scriptures which are able to make man wise for salvation, teaching them to cry: ALLELUIA!

OIKOS II

WHEN thou left thy home and travelled to Constantinople, thou laboured in the midst of worldly distractions. Yet thou didst not forsake the Faith which dwelt first in thy grandmother and mother and also dwelt in thee, steadfastly dedicating thyself to prayer and to the sayings of the Fathers, which thou wrote on packages and wrappings so that others might read them and receive spiritual profit. Wherefore, to one who was in the world but not of it, we the faithful cry aloud in thanksgiving:

Rejoice; most holy temple of the activity of God!

Rejoice; divinely inscribed book of new morals!

Rejoice; for thou made thyself like unto the saints in
perfection!

Rejoice; for thou wisely spurned material things!

Rejoice; splendid victory of the Faith!

Rejoice; honoured clarion of grace!

Rejoice; O Father Nektarios, model of patience and
lover of virtue!

KONTAKION III

A S a fervent lover of the monastic life, thou often visited the
Monastery of the Holy Fathers, conversing there about the spiritual
struggle with its holy founder, Elder Pachomios. As thou aspired to the
angelic habit, thou were tonsured and dedicated thyself to prayer on behalf
of the people as thou sang: ALLELUIA!

OIKOS III

W HOLLY consumed with the love of heavenly knowledge, thou
received a blessing to continue thy theological education to which
thou devoted thyself with zeal and self-denial. Whilst living in Athens,
thou studied day and night, knowing no other roads but that to the school
and to the Church. Wherefore, as to our instructor in heavenly theology,
we thy children joyfully cry:

Rejoice; great pillar of piety!

Rejoice; city of refuge for the faithful!

Rejoice; firm stronghold of Orthodoxy!

Rejoice; venerable vessel and praise of the Holy Trinity!

Rejoice; thou who shone forth in these latter times like a
never-setting sun!

Rejoice; thou who pour forth the nectar of grace upon all
  believers!

Rejoice; O Father Nektarios, model of patience and
  lover of virtue!

KONTAKION IV

A RRAYED in true holiness and pure morals, Patriarch Sophronios of
Alexandria saw in you great potential for service to Christ's Holy
Church. Thou wast ordained to the sacred priesthood and elevated to the
office of Bishop. O wise one, thou offered thy life to Christ as a pure
sacrifice, ever chanting: ALLELUIA!

OIKOS IV

I N thy position as Metropolitan of Pentapolis, thou wast deeply loved by
the faithful, for clothed in the vesture of the hierarchy, thou adorned
thy life with humility. Ever disdainful of material possessions, thou
opened thy hand freely and distributed thine alms to the poor. Like thy
Master, thou willingly came not to be served but to serve and to give thy
life as a ransom for many. Conquered by thy love, we who honour thy
holy memory cry unto thee thus:

Rejoice; model of lambs and shepherds!

Rejoice; pure and honourable abode of holiness!

Rejoice; worthy converser with angels!

Rejoice; good guide of men!

Rejoice; for through thee we are delivered from bodily
  passions!

Rejoice; for through thee we are filled with spiritual delights!

Rejoice; O Father Nektarios, model of patience and
  lover of virtue!

KONTAKION V

WHEN the enemy of our souls saw thee labouring in humility, he could not abide thy holy presence among the people. Raising up slanders, inciting rumours, he sought to destroy thy good name and to lead thee to bitterness and anger. But thou overcame all of his devices, for in all things thou didst meekly chant unto God: ALLELUIA!

OIKOS V

LACKING even thy daily bread, slandered on all sides, thou prayed for thy accusers, begging the Father to forgive them. Refusing to speak one word in thy defence, thou joyfully suffered according to the will of God, committing thyself to Him in doing good, as to a faithful Creator. Wherefore, amazed by thy long-suffering and steadfast endurance, we thy children exclaim:

Rejoice; treasury of great mercy!

Rejoice; inexhaustible bread for the hungry!

Rejoice; container of great virtues!

Rejoice; model of spiritual meekness!

Rejoice; thou who said, "Father, forgive them, for they know not what they have done!"

Rejoice; thou who repaid evil with good!

Rejoice; O Father Nektarios, model of patience and lover of virtue!

KONTAKION VI

HAVING within thou a strong desire for the life of stillness on the Holy Mountain, thou could not abandon the people but heeded their call to remain in the world and to proclaim the words of salvation. Freely thou received and freely thou gave, calling all men to exclaim: ALLELUIA!

OIKOS VI

WITH the words of thy mouth thou dropped heavenly sweetness into the hearts of those who accepted your words with faith, directing the minds of the faithful to seek those things which are above. The sacred writings of thy teachings continually gladden the souls of the pious; for moved by the Holy Spirit, O Father, thou wisely recorded words of grace and instruction for those who cry to thee:

Rejoice; faithful servant of the Most Holy Trinity!

Rejoice; habitation adorned of the Holy Spirit!

Rejoice; light that illumines all the ends of the earth!

Rejoice; thou who delivers people from the abyss of sin!

Rejoice; thou who exalts truth!

Rejoice; thou who dispels falsehood!

Rejoice; O Father Nektarios, model of patience and
lover of virtue!

KONTAKION VII

INVITED to assume the direction of the Rizarios Ecclesiastical School, thou brought peace where there once existed confusion, for thou treated all as a loving father. Wherefore thy students in gratitude sang to God: ALLELUIA!

OIKOS VII

STRONG in the grace that is in Christ Jesus, having received the words of Life, thou committed these to faithful men who, because of thy good instruction and spiritual example, were enabled to teach them to others. Enduring hardships as a good soldier of Christ, thou didst not entangle thyself in the affairs of this life but thought only how to please the Master. Therefore, as to a worker who does not need to be ashamed, rightly dividing the word of truth, we cry out to you in words such as these:

Rejoice; teacher of the divine commandments!

Rejoice; thou who makes wise the unwise by thy teachings!

Rejoice; new Paul, who has bequeathed to us the pattern of
sound words!

Rejoice; new Jude, who has given us the exhortation to
contend earnestly for the faith!

Rejoice; new Chrysostom, who has poured forth upon the
Church the heavenly nectar of piety!

Rejoice; new Damascene, who has defended the faithful from
impious doctrines!

Rejoice; O Father Nektarios, model of patience and
lover of virtue!

KONTAKION VIII

WISELY adorned with understanding and meekness, thou
brought together venerable virgins in godliness, leading them
to Christ by thy words and the works of thy blameless life, teaching
them to sing: ALLELUIA!

OIKOS VIII

LISTENING to thy prayers and earnest supplications, the Lord Who
dost the will of those who fear him, led thee to the island of Aegina
where thou rebuilt the monastery which had been abandoned. Who can
describe thy labours and toils? Exercising vigilance in all things, thou
showeth forth a model of divine virtue. Thy spiritual daughters in
thanksgiving cry to thee thus:

Rejoice; pure and honourable abode of holiness!

Rejoice; all-luminous lamp, beloved by all!

Rejoice; worthy converser with angels!

Rejoice; good guide of men!

Rejoice; pious rule of faith!

Rejoice; holy purification of mortals!

Rejoice; O Father Nektarios, model of patience and
　　　lover of virtue!

KONTAKION IX

WORLDLY-MINDED men cannot understand thy patience, for despite the many cares of the monastery, thou didst not cease writing edifying books for Christians living in the world. Wherefore, amazed at the great wisdom which thou wast given, we cry to God: ALLELUIA!

OIKOS IX

HAVING settled at the Monastery in Aegina, thou became all spirit and led an altogether spiritual life. Venerable, meek, kindly, humble, extremely compassionate, and charitable, thou carried on the good fight in order to lay hold of that which for which Christ Jesus laid hold of thee. In thy pious ways, thou blamelessly followed Dionysios, the godly pastor of Aegina. Now as thou partake of heavenly glory with him, receive from us these praises:

Rejoice; thou who despiseth the world and its delusive
　　　pleasures!

Rejoice; thou who receiveth in exchange heavenly blessings!

Rejoice; thou who completely subdued thy flesh to thy spirit!

Rejoice; thou who subjected thy spirit to thy sweetest Lord
　　　Jesus!

Rejoice; lover of the holy Fathers!

Rejoice; instructor in the prayer of the heart!

Rejoice; O Father Nektarios, model of patience and
lover of virtue!

KONTAKION X

NEVER neglecting mental prayer but always crying from the depths of
thy heart, "Lord Jesus Christ, have mercy on me," all bore witness
that thou hadst become completely spiritualized. Noticing in thou an
exceptional sweetness which radiated from thy serene countenance, the
faithful joyfully exclaimed: ALLELUIA!

OIKOS X

KNOWING that the Most Holy Virgin is a bulwark for all saints and a
joy to monastics, thou often offered thine intercessions to her with
tears and committed thyself to her motherly protection. Writing beautiful
hymns, thou gavest to the faithful the gift of thy love teaching them to sing,
"Rejoice, O unwedded Bride!" Therefore, we cry to thee:

Rejoice; precious chosen one of Christ!

Rejoice; unblemished fragrance of God!

Rejoice; thou who showeth flaming love for the Lord!

Rejoice; thou who always honoured His Holy Mother!

Rejoice; boast of the Orthodox Church!

Rejoice; thou who workest many miracles through the
power of God!

Rejoice; O Father Nektarios, model of patience and
lover of virtue!

KONTAKION XI

WHEN the time came for you to depart to Christ to receive
the Crown of righteousness laid up for thee in heaven, you
endured severe pain and suffering with exemplary patience. Always

thanking the Heavenly Father and blessing His all-holy name, you continually cried: ALLELUIA!

OIKOS XI

THE LORD, Who always glorifies those who glorify Him, did not allow your virtue to be hidden but desiring that those on earth know the glory He has given you in the heavens has revealed your relics as a well-spring of healings and miracles. For immediately after your repose, as your body was being prepared for burial, the Lord worked wonders through your sweater, raising up a man who had been paralyzed for many years. Therefore, together with him we also gratefully cry to you:

Rejoice; speedy helper of those in need!

Rejoice; constant stream of mercy by which we are cleansed!

Rejoice; physician of soul and body!

Rejoice; new pool of Siloam, healing the infirm!

Rejoice; sweet myrrh of compassion!

Rejoice; miracle worker of the faithful!

Rejoice; O Father Nektarios, model of patience and
    lover of virtue!

KONTAKION XII

MULTITUDES of the faithful from all lands continually flee to thy shrine, O holy one, and from thy precious relics faithfully obtain divine grace and answers for their every petition. O Father, as thou know how, fulfil you also the petitions of those who now cry: ALLELUIA!

OIKOS XII

SINGING praises we glorify thee, O all-praised Nektarios; for in thee God Who is glorified in the Trinity is wonderfully glorified. But even if we were to offer thee a multitude of psalms and hymns composed from the soul, O holy wonderworker, we should do nothing to equal the gift of thy miracles, and amazed by them we cry unto thee:

Rejoice; thou who conquered all the snares of the Evil One!

Rejoice; thou who wast sanctified both in soul and body!

Rejoice; speedy helper of those in need!

Rejoice; restoration of health to the sick!

Rejoice; healer of diseases by the Grace of God!

Rejoice; helper of those that suffer cruelly!

Rejoice; O Father Nektarios, model of patience and
    lover of virtue!

Kontakion XIII

A S a partaker in the life of heaven and a dweller with the angels, O Father Nektarios, in that thou laboured to please God, accept our present offering, and unceasingly intercede for thy flock and for all the Orthodox who honour thee, that we may be healed of all diseases of both body and soul, that together with thee in the eternal Kingdom we may unceasingly cry: ALLELUIA! *(Thrice)*

And again, Oikos I and Kontakion I are read.

Oikos I

I N the world thou were shown to be a man of heavenly mind, O Nektarios, hierarch of Christ; for having passed through life in holiness, thou were shown to be blameless, venerable, and God-pleasing in all things. Wherefore, thou hear from us such praises as these:

Rejoice; thou by whom the faithful are edified!

Rejoice; thou of whom the enemy is afraid!

Rejoice; emulator of the venerable fathers!

Rejoice; divine teacher of the Orthodox!

Rejoice; thou for whom the Church joins chorus!

Rejoice; thou in whom Aegina rejoices!

Rejoice; O Father Nektarios, model of patience and
      lover of virtue!

KONTAKION I

I N joy of heart let us hymn with songs the newly revealed star of
Orthodoxy, the newly erected bulwark of the Church; for, glorified by
the activity of the Spirit, he pours forth the abundant grace of healings
upon those who cry:

Rejoice; O Father Nektarios, model of patience and
      lover of virtue!

AKATHIST TO SAINT NICHOLAS II, TSAR, AND EMPEROR OF ALL RUSSIA, THE PASSION-BEARER

KONTAKION I

O PASSION-BEARER chosen from birth and incarnation of the love of Christ, we sing thee praises as one who did love all the fatherland. As thou hast boldness before the Lord, enlighten our darkened minds and hearts that we may cry to thee:

> Rejoice; O Nicholas, God-crowned Tsar and great
> passion-bearer!

OIKOS I

THE Creator of angels did send thee to the Russian land as an angel of meekness and instructor to thy people, as He did choose thee after the example of His Only Begotten Son to be a sacrifice of redemption for the sins of the people. And we, marvelling at the Providence of the Almighty towards thee, cry out with contrition:

Rejoice; O likeness of Christ!

Rejoice; sacrifice of whole burnt offering!

Rejoice; adornment of the Tsars of Russia!

Rejoice; thou who gavest an example of meekness and
forgiveness to all!

Rejoice; true hope of the offended!

Rejoice; unshakable foundation of faith!

Rejoice; O Nicholas, God-crowned Tsar and great
passion-bearer!

KONTAKION II

THE All good Mother of God, seeing her chosen place, the Russian land, defiled by the abomination of corruption, chose thee from thy birth as a most pure one who would be for the cleansing of Russia, that all might as a funeral lamentation make a hymn to thee: ALLELUIA!

OIKOS II

THE pre-eternal Mind did foreknow thy salvation and thy life, prefigured by Job the Much Suffering, joining thy birth and the memory of the righteous one. And we, recalling our sins and lawless deeds, with trembling of heart and contrition of soul cry out to thee thus:

Rejoice; thou who didst endure abuse and trials from thine
own people!

Rejoice; thou who didst preserve the Faith to the end!

Rejoice; example of meekness!

Rejoice; guardian of the worship of God!

Rejoice; rule of humility!

Rejoice; O Nicholas, God-crowned Tsar and great
passion-bearer!

KONTAKION III

THE power of the Most High did overshadow thee, O God-crowned Nicholas, who didst fight back to enlighten the West in its false wisdom, that the world might cry out to God: ALLELUIA!

OIKOS III

HAVING fervour for the enlightenment of those gone astray, thou, O right believing Tsar, was zealous for the erection of churches, the glorification of the relics of the Saints who pleased God, the planting of Christian enlightenment, and the protection of the unfortunate against violence, and so the Christian world cried out to thee thus:

Rejoice; namesake of St. Nicholas upon the earth!

Rejoice; fellow intercessor with St. Seraphim in Heaven!

Rejoice; planter of Orthodoxy!

Rejoice; bearer of the Light of Christ!

Rejoice; teacher of Christian patience!

Rejoice; intercessor for Orthodox Christians!

Rejoice; O Nicholas, God-crowned Tsar and great
passion-bearer!

KONTAKION IV

THOU didst not fear the storm of folly and abuse, O Passion-bearer Nicholas, when thou didst renounce agreement with the enemies for the destruction of the fatherland; and thou didst endure censure, imprisonment, and death, crying to the Almighty: ALLELUIA!

OIKOS IV

HEARING of the tumults of the Russian land and beholding the destruction of Christians, thou didst unceasingly pray, that the alleged Mother of God save Orthodox Russia. Wherefore, we cry out to thee:

Rejoice; fragrant incense of prayer!

Rejoice; inextinguishable lamp of faith!

Rejoice; admonisher of the violent by the meekness!

Rejoice; consoled of the disconsolate amid sorrows!

Rejoice; lover of heavenly things!

Rejoice; O Nicholas, God-crowned Tsar and great passion-bearer!

KONTAKION V

THOU hast been revealed as a God-guided star for Russians in the diaspora, O Tsar Nicholas; for, gathering them together in thy name, thou dost show the path to the rebirth of the Russian land, that we may hear angels crying out: ALLELUIA!

OIKOS V

SEEING that thy meekness and humility accomplished nothing, thou didst place all thy hope in the Most Pure Mother of God and give thyself entirely into the hands of the Almighty, that even the senseless might be instructed to sing to thee:

Rejoice; vanquisher of pride!

Rejoice; invincible rampart of the infirm!

Rejoice; enlightenment of the proud!

Rejoice; overflowing love for thy people!

Rejoice; fervent sacrifice for the Russian land!

Rejoice; O Nicholas, God-crowned Tsar and great
passion-bearer!

KONTAKION VI

THE ends of the world preach thy glory, and thy word hath gone forth into all the earth; for there is no sacrifice thou wouldst not have offered for the good of the Russian land, thereby teaching thy people to sing in thanksgiving to God: ALLELUIA!

OIKOS VI

THOU didst shine forth greater than the sun for the Russian land, O Tsar Nicholas, revealing thine intercession for the Orthodox people even unto death, that all might be converted to Christ and hasten to thee. Therefore, we hymn thee thus:

Rejoice; O light that hath come out of the East!

Rejoice; example to Orthodox kings!

Rejoice; unquenchable shining of righteousness!

Rejoice; unsetting luminary of meekness!

Rejoice; fatherly exhortation to sinners!

Rejoice; fervent glorification of the righteous!

Rejoice; O Nicholas, God-crowned Tsar and great
passion-bearer!

KONTAKION VII

WISHING to strengthen Orthodox Faith on earth, thou didst move thy whole kingdom to the defence of the wronged land of Serbia, that all might cry out to God: ALLELUIA!

OIKOS VII

THE LORD did manifest thee as a new Noah, a builder of salvation for the Russian people, that all, remembering thy labours, might cry out ceaselessly thus:

Rejoice; helmsman of the Russian ship!

Rejoice; consoler of the Slavs in misfortunes!

Rejoice; guide of Russians!

Rejoice; proclaimer of the love of peace!

Rejoice; planter of Christian virtues!

Rejoice; O Nicholas, God-crowned Tsar and great
    passion-bearer!

KONTAKION VIII

WE see strange wonder in thee, O Nicholas, who many times wast saved by the right hand of the Most High and was crowned by a martyr's crown with thy children and kinsmen, that we might cry out to God the Provider of all things: ALLELUIA!

OIKOS VIII

THOU was entirely a defender for all Christians, O divinely chosen Nicholas, and didst show a double intercession for the Slavic peoples, moving them to sing to thee in praise:

Rejoice; defence of the offended!

Rejoice; exhortation to offenders!

Rejoice; refuge of the grieving!

Rejoice; intercessor for the persecuted!

Rejoice; peacemaker in thy life!

Rejoice; champion of Christians after thy murder!

Rejoice; O Nicholas, God-crowned Tsar and great
passion-bearer!

KONTAKION IX

B y many wonders did the Lord reveal His good will to the Russian
people, until they did grieve Him mightily; but being called by thee
in repentance, we cry out together unto God: ALLELUIA!

OIKOS IX

E LOQUENT orators, like voiceless fish, cannot express the height of
thy patience; but we, beholding the abyss of our fall, cry out
in contrition of spirit:

Rejoice; unvanquishable patience!

Rejoice; unwavering faithfulness of Christians!

Rejoice; wise teacher of the foolish!

Rejoice; thou who didst give an example to the faithful in
thy life and martyr's death!

Rejoice; thou who didst suffer for the sins of thy people!

Rejoice; O Nicholas, God-crowned Tsar and great
passion-bearer!

KONTAKION X

CHRIST the Knower of hearts, Who founded His Church on the blood of martyrs, desiring to save all men, did place thee, O Passion-bearer Nicholas, as the foundation of the new house of the Russian realm, that all within it might cry out to God: ALLELUIA!

OIKOS X

THOU art a rampart for all who hasten to thee with faith, and an inextinguishable protection for the Orthodox world, and thou dost teach all the faithful to glorify thee thus:

Rejoice; manifestation of heavenly things on earth!

Rejoice; new strength for those grown faint in virtues!

Rejoice; dawn that hath shone forth on the land of Russia!

Rejoice; river that doth nourish all her boundaries!

Rejoice; teacher of the humility of wisdom!

Rejoice; planter of faith and love!

Rejoice; O Nicholas, God-crowned Tsar and great passion-bearer!

KONTAKION XI

OFFERING a hymn to the Most Holy Trinity even unto thy death, thou didst finish thy course and keep the Faith, by which thou dost move all Orthodox Christians to sing: ALLELUIA!

OIKOS XI

THOU wast sent by the Giver of Light to the Russian land like an immaculate lamb, and thou didst lay down thy life for the redemption of our sins, that we all might ceaselessly glorify thee thus:

Rejoice; sacrifice beloved of God!

Rejoice; unquenchable abundance of love!

Rejoice; praise of the faithfulness of Christ!

Rejoice; invisible blowing of the Spirit!

Rejoice; mirror of wisdom!

Rejoice; hope of the hopeless!

Rejoice; O Nicholas, God-crowned Tsar and great
   passion-bearer!

KONTAKION XII

DIVINE grace which health the infirm did foreknow thee as an imperishable healing for thy subjects who cry out to God: ALLELUIA!

OIKOS XII

HYMNING thy sufferings, O Passion-bearer Nicholas, we bow down before thy patience, for the power of the Almighty Trinity was manifest in thee, that we might all with one accord cry out:

Rejoice; beloved child of Christ!

Rejoice; thou who didst conduct thine immaculate
   children and faithful servants to Christ!

Rejoice; thou who didst aid the Queen to be righteous and
   a martyr!

Rejoice; thou who didst truly direct thy people!

Rejoice; thou who didst not bring abuse to the honour
   of thy fatherland!

Rejoice; thou who didst gain the Kingdom of Heaven!

Rejoice; O Nicholas, God-crowned Tsar and great
passion-bearer!

KONTAKION XIII

O MOST wondrous and most glorious Passion-bearer Nicholas, look down upon thy earthly kingdom and thy people, for we have no answer for our sins, and entreat the Almighty that He may not enter into judgment with us, but might vouchsafe us ceaselessly to cry out: ALLELUIA! *(Thrice.)*

And again, Oikos I and Kontakion I are read.

OIKOS I

THE Creator of angels did send thee to the Russian land as an angel of meekness and instructor to the people, and He did choose thee after the example of His Only Begotten Son to be a sacrifice of redemption for the sins of the people. And, we, marvelling at the Providence of the Almighty towards thee, cry out with contrition:

Rejoice; O likeness of Christ!

Rejoice; sacrifice of whole burnt offering!

Rejoice; adornment of the Tsars of Russia!

Rejoice; thou who gavest an example of meekness and
forgiveness to all!

Rejoice; true hope of the offended!

Rejoice; unshakable foundation of faith!

Rejoice; O Nicholas, God-crowned Tsar and great
passion-bearer!

KONTAKION I

O PASSION-BEARER chosen from birth and incarnation of the love of Christ, we sing thee praises as one who did love above all thy fatherland. As thou hast boldness before the Lord, enlighten our darkened minds and hearts that we may cry to thee:

Rejoice; O Nicholas, God-crowned Tsar and great
passion-bearer!

TROPARION
(Tone VI)

THOU didst meekly endure the loss of an earthly kingdom, and bonds and many sufferings from the fighters against God, witnessing of Christ even unto death, O great Passion-bearer and God-crowned Tsar Nicholas. Wherefore Christ God did crown thee and thy Queen and children with a martyr's crown in Heaven; do thou entreat Him to have mercy on the Russian land and to save our souls.

A PRAYER TO THE HOLY TSAR-MARTYR NICHOLAS

O HOLY passion-bearer Tsar Martyr Nicholas! The Lord has chosen thee as His anointed one to judge with mercy and righteousness thy people and to be the guardian of the Orthodox Kingdom.

THIS royal service and the care for souls thou hast completed with the fear of God. Testing thee as gold in the furnace, the Lord has allowed bitter sorrows to come upon thee, as to the much suffering Job, by depriving thee of thy royal throne, and sending upon thee martyric death. Having meekly endured all this, like a true slave of Christ, thou art partaking of the highest glory at the Throne of the God of All, together with the Holy Martyrs, the holy Tsarina Alexandra, the holy youth Crown Prince Alexis, and the holy Princesses Olga, Tatiana, Maria and Anastasia and with the faithful servants of thine, as well as with the holy Martyr Grand Duchess Elizabeth and with all the Royal Martyrs and the Holy Martyr Barbara.

FOR as having great boldness before Christ King, for whose sake thou hast endured everything, pray with us, that the Lord might forgive the sin of thy people, who did not stop thy slaughter, as King and Anointed One of God, that the Lord will deliver the suffering land of Russia from the fierce and godless ones, who came upon it because of our sin and apostasy, and that He will restore the throne of Orthodox Tsars, and to us will grant forgiveness of sins and will instruct us on every good deed, that we might acquire humbleness, meekness and love, as these Martyrs have done, that we will be vouchsafed the Heavenly Kingdom, where together with thee and all the Holy New Martyrs and Confessors of Russia, we might glorify Father, Son, and Holy Spirit, both now and ever and to the ages of ages. AMEN.

*Holy Royal Martyrs Tsar Nicholas and Family
Pray Unto God For Us!*

Glory Be to God for All Things!

AKATHIST TO VENERABLE NILUS, WONDERWORKER OF SORA

KONTAKION I

FOR thee, the chosen conqueror of noetic foes, who spurned the false world and carnal pleasures, and, following the words of the psalmist, sought God in the wilderness, have we composed praises. As thou hast boldness before the Lord, pray thou, O venerable one, on behalf of us who honour thy most sacred memory with faith and love, that we may cry to thee:

Rejoice; O venerable Nilus, wonderworker of Sora!

OIKOS I

EMULATING the life of the angels and patterning thyself on those who were great among the fathers, thou didst cut thyself off wholly from the confusion of the world, and, manfully arming thyself for the struggle of asceticism, didst carefully follow the way of the commandments of God, O blessed one; wherefore, we who honour thy most sacred memory with faith do bless thee with these praises:

Rejoice; O emulator of the life of the angels!

Rejoice; follower of the life of the fathers of old!

Rejoice; courageous vanquisher of invisible foes!

Rejoice; earnest fulfiller of the commandments of God!

Rejoice; careful preserver of the divinely inspired Traditions of the fathers!

Rejoice; codifier of rules for the monastic life of asceticism!

Rejoice; most pure mirror of the virtues!

Rejoice; sweet-sounding timbrel of the Holy Spirit!

Rejoice; image of profound humility!

Rejoice; zealous doer of the will of God!

Rejoice; for through thee have we learned to tread the straight path!

Rejoice; for through thy mediation for us before God we hope to receive salvation!

Rejoice; O venerable Nilus, wonderworker of Sora!

KONTAKION II

BEHOLDING thy humble mindedness more lustrous than gold, we boldly say of thee that thou art truly a disciple of Christ and a fellow heir to His kingdom; wherefore, O most blessed one, trusting that, through thy mediation to Him for us, we shall receive the remission of sins, we cry aloud: ALLELUIA!

OIKOS II

DESIRING to enrich thyself with an understanding of the most divine Scriptures, thou didst abide continually in the study thereof, O wise one, whereby thou didst give thy soul to drink of the waters of piety, wherewith thou fillest us also, who with love chant unto thee such things as these:

Rejoice; treasury of divine understanding!

Rejoice; granary filled to overflowing with the works of faith!

Rejoice; vine of the Master, heavy laden with His
goodly harvest!

Rejoice; thou who learned to fulfil the will of God!

Rejoice; river overflowing with the water of grace divine!

Rejoice; thou who wast vouchsafed to receive the knowledge
of the divine Scriptures!

Rejoice; thou who with the water of thy discourses gavest
drink unto those who thirsted for salvation!

Rejoice; thou who becamest a model of salvation for those
who followed thee!

Rejoice; splendid adornment of monks!

Rejoice; thou who in thyself showed them the way to
salvation!

Rejoice; thou who trained them for victory in the noetic
    battle!

Rejoice; thou who set at nought all the wiles of the enemy!

Rejoice; O venerable Nilus, wonderworker of Sora!

KONTAKION III

G IRDED about with the power of the Most High, thou didst boldly go
forth to do battle with the enemy; and contending mightily, thou
didst vanquish the captains of the demons, and with the streams of thy
tears didst drown the infernal pharaoh, showing thyself as a model of
victory for all who desire to follow thee in courageous combat, chanting
victoriously unto the Lord: ALLELUIA!

OIKOS III

H AVING within thee exalting humility of mind, thou didst mount
to the summit of the virtues; and furnished with wings of divine
knowledge, thou didst easily soar above the snares of the enemy;
wherefore, thou hast entered the heavenly bridal-chamber with glory, O
divinely wise one. And we, marvelling at the height of thy virtuous life,
cry aloud with love:

Rejoice; true emulator of the humility of Christ!

Rejoice; thou who thereby didst attain unto everlasting rest!

Rejoice; thou who didst obtain wings of humble
    mindedness and divine knowledge!

Rejoice; thou who wast upborne to the heavens by humility
    and love!

Rejoice; thou who didst arm thyself with the sword of
    humility and the shield of patience!

Rejoice; thou who in lowliness of spirit didst serve Him
    Who exalteth those of low estate!

Rejoice; thou who didst earnestly emulate Christ Who
abased Himself for our sake!

Rejoice; thou who for this received great grace from Him!

Rejoice; thou who by meekness and humility didst crush all
the snares of the enemy!

Rejoice; thou who didst mystically learn to hymn God
unceasingly within thy heart!

Rejoice; thou who didst make thy heart a habitation
for God!

Rejoice; thou who didst offer up unceasing prayers, like
incense of sweet savour, unto the Lord Who
loved thee!

Rejoice; O venerable Nilus, wonderworker of Sora!

KONTAKION IV

HAVING within me a tempest of vain thoughts, I am unable to lift up
my mind to the heights of thy corrections and sing thy praises
worthily, O father; yet accept me, who with heartfelt love hymn thee, and
mediate salvation for me, who cry: ALLELUIA!

OIKOS IV

HEARKENING to thy salvific Traditions and wise instructions, thy
disciples joyously hastened after thee, and, guided by thee, came to
know lofty and hidden things, chanting to thee in thanksgiving:

Rejoice; thou who transmitted the Traditions of salvation
unto thy disciples!

Rejoice; thou who clearly indicated to them the goodly path
to salvation, and not the path of error!

Rejoice; thou who didst keep the commandments of God
with care!

Rejoice; thou who didst teach those who followed thee to
keep them as well!

Rejoice; thou who didst zealously implement the salvific
traditions of the fathers!

Rejoice; thou who hast taught us faithfully to follow them!

Rejoice; wise teacher of those who truly desire to live the
monastic life!

Rejoice; earnest lover of the wonderworking fathers of old!

Rejoice; thou who hast been reckoned among their choir
in the mansions of heaven!

Rejoice; thou who after thy repose hast been given the gift
of miracles!

Rejoice; for through thee do we receive the healing of bodily
ailments!

Rejoice; for by thy mediation we hope to receive the
forgiveness of sins!

Rejoice; O venerable Nilus, wonderworker of Sora!

KONTAKION V

SEEING thee as a radiant star shining forth in the wilderness, we
rejoice, and, attracted by the brilliance thereof, hastening together we
earnestly celebrate thy memory, O venerable one, keeping splendid
festival and chanting unto God in thanksgiving: ALLELUIA!

OIKOS V

W E perceive thee as a radiant lamp shining brightly in the trackless wilderness, for, even though, because of thy humility of mind, thou art covered as with a bushel, yet hast thou not been able to hide, having been set aloft upon the summit of the virtues. Wherefore, illumined by thy miracles, we cry out to thee such things as these:

Rejoice; thou who wast illumined by the light of the
threefold Sun!

Rejoice; thou who learned wisdom from the Well-spring
of wisdom!

Rejoice; thou who by God hast been given the greatly
increased talent!

Rejoice; thou who hast been shown to be a chosen
husbandman of the vineyard of Christ!

Rejoice; thou who most abundantly watered the field of thy
soul with tears of compunction!

Rejoice; thou who didst produce manifold fruits of
the virtues!

Rejoice; flower of paradise which budded forth in
the wilderness!

Rejoice; thou who perfumest us with the fragrant myrrh of
the virtues!

Rejoice; luminary burning brightly in the firmament of the
Church of Christ!

Rejoice; thou who hast driven away the gloom of ignorance
and dark oblivion!

Rejoice; thou who hast made clear to us the
understanding of the writings of the fathers!

Rejoice; thou who didst manifestly reveal the mysteries
hidden in them!

Rejoice; O venerable Nilus, wonderworker of Sora!

KONTAKION VI

THOU wast truly a preacher of the truth, O Nilus our ever-memorable
father, clearly showing forth the path which leadeth to the kingdom
on high, and showing thyself to be a paragon of true monasticism for those
who desire to become heirs thereto, teaching them by word and deed to
shun the tumults of the world, and ever moving them to chant the divine
hymn: ALLELUIA!

OIKOS VI

SINCE thine honoured repose, thou hast shone forth with the light of
miracles, appearing in faraway lands, and delivering men from bitter
captivity, O Nilus our wonder-working father; wherefore, saved by thee
from misfortunes, we, thy servants, cry out to thee in thanksgiving:

Rejoice; deliverer of captives!

Rejoice; speedy intercessor for those who invoke thine aid!

Rejoice; thou who helpest those in tribulation!

Rejoice; thou who all-gloriously freest them from the assault
and violence of unclean spirits!

Rejoice; thou who dost transform sorrows and griefs into joy!

Rejoice; thou who breakest asunder the insidious snares of
the demons!

Rejoice; for thou dost quickly anticipate the need of those
who call upon thee!

Rejoice; for from diverse misfortunes and perils dost thou
rescue those who love thee!

Rejoice; thou who givest consolation to those who languish
in despondency!

Rejoice; thou who drivest away the dark clouds of sorrows!

Rejoice; physician of bodily illnesses!

Rejoice; mediator of the good things of heaven!

Rejoice; O venerable Nilus, wonderworker of Sora!

KONTAKION VII

WHEN the time came for thee to leave this world and depart unto
the Lord, thy disciples, assembling and shedding tears, said:
"Leave us not orphaned, O father!" And with them, we cry aloud unto
thee: "Forget us not, but visit, console and provide for thy servants, who
honour thee with love and cry out to God: ALLELUIA!"

OIKOS VII

A NEW and all-glorious miracle didst thou show forth when, shining
with the brilliance of lightning and spreading an ineffable sweet
fragrance, thou didst appear to a God-loving man who was held captive,
commanding him to paint the likeness of thine image. And we, marvelling
thereat, cry out to thee such things as these:

Rejoice; O all-glorious worker of miracles!

Rejoice; fulfiller of the good pleasure of God toward men!

Rejoice; thou who thereby didst make know thine own
holiness and boldness toward God!

Rejoice; thou who through this hast revealed unto us the
grace which thou hadst received from God!

Rejoice; thou who by thine appearance brought gladness
unto one who languished captive amid sorrow!

Rejoice; thou who promised him speedy liberation
    from captivity!

Rejoice; thou who gavest him the image of thy countenance!

Rejoice; thou who didst arrange for him an all-glorious
    deliverance from captivity!

Rejoice; thou who returned him, rejoicing, to his homeland!

Rejoice; for even the angels are astonished by the favour
    shown thee by God!

Rejoice; for the fame of thy miracles hath gone forth into
    all the earth!

Rejoice; thou who hast amazed all by thine all-glorious
    wonder-working!

Rejoice; O venerable Nilus, wonderworker of Sora!

KONTAKION VIII

BEHOLDING the strange and all-glorious miracle wrought by thee, O Nilus our father most rich, we beseech thee: Entreat God Who worketh miracles through thee, that we also may withdraw from this vain and deceitful world, may sail safely across the deep of life, and, by thy mediation, may attain unto the calm haven, forever chanting in thanksgiving: ALLELUIA!

OIKOS VIII

THOU wast wholly full of divine love, O most blessed one; and, in nowise yielding to the love of the flesh and the world, thou didst live out thy life in chastity and holiness like one of the incorporeal beings; wherefore, thou didst receive from God the grace to work all-glorious miracles. For which cause accept these praises, offered unto thee from our zeal:

Rejoice; spacious abode of divine love!

Rejoice; dwelling-place of the Holy Trinity!

Rejoice; mighty and valorous conqueror of noetic foes!

Rejoice; ally of those who call upon thee for aid in
vanquishing them!

Rejoice; citizen of the wilderness!

Rejoice; thou who art mighty and wondrous in patience!

Rejoice; great lover of stillness!

Rejoice; wise establisher of rules for the solitary
monastic life!

Rejoice; guide to salvation for monastics!

Rejoice; participant in the choir of the venerable!

Rejoice; for with all the saints thou enjoyest everlasting
gladness!

Rejoice; for with them thou hast joyously inherited the
mansions of heaven!

Rejoice; O venerable Nilus, wonderworker of Sora!

KONTAKION IX

ALL of angelic and human nature marvelled at thy wondrous way of
life in the flesh, O Nilus our God-bearing father; for, having fought
the fight of asceticism, thou didst finish the race without stumbling.
Wherefore, thou hast been invested by God with the crown of
righteousness, making thine abode with the choirs of the saints in the
mansions on high, ever chanting: ALLELUIA!

OIKOS IX

THE speech of those wise according to the flesh was shown to be
foolish when the foolish were made wise through the activity of the

Holy Spirit and tamed their audacious tongues; wherefore, O God-bearer, not worldly wisdom, but the activity of the Holy Spirit made thee also wise and showed thee to speak eloquently of things divine. And we, fashioning hymnody of praise for thee, chant:

Rejoice; thou who wast given wisdom from on high!

Rejoice; splendid receptacle of the knowledge of God!

Rejoice; radiant lamp shining with divine effulgence!

Rejoice; thou who wast illumined by the grace of the
Holy Spirit!

Rejoice; thou who for monastics set down in writing the
mystic law!

Rejoice; thou who transmitted to them salvific traditions!

Rejoice; mediator of everlasting blessedness!

Rejoice; sure instructor of salvation!

Rejoice; guide to the reception of the good things of heaven!

Rejoice; thou who shattered the horn of pride!

Rejoice; for by thy supplications for us are we delivered from
diverse misfortunes!

Rejoice; for by thine intercession unto God are we freed
from the temptations of the enemy!

Rejoice; O venerable Nilus, wonderworker of Sora!

KONTAKION X

THOU wast a true guide for those who desire to be saved, O most blessed father, directing them with the commandments of Christ the

Saviour and the saving Traditions of the God-bearing fathers. Wherefore, we also, desiring to follow after them, chant with reverence, directed by thy prayers: ALLELUIA!

OIKOS X

THOU wast a bulwark and tower of confirmation for thy disciples, showing forth in thyself a model of courageous struggle, and confirming by deed and word the way whereby they might counter the battle of the enemy mightily. And we, who are weak, looking to thee for mediation in our behalf, offer thee this praise, crying:

Rejoice; tower of patience!

Rejoice; model of valiant struggle!

Rejoice; brave warrior of the army of Christ!

Rejoice; citizen of the heavenly Jerusalem!

Rejoice; thou who sowed tears of compunction on the earth!

Rejoice; thou who in the heavens partakest of the fruits of eternal consolation!

Rejoice; thou who endured the afflictions of the wilderness with good cheer!

Rejoice; thou who soared aloft from the wilderness to the mansions of paradise!

Rejoice; thou who didst keep vigil in unceasing prayers!

Rejoice; thou who didst have thy mind ever uplifted to God!

Rejoice; thou who suffered for Christ in the mortification of the flesh!

Rejoice; thou who wast vouchsafed divine glory by Him!

Rejoice; O venerable Nilus, wonderworker of Sora!

Kontakion XI

A CCEPT us who offer thee hymnody of praise, O father, and deliver us
from the tyranny of the passions and the storm of evil thoughts; for
thee have we, thy servants, acquired as a helper, a fervent intercessor and
advocate before God for us who hope, through thee, to receive
deliverance and salvation from evils, and who cry: ALLELUIA!

Oikos XI

O BLESSED one, Christ hath shown thee to be a radiant beacon for
monastics, enlightening us with the immaterial fire of the virtues and
illumining with beams of humility of mind and shining with the effulgence
of miracles upon us who cry out to thee such things as these:

Rejoice; radiant beacon of monastics!

Rejoice; shining lamp of ascetics!

Rejoice; brilliant star shining with the light of the Trinity!

Rejoice; thou who dost share in the never-waning light!

Rejoice; rain-laden cloud who poured forth torrents of tears!

Rejoice; thou who with lightning-flashes of grace dost
illumine those who love thee!

Rejoice; thou who affrighted the enemy as with claps
of thunder!

Rejoice; thou who drowned them with the downpours of
thy tears!

Rejoice; thou who calmly reached the end of thy life
in humility!

Rejoice; thou who for all wast an image of Christ-like
meekness!

Rejoice; thou who hast shone forth miracles since thy
    repose!

Rejoice; thou who with power hast shone forth the loftiness
    of thy manner of life!

Rejoice; O venerable Nilus, wonderworker of Sora!

KONTAKION XII

A S Master and Lord of all, the great Bestower of gifts desired to give
thee grace and to show thee forth on earth as all-glorious; and He
hath likewise glorified thee in heaven, enriching thee with the gift of
miracles. He hath sanctified and glorified thee, and taught us to chant in
thanksgiving for thee the hymn: ALLELUIA!

OIKOS XII

H YMNING thy corrections, struggles and battles, thy profound
humility of mind and thine honoured passing from earth to heaven,
we praise also the grace of miracles which thou hast received from God,
Who hath sanctified and glorified thee, and hath taught us to cry out to
thee:

Rejoice; thou who hast finished well the course of
    ascetic struggles!

Rejoice; thou who hast inherited the all-joyous abode
    of paradise!

Rejoice; thou who shone with the brilliance of the virtues
    on earth!

Rejoice; thou who in the heavens hast received the reward
    for thy manifold labours!

Rejoice; splendid adornment of the wilderness!

Rejoice; thou who wast vouchsafed to behold most
    gladsome joy!

Rejoice; most luminous mirror of the monastic life!

Rejoice; bulwark and mighty rampart for us who love thee,
    against the assaults of the adversary!

Rejoice; for through thee do we avoid diverse temptations!

Rejoice; for through thine intercession before God for us do
    we find speedy aid amid diverse misfortunes!

Rejoice; bestower of bodily health!

Rejoice; mediator of salvation for our souls!

Rejoice; O venerable Nilus, wonderworker of Sora!

KONTAKION XIII

O OUR most blessed and venerable father Nilus, accept from us this hymnody offered thee with love, and deliver us from divers misfortunes, perils and the torment which is to come, that by thy mediation we may be vouchsafed to chant eternally with thee to the triune God this hymn of thanksgiving: ALLELUIA! *(Thrice.)*

And again, Oikos I and Kontakion I are read.

OIKOS I

E MULATING the life of the angels and patterning thyself on those who were great among the fathers, thou didst cut thyself off wholly from the confusion of the world, and, manfully arming thyself for the struggle of asceticism, didst carefully follow the way of the commandments of God, O blessed one; wherefore, we who honour thy most sacred memory with faith do bless thee with these praises:

Rejoice; O emulator of the life of the angels!

Rejoice; follower of the life of the fathers of old!

Rejoice; courageous vanquisher of invisible foes!

Rejoice; earnest fulfiller of the commandments of God!

Rejoice; careful preserver of the divinely inspired Traditions of the fathers!

Rejoice; codifier of rules for the monastic life of asceticism!

Rejoice; most pure mirror of the virtues!

Rejoice; sweet-sounding timbrel of the Holy Spirit!

Rejoice; image of profound humility!

Rejoice; zealous doer of the will of God!

Rejoice; for through thee have we learned to tread the straight path!

Rejoice; for through thy mediation for us before God we hope to receive salvation!

Rejoice; O venerable Nilus, wonderworker of Sora!

KONTAKION I

FOR thee, the chosen conqueror of noetic foes, who spurned the false world and carnal pleasures, and, following the words of the psalmist, sought God in the wilderness, have we composed praises. As thou hast boldness before the Lord, pray thou, O venerable one, on behalf of us who honour thy most sacred memory with faith and love, that we may cry to thee:

Rejoice; O venerable Nilus, wonderworker of Sora!

PRAYER I

O OUR most venerable father Nilus, accept this hymn of praise, which is offered to thee with faith and love, and, mercifully bowing down from the heights of heaven, as a solicitous father entreat the Lord and

Master of all creation, that He grant forgiveness of sins, amendment of life, and a peaceful Christian end, untroubled by the spirits of evil, unto those who honour thee. At that time stand thou forth, O most blessed father, driving the fear of death away from thy children who love thee, and easing the separation of their souls from their bodies and their passage through the dread way-stations. And by thy mighty supplication and merciful intercession before the Lord for us, vouchsafe that on the day of the dread judgment we may receive a place on the right hand with all who have pleased God. AMEN.

PRAYER II

O VENERABLE father Nilus, blessed of God, our divinely wise instructor and teacher! Having withdrawn from the turmoil of the world for the sake of God's love, thou didst choose to make thine abode in the trackless wilderness and impenetrable forests. And having increased the children of the wilderness like a right fruitful branch, thou didst show thyself to them as an image of every monastic virtue by word, writing, and manner of life. And having lived on earth like an angel in the flesh, thou now dwellest in the mansions of heaven, where the cry of those who keep festival is unceasing, and, standing with the choirs of saints before God, thou dost continually offer up praises and glorification unto Him. We beseech thee, O thou who art blessed of God: Instruct us also who live under thy protection, that we may follow in thy steps without wavering; that we may love the Lord God with all our heart, please Him alone and think of Him alone, manfully and skilfully trampling underfoot those thoughts which drag us down, and may ever vanquish the assaults of the enemy; that we may love all the restraints of the monastic life, and come to hate the beautiful things of this world out of love for Christ, and plant in our hearts every virtue wherein thou didst labour. Entreat Christ God, that He illumine the minds and hearts of all Orthodox Christians who dwell in the world, that they may see salvation, that He establish them in faith and piety, and in the doing of His commandments, protect them from the deception of this world, and grant unto them, and to us remission of sins, and bestow upon them, according to His true promise, all things they need for this transitory life. Yea, let those who abide in the wilderness and in the world live a life of inner stillness, in all piety and honour, and glorify Him with mouth and heart, together with His unoriginate Father, and His all-holy, good and life-creating Spirit, always, now and ever, and unto the ages of ages. AMEN.

AKATHIST TO SAINT RAPHAEL
OF BROOKLYN

KONTAKION I

O HOLY Father, called from thy native land to the distant shores of the New World, thou didst take up thy cross and follow after Christ. Wherefore, as to one who hath crucified himself on behalf of his flock, as to our faithful guardian and protector, we fervently cry:

Rejoice; O Father Raphael, good shepherd of the lost sheep
  in America!

OIKOS I

THOU didst begin thy life in exile, O holy Father Raphael. Child of pious Orthodox parents, successor to the holy Hieromartyr Joseph, even in thy mother's womb thou didst enjoy no repose. Thus was thy life of travel mystically foretold. Thou wast chosen to bring the light of holy Orthodoxy to the scattered flock of Christ in the New World, who together with us honour thee in these words of praise:

> Rejoice; thou who like thy Master wast born in a city not thine own!

> Rejoice; recipient of the name of the great Archangel!

> Rejoice; thou who didst say, "Man meant it to me for evil, but God for good!"

> Rejoice; thou who wast anointed with the blood of the martyrs!

> Rejoice; thou who didst traverse the world in ministry to the faithful!

> Rejoice; thou who didst lead all men to the worship of the Holy Trinity!

> Rejoice; O Father Raphael, good shepherd of the lost sheep in America!

KONTAKION II

A FERVENT student, from thy youth thou didst dedicate thyself to acquiring knowledge of the truth. Excelling in thy studies, thou didst not despair when thy father in his poverty could no longer afford to send thee to school. But turning thyself to prayer and to the protection of the holy Archangel, thou didst continually cry: ALLELUIA!

OIKOS II

HEARING thy prayers and ardent sighs, God raised up for thee an earthly patron who successfully interceded with the Patriarch to accept thee as a student. Wherefore, as to one who in true humility wast exalted by the hand of God, we joyfully cry:

Rejoice; thou who in thy poverty didst learn true humility!

Rejoice; thou who in thy distress didst turn thyself to thy
heavenly Patron!

Rejoice; thou who wast exalted to become a shepherd of
Christ's rational flock!

Rejoice; thou who having been exalted didst humble thyself
to search for the lost sheep!

Rejoice; consoler of the afflicted!

Rejoice; defender of the downtrodden!

Rejoice; O Father Raphael, good shepherd of the lost sheep
in America!

KONTAKION III

CONTINUING thine education, thy tender soul was nourished by the riches of patristic theology. Plumbing the depths of Holy Scripture, thou wast instructed by the Holy Spirit. And thou didst show thyself to be a worthy proclaimer of the Holy Gospel, teaching all to sing: ALLELUIA!

OIKOS III

THE words of the Apostle who was baptized in the town of thy fathers resounded in thine ears: "How shall they believe in Him of Whom they have not heard? And how shall they hear without a preacher?" Thou couldst not forget thine own people, living in thy homeland and scattered throughout the world, but didst raise thy voice, enlightening them with the Light of Christian Truth. Taught by thy words and instructed by thine example, the faithful thankfully celebrate thy memory and sing:

Rejoice; thou who didst excel in learning and didst thereby astonish the wise of this world!

Rejoice; thou who didst grieve over the ignorance of the people!

Rejoice; thou who with Orthodox doctrine didst instruct those seeking salvation!

Rejoice; thou who didst not disgrace this teaching by thy manner of life!

Rejoice; thou who wast patient and gentle with the weak and suffering!

Rejoice; thou who like thy Master wast firm with the obstinate!

Rejoice; O Father Raphael, good shepherd of the lost sheep in America!

KONTAKION IV

NOT content with thy knowledge of Scripture and the holy Fathers, thou didst continue thine education in the land of Russia. Like the Apostle Andrew, traveling to the ancient city of Kiev, thou didst exclaim: ALLELUIA!

OIKOS IV

RECEIVING the grace of the priesthood, thou wast appointed the head of the Antiochian metochion in Moscow. Seeing in this the hand of God, thou didst accept this new position as an opportunity to do good to others. Never thinking of thyself but always of thy people, thou didst bring many from Syria to Russia to be instructed in theology. Wherefore, the faithful rejoiced and justly honouring thy labours, magnified thee thus:

Rejoice; thou who didst renounce all care for thyself!

Rejoice; thou who didst concern thyself only with the cares of others!

Rejoice; for freely thou didst receive and freely thou didst give!

Rejoice; thou who didst beget many children for the Church of Christ!

Rejoice; protection of the poor!

Rejoice; ardent haven for widows and orphans in their affliction!

Rejoice; O Father Raphael, good shepherd of the lost sheep in America!

KONTAKION VI

HEARING of thy labours and love for thy people, the children of Antioch in America petitioned thee to come to the New World to pastor them in their place of immigration. Thou didst receive their words as a divine invitation, knowing them to be scattered, deprived of spiritual consolation. Journeying therefore from the East to the West, thou didst pour thyself into the life-sustaining prayers of the Church, and through them, didst find the guidance and inspiration to gather the lost sheep to which thou wast being sent, ever chanting: ALLELUIA!

OIKOS VI

UPON thine arrival, thou didst devote thyself to the ministry thou hadst been given, establishing a holy place in which to offer prayers on behalf of the people. Thou didst furnish the entire chapel of thine own substance, offering it without cost to the faithful. Together with them, remembering thy holy example, we glorify God for bringing thee to this land and honour thee with these words:

Rejoice; for thy dedication equalled that of the Apostles!

Rejoice; for thy perseverance was a gift of the Holy Spirit!

Rejoice; thou who hast won the heights through humility!

Rejoice; thou who hast acquired riches through poverty!

Rejoice; thou who didst care for the helpless!

Rejoice; thou who didst distribute thine own funds to
      the poor!

Rejoice; O Father Raphael, good shepherd of the lost sheep
      in America!

KONTAKION VI

LIVING among the people, they became witnesses of how devoutly and justly and blamelessly thou didst act among them, exhorting, comforting and charging everyone as a father does his own children. Truly, through thee the word of the Gospel came in power and in the Holy Spirit with much assurance, so that the faithful became followers of thee and of the Lord, chanting joyfully: ALLELUIA!

OIKOS VI

NEWS of small communities of Orthodox Christians began to reach thee. Hearing their call, "Come, and help us," thou didst decide to make the first of many missionary journeys. Traveling from the East Coast to the West, thou didst stay in no place for more than four days. Finding Orthodox Christians, thou didst administer the holy Mysteries and preach the Word of God to the spiritually hungry. Receiving thee as if thou wast Christ Himself, the faithful welcomed thee with words such as these:

Rejoice; Bringer of new Life to many children through
      holy baptism!

Rejoice; Giver of the seal of the gift of the Holy Spirit
      through anointing with Chrism!

Rejoice; Restorer of penitents to the holy Church through
the mystery of Confession!

Rejoice; Uniter of spouses together in the Lord!

Rejoice; worthy Celebrant of the Divine Liturgy!

Rejoice; fiery Proclaimer of pastoral theology!

Rejoice; O Father Raphael, good shepherd of the lost sheep
in America!

KONTAKION VII

HAVING been spiritually formed by the Church's cycle of prayers,
thou didst prepare liturgical texts for use by thy people.
Bringing them true consolation in the divine prayers, thou didst teach
them to sing: ALLELUIA!

OIKOS VII

SEEING the need of the scattered Orthodox people for true pastoral
ministry, thou didst devote thyself to finding priests to care for their
souls.   Bringing priests from the Old World to America and
recommending faithful men for ordination, thou didst accept the spiritual
welfare of thy people as thine only concern.   Accept therefore from us
such praises as these:

Rejoice; beacon of Orthodoxy!

Rejoice; golden trumpet of the Holy Spirit!

Rejoice; new Paul, who didst take upon thyself the burden
of care for the churches!

Rejoice; new John, who didst command all men to love
one another!

Rejoice; new Juvenal, who didst desire everywhere to preach
the holy Gospel!

Rejoice; new Herman, who didst always care for the least of
the brethren!

Rejoice; O Father Raphael, good shepherd of the lost sheep
in America!

KONTAKION VIII

WHEN the holy hierarch and confessor Tikhon was sent to America,
thou didst receive him as the true shepherd of the flock of
Orthodox Christians. Knowing that in Christ all are one, whether Arab,
Greek, or Russian, thou didst rejoice in God, chanting: ALLELUIA!

OIKOS VIII

AS a healer of souls and a peacemaker, whether in an established
Temple, a storefront or a family's living room, thou didst gather the
people for prayer. Carrying on the apostolic ministry of reconciliation,
uniting brother to brother, healing wounds, thou didst establish over them
the banner of love. Wherefore, as to one who hast shown himself to be a
son of God, we joyfully chant to thee these praises:

Rejoice; thou who didst exhort the people of God not to
receive His grace in vain!

Rejoice; thou who didst in all things approve thyself as a
minister of God!

Rejoice; thou who didst live as unknown and yet well known!

Rejoice; thou who, though dying, didst live!

Rejoice; as sorrowful, always rejoicing!

Rejoice; as poor, thou didst make many rich!

Rejoice; O Father Raphael, good shepherd of the lost sheep
in America!

KONTAKION IX

L OVING GOD above all, and being sent to serve Him among the least brethren, like an apostle thou didst offer prayers day and night for their salvation. Thou didst raise up a holy Temple for the Orthodox Arabs, dedicating it to Holy Nicholas, Wonder-worker of Myra in Lycia. Now together with him in heaven thou dost exclaim: ALLELUIA!

OIKOS IX

I T is impossible for the worldly-minded to comprehend thy humility. For when thou wast presented with a pectoral cross in appreciation for thy manifold labours, thou didst object, saying: "I am an unprofitable servant, having only done what was my duty. Can we servants of God and spiritual pastors expect anything in life except labour and grief?" In amazement at thy self-abasement, with joy and wonder we cry to thee thus:

Rejoice; thou who wast filled only with love for God and all men!

Rejoice; thou whose eye was single!

Rejoice; thou who camest not to be served but to serve!

Rejoice; thou who didst give thy life as a ransom for many!

Rejoice; Angel of spiritual comfort for those in tribulation!

Rejoice; Model of spiritual meekness!

Rejoice; O Father Raphael, good shepherd of the lost sheep in America!

KONTAKION X

D ESIRING to save a multitude of people through thy care, the All-merciful Lord chose thee and appointed thee to bear much fruit. Labouring abundantly, thou didst travel from city to city, from village to village, defending the Orthodox from the assaults of the enemy, teaching them to chant in Orthodox fashion: ALLELUIA!

OIKOS X

THE love of thy people for thee and thy love for them greatly impressed the holy hierarch Tikhon. He saw in thee the image of a true shepherd—, one who served not by compulsion, but willingly, not for dishonest gain but eagerly; one who was not a lord but a humble servant. Traveling to Russia, he forcefully entreated the Holy Synod to allow him to consecrate thee as his Vicar Bishop. Bearing within thee the abundant grace of the Holy Spirit, thou wast the first to be consecrated to the sacred episcopacy in the New World. Wherefore, grateful to God, we the faithful chant with joy to thee:

> Rejoice; O high priest of God Most High, who received
> divine grace in abundance at thy consecration!

> Rejoice; most luminous lamp, burning and shedding light!

> Rejoice; thou who hast illumined the whole world with the
> rays of thy virtues!

> Rejoice; thou who offered the divine Sacrifice at the throne
> of Christ!

> Rejoice; hierarch adorned with the understanding of
> Orthodoxy!

> Rejoice; thou who gavest drink to the faithful with the
> streams of the doctrine of salvation!

> Rejoice; O Father Raphael, good shepherd of the lost sheep
> in America!

KONTAKION XI

CONSECRATED as a hierarch of the Russian Orthodox Church, with the blessing of the Patriarch and Holy Synod of Antioch, thy ministry extended to all Orthodox Christians. As a self-proclaimed Syro-Arab by birth, Greek by education, American by residence, Russian at heart and

Slav in soul, thou didst minister to all, teaching the Orthodox in the New World to proclaim with one voice: ALLELUIA!

OIKOS XI

THINE archpastoral burden weighed upon thee; thine omophorion was very heavy. Thy flock was confused, surrounded by many false teachings. Possessing the spirit of understanding and of wisdom, thou didst enlighten the minds of the deceived, proclaiming the Word, preaching in season and out of season, by exhortation and letter. We who are the recipients of thy counsel and the beneficiaries of thy wisdom cry out to thee thus:

Rejoice; thou who didst share the ministry of the Apostles!

Rejoice; thou who didst tend the flock according to the words of the Apostle Peter!

Rejoice; steadfast uprooter of heresy!

Rejoice; impartial observer of the canons of the Church!

Rejoice; destroyer of impious doctrines!

Rejoice; skilful helmsman of the Church!

Rejoice; O Father Raphael, good shepherd of the lost sheep in America!

KONTAKION XII

KNOWING the grace of God which hath been given unto thee, O most glorious hierarch Raphael, we who are weak and heavy-laden with the burden of our sins flee to thee as our refuge and mighty defender. Pray fervently unto the Lord that He will preserve His Holy Church from unbelief and schism, from danger and temptation, that we may chant to God who through thee doeth good things for us: ALLELUIA!

OIKOS XII

As a faithful servant of thy Master, it was given to thee to suffer at the end of thine earthly life. Wherefore, as to a faithful servant who didst glorify Christ both in thy life and in thy death, to thee who hast received a glorious crown in heaven, we gather to offer these unworthy words of praise:

Rejoice; thou who wast overshadowed with divine power!

Rejoice; thou who didst faultlessly preserve the True Faith!

Rejoice; thou who didst reveal thy righteousness in thy
  Repose!

Rejoice; thou who hast received eternal rest in heaven with
  the saints!

Rejoice; great warrior of Orthodoxy!

Rejoice; invincible defender of piety!

Rejoice; O Father Raphael, good shepherd of the lost sheep
  in America!

KONTAKION XIII

O MOST holy and most wonderful Father Raphael, look down from the heights of heaven upon thy flock and accept this, our present offering. Entreat the Lord God that He will pour out upon us His divine grace and the gift of the Holy Spirit, that we, being delivered from all enemies visible and invisible, may forever chant to Him with thee and all the saints: ALLELUIA! *(Thrice)*

And again, Oikos I and Kontakion I are read.

OIKOS I

THOU didst begin thy life in exile, O holy Father Raphael. Child of pious Orthodox parents, successor to the holy Hieromartyr Joseph, even in thy mother's womb thou didst enjoy no repose. Thus was thy life of travel mystically foretold. Thou wast chosen to bring the light of holy Orthodoxy to the scattered flock of Christ in the New World, who together with us honour thee in these words of praise:

Rejoice; thou who like thy Master wast born in a city not
thine own!

Rejoice; recipient of the name of the great Archangel!

Rejoice; thou who didst say, "Man meant it to me for evil,
but God for good!"

Rejoice; thou who wast anointed with the blood of
the martyrs!

Rejoice; thou who didst traverse the world in ministry to
the faithful!

Rejoice; thou who didst lead all men to the worship of the
Holy Trinity!

Rejoice; O Father Raphael, good shepherd of the lost sheep
in America!

KONTAKION I

O HOLY Father, called from thy native land to the distant shores of the New World, thou didst take up thy cross and follow after Christ. Wherefore, as to one who hath crucified himself on behalf of his flock, as to our faithful guardian and protector, we fervently cry:

Rejoice; O Father Raphael, good shepherd of the lost sheep
in America!

PRAYER TO ST. RAPHAEL

Let us pray to our holy Father Raphael.

O holy hierarch Father Raphael, pray unto God for us.

O WISE and loving hierarch of the Church of Christ God, good shepherd of the lost sheep in America, sustenance for our souls, admonition for the lost, defence against foes, uniter of the Orthodox world, proclaimer of the truth, uplifter of the oppressed, guardian of the faith, father to orphans, protector of widows, friend of the poor, reconciler of foes, great light from Antioch, new Moses who didst lead thy people out of the wilderness into the Promised Land, new Elias who hast placed within the holy Church a double portion of thy spirit, new Ezra who didst build up the Temple of God, new Apostle of Christ our God, lover of the holy prayers and divine services, adornment of the holy Church, seeker of the lost, joy of all the Orthodox, son of Antioch, boast of America, O holy Father Raphael: Mercifully hearken unto these supplications which are offered unto thee by thy grateful children. O high priest of the Most High God, lift up thy hands and bless us, O thou who art thrice-blessed of the All-holy Trinity. O comforter of the oppressed who art a bearer of the heavenly King, the Comforter and Spirit of Truth, take us to thy bosom and shelter us from all harm. O shepherd who art a servant of the Lamb and a sheep of His flock, take up thy staff and guide us to secure and verdant pastures. O father who art a son and heir of the Unoriginate Father, lift up thine arms and intercede with him that the Church may be preserved in tranquillity; that her God-appointed hierarchs may be granted peace, safety, honour, health and length of days, rightly dividing the word of truth; that her priests may be clothed with righteousness; that her God-fearing monastics may shine forth as paradisiacal lights upon the world; and that her Christ-loving people may be granted mercy, life, peace, health, salvation and visitation, pardon and forgiveness of sins. Beseech thou him that we may be granted to live a peaceful life in this age, and to see the good things in the age which is to come, always glorifying the unoriginate Father, the only-begotten Son and the all-holy and good and life-giving Spirit, the consubstantial Trinity, unto the ages of ages. AMEN.

AKATHIST TO OUR RIGHTEOUS FATHER JACOB NETSVETOV, ENLIGHTENER OF ALASKA

KONTAKION I

O HOLY Father Jacob whose children number more than the stars in the northern sky, whose life and teachings have become a ladder reaching from earth to heaven: Having wrestled with temptation and fought the good fight, thou hast become our valiant intercessor before the Lord our God.

P RAY to Him for us who venerate your sacred memory and who strive to continue thy holy work as the New Israel in the New World of America, That we may sing with love and joy to thee, the messenger of reconciliation and peace:

> Rejoice; O Holy Father Jacob, Baptizer, and Enlightener of
> the Native Peoples of Alaska!

OIKOS I

ORN on the Island dedicated to the Holy Great Martyr George, O
Father Jacob, thou hast become a warrior for Christ, vanquishing
every temptation that arose within thy heart and soul, bringing peace to a
land where only violence had reigned, reconciling hostile tribes by
preaching to them the Gospel of peace and forgiveness. Thou became a
father of many nations as thou baptized and enlightened thousands of
people who had never known Jesus Christ, pastoring your scattered flock
in the Aleutian Islands, the Yukon Delta and at New Archangel. In thy
humility, devotion, piety, and perseverance, thou hast become the image
of the perfect evangelist to us who stand before thy holy icon and offer
these praises to thee:

Rejoice; First flower of the Alaskan wilderness!

Rejoice; First son of the Aleut nation called to the Holy
Priesthood!

Rejoice; Joy of the Pribilof Islands!

Rejoice; Father of Atka and the Aleutian Archipelago!

Rejoice; Candle illuminating the Arctic night!

Rejoice; Light, kindling the flame of the Christian Faith in
the north!

Rejoice; O Holy Father Jacob, Baptizer, and Enlightener of
the Native Peoples of Alaska!

KONTAKION II

ROM thy youth, O blessed Jacob, thy parents guided thee on the path
of salvation. Thy childhood amongst thy mother's Aleut kinsmen
prepared thee well for thy future missionary labours. Fluent in their
ancient language, thou also offered prayers to God in thy father's Slavic
tongue. At an early age, thou joined the Aleut and Russian faithful,
gathered in the chapel of St. George, singing: ALLELUIA!

OIKOS II

S ETTING sail for Kamchatka, thou continued across the frozen tundra of Siberia to the shores of Lake Baikal, to enrol at the seminary in glorious Irkutsk. Thou mastered theology in the city of St. Innocent, Enlightener of Siberia's Native Peoples, and studied his respectful approach to their languages and cultural traditions. Returning to Russian America with thy young bride, Anna Simeonova, thou commenced thine evangelical work at Atka, where today thou art remembered with love:

Rejoice; Father of the Atkan church and its benefactor!

Rejoice; Baptizer of Aleut children and people!

Rejoice; Teacher of the Orthodox Faith in Russian America!

Rejoice; Beautiful adornment of the land of thine ancestors!

Rejoice; Heroic missionary to the Peoples of the North!

Rejoice; Humble architect of the Orthodox Church in the Aleutian Islands!

Rejoice; O Holy Father Jacob, Baptizer, and Enlightener of the Native Peoples of Alaska!

KONTAKION III

L EARNING of the labours of thy friend and mentor St. Innocent, thou devoted thyself to mastering his Aleut translation of the Gospel of St. Matthew. Adapting the text to the Atkan dialect, thou proclaimed the Good News to thy flock who sang: ALLELUIA!

OIKOS III

F OLLOWING the example of St. Innocent, the future Metropolitan of Moscow, thou established a school at Atka where children could learn to read in both Aleut and Russian. Thou translated Sacred Scripture and deepened their knowledge of God and His creation by thy dedicated instruction. Enlightened by thy teaching at church and in school, the people of Atka praise thee with these words of thanksgiving:

Rejoice; Apostle to the New World!

Rejoice; Son of both Russia and America!

Rejoice; Faithful servant of Jesus Christ!

Rejoice; Adopted son of the Theotokos!

Rejoice; Thy teaching endures as our spiritual legacy!

Rejoice; Thy example inspires our evangelical labours!

Rejoice; O Holy Father Jacob, Baptizer, and Enlightener of the Native Peoples of Alaska!

KONTAKION IV

RECOGNIZING thy talents and devotion, the Holy Synod enlarged thy district to include the Kurile Islands, far to the west. Sailing across the Bering Straits to evangelize the Native people there, thou celebrated Divine Services aboard ship and in thy tent-church, singing: ALLELUIA!

OIKOS IV

O BLESSED Father Jacob! Thou endured the hazards of travel in the north throughout thy entire life. Like the Holy Apostle Paul, thou experienced storms at sea as well as temptation and persecution on land. Thou were constantly ill, bedridden for many days, unable to stand or to walk. Thou persevered through many hardships to bring the Light of Christ to thy flock in remote villages and settlements, by the power of the glorified and resurrected Lord; thou continued thy apostolic ministry in Alaska, where thou are remembered today in songs of praise:

Rejoice; Thou suffered many temptations and fears!

Rejoice; Thou triumphed over them by the Grace of God!

Rejoice; Thou sailed tempestuous seas like the Holy
  Apostles!

Rejoice; Thou received the power of the Holy Spirit as they
  did on Pentecost!

Rejoice; Long-suffering servant of the Lord!

Rejoice; Patient pastor and humble teacher!

Rejoice; O Holy Father Jacob, Baptizer, and Enlightener of
  the Native Peoples of Alaska!

KONTAKION V

RETURNING again to thy home at Atka, thee offered thanks to God for thy safe journey. Warmed by the love of thy flock and thy family, thou renewed thy dedication to the service of the Lord, constructing a holy church and writing the icons for it thyself as the temple was dedicated in the name of St. Nicholas of Myra in Lycia, thou sang thankfully to God: ALLELUIA!

OIKOS V

THY life, O holy Father, was filled with disappointment, hardship, and tragedy. Thy wife Anna became ill and died at the hospital in Sitka. Thy house at Atka burned and thy nephew Vasiliy, whom you loved as a son, also suddenly died, leaving thee homeless and alone. Thy desire was to enter monastic life, but there was no one to replace thee. Thou obediently remained in the Aleutians for twenty years, where today thou art remembered with gratitude:

Rejoice; Thou accepted and endured all things as decreed
  by the Lord!

Rejoice; Thou loved Him with all thy mind, soul, and heart!

Rejoice; Thou persevered in times of tribulation and need!

Rejoice; Thou triumphed over temptation, depression,
and fear!

Rejoice; Lamp, illuminating the household of Faith!

Rejoice; Light glowing with love and humility!

Rejoice; O Holy Father Jacob, Baptizer, and Enlightener of
the Native Peoples of Alaska!

KONTAKION VI

TRAVELING throughout the Aleutians by kayak, thou erected thy tent-church in camps, temporary settlements and villages, preaching, teaching, encouraging, and confirming thy spiritual children in the Orthodox Faith. They were amazed at thy energy and dedication and loved thee as their faithful guide and father, praising God with the song: ALLELUIA!

OIKOS VI

HAVING established the True Faith in thy native land, thou wast transferred to another region and entrusted with an even greater task. St. Innocent, as thy bishop, appointed thee to the new mission station on the Yukon River, where thou began the evangelization of the Yup'ik Eskimos. Thou studied their language and began the work of enlightening them with the help of many Aleuts who had settled among them. Throughout western Alaska, the Yup'ik people celebrate thy memory with these words:

Rejoice; Enlightener of the Yukon Delta!

Rejoice; Joy of the Aleut and Eskimo nations!

Rejoice; Educator and guide to the Peoples of the North!

Rejoice; Instructor and teacher of children and elders!

Rejoice; Baptizer of the Yukon and Kuskokwim!

Rejoice; Sanctifier of the forests, lakes, and tundra!

Rejoice; O Holy Father Jacob, Baptizer, and Enlightener of
the Native Peoples of Alaska!

KONTAKION VII

THOU founded the parish of the Elevation of the Holy Cross and
built the first Christian temple on the banks of the
Yukon. Writing many icons for the church thyself, thou glorified
God for the fervent faith of thy spiritual children whom thou taught
to sing: ALLELUIA!

OIKOS VII

THE Athabaskan Indians, whose homeland lies in the heartland of
Alaska, heard of thy mission work among their Eskimo neighbours
and invited thee to visit them. Paddling upstream, thou reached their
settlement at Shageluk in three days, and preached the Word of God to
them. Thou counted over a hundred canoes, kayaks, and boats
converging on the river, where thou baptized more than three hundred
souls. Their descendants today glorify thee:

Rejoice; Heroic missionary to the Indian peoples!

Rejoice; Herald of peace, forgiveness, and reconciliation!

Rejoice; Thou brought the divine message of love to
warring enemies!

Rejoice; Thou united them to Christ and to each other as
they accepted the Orthodox Faith!

Rejoice; They requested Holy Baptism in the Shageluk
River!

Rejoice; They received the Heavenly Bread and the Cup of
Life from thy hands!

Rejoice; O Holy Father Jacob, Baptizer, and Enlightener of
the Native Peoples of Alaska!

KONTAKION VIII

UNITED in truth and in love, the Athabaskan peoples embraced the
Orthodox Faith and ended centuries of inter-tribal strife and
violence. Thou became blessed as a child of God, preaching the Gospel
of Peace and reconciling former enemies who exclaimed in wonder and
joy: ALLELUIA!

OIKOS VII

TRAVELING across the frozen tundra by dog sled, you struggled to visit
the Eskimo settlements in the delta region. You discovered the site
of St. Juvenaly's martyrdom and asked his intercessions for your apostolic
labours. Your missionary endeavours required you to risk your health and
safety as you persevered for nearly twenty more years on the shores of the
Bering Sea, where we celebrate your memory in song:

Rejoice; Evangelist illuminating the northern sky!

Rejoice; Missionary to distant lands and peoples!

Rejoice; Physician of souls and bodies!

Rejoice; Archpriest, true shepherd, and humble pastor!

Rejoice; Missionary of reconciliation!

Rejoice; Preacher of the Good News of eternal salvation!

Rejoice; O Holy Father Jacob, Baptizer, and Enlightener of
the Native Peoples of Alaska!

KONTAKION IX

ILL-STRICKEN with fever and bodily weakness, with no one to care for
thee, bedridden for weeks, unable to stand or walk, thou remained
steadfast in faith, persevering in hope, constant in prayer. Rising from thy

bed, thou managed to celebrate the divine services of Holy Week and Pascha. Transformed and renewed by the joy of the Resurrection, thou cried out to God: ALLELUIA!

OIKOS IX

SAINT INNOCENT, thy bishop, appreciated thy talents and dedication, conferred and consulted with thee about the progress of the mission in Alaska and recognized thine accomplishments. Others were jealous or ignorant of thy true character and unjustly attacked thee. Knowing of thy remarkable humility and patience, we sing with love to thee:

Rejoice; Thou prayed for those who criticized and slandered thee!

Rejoice; Thou followed the Lord's command and example and forgave them all!

Rejoice; Thou blessed those who cursed thee!

Rejoice; Thou did good to those who attacked and offended thee!

Rejoice; Perfect image of Christian charity!

Rejoice; Icon of Christ and His faithful servant!

Rejoice; O Holy Father Jacob, Baptizer, and Enlightener of the Native Peoples of Alaska!

KONTAKION X

AS formerly at Atka, the Eskimo children at the Yukon mission attended your school, where they learned to read the Holy Scriptures and sing sacred hymns in their own language. Celebrating the Liturgy in Slavonic, Greek, and Yup'ik, thou taught all to praise God also in Hebrew: ALLELUIA!

OIKOS X

FOR nearly forty years thou dwelt in the Alaskan wilderness, serving Jesus Christ as a modern apostle. Thou brought healing to the sick as an elder of the Church, fulfilling the instructions of thine apostolic namesake, James. Because of thy missionary labours and the miraculous cures that accompanied thy ministry, accept these hymns of thanksgiving from our unworthy lips:

Rejoice; Physician of bodies and healer of souls!

Rejoice; Teacher of pastors and guide of the Faithful!

Rejoice; Thou were inspired by the joy of the Resurrection!

Rejoice; Thou ascended the ladder that reaches to Heaven!

Rejoice; Thou endured evil attacks and forgave all your foes!

Rejoice; In forgiving thine enemies, thou were forgiven thy sins!

Rejoice; O Holy Father Jacob, Baptizer, and Enlightener of the Native Peoples of Alaska!

KONTAKION XI

HAVING founded and nurtured the parish on the Yukon, thou trained local leaders to succeed thee and continue thy holy work. Some became singers, others readers, and still others priests, who sang with the angels: ALLELUIA!

OIKOS XI

SUMMONED to Sitka to answer unjust accusations against thee, thou left the land of the Eskimo people and entered the territory of the Tlingit. Thou spent the last years of thine earthly life serving them in their chapel and preaching the Word of God to them. Today, they join us in singing these praises to thee:

Rejoice; Apostle to all Alaska!

Rejoice; Father of the Native Peoples!

Rejoice; Teacher and guide by your words and example!

Rejoice; Thy heroic life inspires us all!

Rejoice; True son of St. Herman and St. Innocent!

Rejoice; Faithful and humble servant of our Lord
Jesus Christ!

Rejoice; O Holy Father Jacob, Baptizer, and Enlightener of
the Native Peoples of Alaska!

KONTAKION XII

WHILEST in Sitka, thou located the grave site of thy beloved wife and erected a fitting memorial to her. Thou lived in the All-Colonial School during thy final years, offering thy knowledge and wisdom to another generation of future missionaries. With simplicity and humility, thou prepared new labourers for the plentiful harvest. Through them, we have become your spiritual children, and praise God for your faithful ministry in Alaska, singing: ALLELUIA!

OIKOS XII

O HOLY Father Jacob, thou fell asleep in the Lord and were buried in a place of honour, at the doors of the Tlingit chapel thou hadst served. The Aleuts, Russians, Creoles, Athabascan, as well as the Yup'ik and Tlingit nations today celebrate thy memory:

Rejoice; Spiritual Father of many nations!

Rejoice; Humble pastor and preacher of peace!

Rejoice; The seas, forests, mountains, and tundra sing
thy praises!

Rejoice; Heaven and earth celebrate thine apostolic
 accomplishments!

Rejoice; Our intercessor, guide, and healer!

Rejoice; Our example and inspiration!

Rejoice; O Holy Father Jacob, Baptizer, and Enlightener of
 the Native Peoples of Alaska!

KONTAKION XIII

B EYOND Alaska thou were forgotten for more than a hundred years,
but thy spiritual children kept the memory of thy heroic apostolic
ministry alive in their hearts. Today thou art glorified by the Orthodox
Church in America as a modern Apostle. Pray, O Holy Father Jacob,
that inspired by thy dedication, patience, humility, and Paschal joy, we
may worthily continue the sacred work to which thee dedicated thine
entire life, that together with thee, in the Kingdom of Heaven we may
join the angelic choir, singing: ALLELUIA! *(Thrice)*

And again, Oikos I and Kontakion I are read.

OIKOS I

B ORN on the Island dedicated to the Holy Great Martyr George, O
Father Jacob, thou hast become a warrior for Christ, vanquishing
every temptation that arose within thy heart and soul, bringing peace to a
land where only violence had reigned, reconciling hostile tribes by
preaching to them the Gospel of peace and forgiveness. Thou became a
father of many nations as thee baptized and enlightened thousands of
people who had never known Jesus Christ, pastoring thy scattered flock in
the Aleutian Islands, the Yukon Delta and at New Archangel. In thy
humility, devotion, piety, and perseverance, thou hast become the image
of the perfect evangelist to us who stand before thy holy icon and offer
these praises to thee:

Rejoice; First flower of the Alaskan wilderness!

Rejoice; First son of the Aleut nation called to the
　　Holy Priesthood!

Rejoice; Joy of the Pribilof Islands!

Rejoice; Father of Atka and the Aleutian Archipelago!

Rejoice; Candle illuminating the Arctic night!

Rejoice; Light, kindling the flame of the Christian Faith in
　　the north!

Rejoice; O Holy Father Jacob, Baptizer, and Enlightener of
　　the Native Peoples of Alaska!

KONTAKION I

O HOLY Father Jacob whose children number more than the stars in the northern sky, whose life and teachings have become a ladder reaching from earth to heaven: Having wrestled with temptation and fought the good fight, thou hast become our valiant intercessor before the Lord our God. Pray to Him for us who venerate thy sacred memory and who strive to continue thy holy work as the New Israel in the New World of America That we may sing with love and joy to thee, the messenger of reconciliation and peace:

Rejoice; O Holy Father Jacob, Baptizer, and Enlightener of
　　the Native Peoples of Alaska!

AKATHIST TO ALL THE SAINTS THAT SHONE FORTH IN THE LANDS OF THE WEST

KONTAKION I

NOW let us praise, as is meet, all the saints that in times of old shone forth in the lands of the West, enlightening these parts through their sufferings and struggles. And let us sing to them, as to those that unceasingly pray for us before God, saying:

Rejoice; all ye Saints, that in the lands of the West confessed
  the true faith!

OIKOS I

THE most holy name of our Saviour hath been glorified wondrously in you, O saints of the West. For, beholding your holy life and deeds for salvation, the peoples of the West learned how to worship the True God and honour you with joy, saying:

Rejoice; Apostles and martyrs, monks and bishops, for ye
  are the praise and joy of all the West!

Rejoice; for ye above all are the most precious fruit of these lands!

Rejoice; for your holy blood washed away all heathen defilement!

Rejoice; for through teachings full of power ye delivered the people from ignorance!

Rejoice; for in the darkness of those times ye shone forth like most radiant beacons of light!

Rejoice; for before the whole world ye were shown to be true guides to the path of salvation!

Rejoice; for in this way ye became fathers in Christ to all the peoples of the West!

Rejoice; for even to this day ye pray unceasingly for us in the heavens!

Rejoice; for ye above all are the strong hope of these places!

Rejoice; for ye are the boast of all the faithful of the West!

Rejoice; for ye teach us how to give true honour to God!

Rejoice; for ye call the whole West to repentance and turn back to God!

Rejoice; all ye Saints, that in the lands of the West confessed the true faith!

KONTAKION II

THE lands of the West were also counted worthy to receive the wonderful Apostles of God, that with unquenchable zeal everywhere preached the Gospel of salvation. And through them, the peoples of the West were born in Christ for the first time, and began to sing to Him as to the true God: ALLELUIA!

OIKOS II

The Holy Apostles made themselves enlighteners of the West through their untiring labours. For they put at naught the dark powers of the enemy and fearlessly spread the light of Christ in all places. And therefore, they confessed the truth even unto blood and became worthy to hear from the mouths of all songs of praise like these:

Rejoice; Apostles of Christ, that strove to bring the Gospel
  to the lands of the West!

Rejoice; for ye above all others are the fathers and protectors
  of these places!

Rejoice; therefore, Holy Peter and Paul, Princes of the
  Apostles, for ye founded the first Church in the West!

Rejoice; for through you pagan Rome began to offer pure
  sacrifice to the True God!

Rejoice; for ye were shown to be fearless before all the
  terrors and persecutions of the unbelievers!

Rejoice; for at the end ye sealed your faith in Christ even
  with your own blood!

Rejoice; Holy Apostle James, son of Zebedee, who hast
  enlightened the Spanish lands!

Rejoice; for thy relics rest in these parts to this day, bringing
  great comfort to all!

Rejoice; thou too, Holy Apostle Simon the Zealot, who
  brought the faith in the Risen Christ to Britain!

Rejoice; for like all the other Apostles thou too didst receive
  death for eternal life!

Rejoice; Holy Aristobulus, who followed Saint Simon in
  preaching!

Rejoice; for thou didst become the first bishop of Britain
and witness of Christ!

Rejoice; all ye Saints, that in the lands of the West confessed
the true faith!

KONTAKION III

THE Apostles of God left worthy disciples and followers in the places
they enlightened, and they were in nothing less than their fathers,
but in all things followed them in labour and zeal. For by the example
of their lives they delivered the heathen from idolatry and brought
them to venerate the One True God, teaching them to sing to Him
unceasingly: ALLELUIA!

OIKOS III

NOW let us all sing with one voice to all those that were worthy to
become followers of the Holy Apostles, furthering their work and
hallowing the lands of the West through their teachings and blood; and let
us all say to them, as to those who even to this day pray for us before the
throne of God, words of praise like these:

Rejoice; all ye who have shown yourselves to be wonderful
disciples of the disciples of Christ!

Rejoice; for alongside your fathers ye struggled fervently for
the enlightenment of the West!

Rejoice; therefore, among all, Holy Clement, for the prince
of the Apostles consecrated thee bishop of Rome!

Rejoice; for thou didst shepherd the flock entrusted to thee
with great wisdom and worthiness!

Rejoice; also, Holy Ignatius, Bishop of Antioch, for thou
too didst receive consecration from the hands of
Saint Peter!

Rejoice; thou bearer of God, for thy writings greatly console
us to this day!

Rejoice; for thy glorious martyrdom is for all an example of
manliness and courage in the face of death!

Rejoice; thou too, Holy Justin lover of wisdom, for through
thy writings thou didst arouse the wrath of the enemies
of Christ!

Rejoice; for not suffering thy divine wisdom, they martyred
thee in the arenas of Rome!

Rejoice; also, Holy Irenaeus, Bishop of Lyon, who from
Asia Minor came to enlighten the lands of Gaul!

Rejoice; for through thy divinely-inspired writings, thou didst
ceaselessly fight against all heresies!

Rejoice; for on account of this, all Christians honour thee as
a great Pillar and Father of the Church!

Rejoice; all ye Saints, that in the lands of the West confessed
the true faith!

KONTAKION IV

NOW let us offer songs of praise to all those that in the lands of
the West suffered for Christ even unto blood, and with their
manliness trampled down death; and to God, Who strengthened them
in torments and tortures beyond all imagination, let us all unceasingly
sing thus: ALLELUIA!

OIKOS IV

WITH joy ye shed your blood for Christ, O venerable martyrs, and
to Him ye offered yourselves as a well-received sacrifice. And
seeing your ineffable patience, the peoples of the West understood that
the God of Glory Himself dwelt within you, and marvelling at such a thing,
with faith began to sing to you thus:

Rejoice; Tatiana and Anastasia, together with Sophia and
her three daughters!

Rejoice; Cecilia and Agnes, who showed yourselves women
unequalled in courage!

Rejoice; Laurence, the archdeacon, together with Sebastian,
the glorious martyr of Christ!

Rejoice; good victors, for through your ineffable passions ye
hallowed pagan Rome!

Rejoice; all ye who filled all the lands of the West with your
struggles!

Rejoice; Agatha and Lucy, praised martyrs, for in Italy ye
fought the good fight!

Rejoice; Valentine and Januarius, enlightened bishops, for
ye sealed your teaching with blood!

Rejoice; Cyprian, the hierarch, together with Perpetua and
Felicity and all those that laid down their lives for
Christ in the African lands!

Rejoice; Maurice, wonderful martyr, for alongside thy
soldiers thou didst fearlessly stand up to death in the
Swiss lands!

Rejoice; Vincent, the deacon, for thou didst hallow Spain
through thine unimaginable torments!

Rejoice; Alban, valiant warrior, for thou didst offer thyself as
the first pure sacrifice of Britain to the true God!

Rejoice; Ursula, bride of Christ, who with thy blood washed
the German lands!

Rejoice; all ye Saints, that in the lands of the West confessed
the true faith!

KONTAKION V

A S THE enemy of our salvation saw that he could not defeat the faith of the disciples of Christ through tortures and persecutions beyond compare, he sent against them hosts of deceitful teachers and shepherds, who with treachery would lead the faithful into delusion. But against them stood up wise Fathers, great both in word and deed, who with the wisdom of the Holy Spirit overcame all heresy and taught the people to give true honour to God, saying: ALLELUIA!

OIKOS V

N ow let us praise with joy all the fearless confessors of the Orthodox Faith, who fought valiantly for the truth in the lands of the West and rooted out all lies from among the people through their holy struggles and deeds; and let us sing to them as to true chosen ones of the All-Merciful God, saying:

> Rejoice; Holy Hosius of Cordoba, for thou didst preside at the First Council of the whole world!

> Rejoice; Holy Hilary, Bishop of Poitiers, for thou too didst fearlessly defend the true faith!

> Rejoice; for on account of this thou didst suffer countless persecutions at the hands of the Arian blasphemers!

> Rejoice; Holy Ambrose, for thou didst rule over the city of Milan with thy divine wisdom!

> Rejoice; for with thy words and writings thou didst turn the throngs to Christ!

> Rejoice; also, Blessed Augustine, for through the prayers of thy mother Monica, God turned thee back from the path of perdition!

> Rejoice; for thou didst become a wise bishop and great fighter against heretics!

Rejoice; Jerome, thou blessed man, for through thy many
writings thou didst enlighten the lands of the West!

Rejoice; Holy Leo, Pope of Rome, for at the Council of
Chalcedon thou didst wonderfully fight for the
Orthodox Faith!

Rejoice; for having godly light, thou didst unfailingly guide
the people entrusted to thee on the path of salvation!

Rejoice; Holy Martin, fearless Pope, for together with Saint
Maximus thou didst confess the truth unto death!

Rejoice; for with joy thou didst suffer for the true faith all the
torments of the impious emperor!

Rejoice; all ye Saints, that in the lands of the West confessed
the true faith!

KONTAKION VI

THE TIMES of dread persecution ended through Divine Providence,
but martyrdom for Christ did not. For those that had up until then
visibly shed their blood for the faith, began to suffer for it invisibly,
through fasting and tears crucifying all their sinful desires and lusts. On
account of this, they made themselves even like unto angels in the flesh,
learning to offer to God unceasing praise: Alleluia!

OIKOS VI

THE LANDS of the West also gave birth to men and women perfect in
holiness, who by their struggles beyond nature won the everlasting
joys of heaven, making themselves to all an unlying example on the path of
salvation. Let us therefore honour first those that shone forth in the land
of Gaul, establishing the monastic life in these parts, and let us joyfully say
to them thus:

Rejoice; Holy Martin, for of all Western people, thou wast
the first to be deigned to taste of the sweetness of
monastic life!

Rejoice; for following thine example, throngs of the faithful
chose to forsake the fleeting glory of this world!

Rejoice; for shining with the gift of wonderworking, thou
didst become Bishop of Tours and the great protector
of the West!

Rejoice; Holy John Cassian, for together with thy friend
Germanus, thou didst drink of the wisdom of the
desert Fathers!

Rejoice; for through thy wonderful writings, thou didst make
thyself the true founder of monastic life in the West!

Rejoice; Holy Honoratus, for on the isle of Lerins thou didst
found Gaul's most famed monastery!

Rejoice; for countless numbers of saints strove there for
salvation, turning Gaul into the Thebaid of the West!

Rejoice; therefore, together with Hilary and Eucherius, with
Vincent and Caesarius and many other holy monks!

Rejoice; also Holy Gregory of Tours, for thou too didst
ceaselessly strive for the fame of the saints of thy lands!

Rejoice; thou too, Holy Germanus, Bishop of Auxerre, who
through thy gifts enlightened both Britain and Gaul!

Rejoice; Blessed Saint Geneviève, for from childhood thou
didst yearn to live as an anchoress!

Rejoice; for thou didst proved thyself a most-powerful
protectress of Paris through thy holy prayers!

Rejoice; all ye Saints, that in the lands of the West confessed
the true faith!

KONTAKION VII

SPRINGING up from the lands of Gaul as from a clear and fresh fountain, monastic life spread everywhere in the West; and in each nation it bore fruit in holy monks full of virtue, who with pure voices and hearts of praise sang to God for themselves and for the whole world: ALLELUIA!

OIKOS VII

NOW LET us all praise with one voice those that strove for Christ in the lands of Britain and Italy, and through their struggles made themselves enlightened apostles of these lands and fathers of monastic life in these places; and let us sing to them as to most wonderful victors in the struggle against the powers of the enemy, saying thus:

Rejoice; Holy Ninian, for it was at Saint Martin's feet that thou didst learn all the secrets of monastic life!

Rejoice; for perfecting thyself in holiness, thou didst become the enlightener of thy home, the land of the Picts!

Rejoice; Holy Patrick, wonderful apostle, for by thy divine zeal thou didst turn the Irish land to God!

Rejoice; for in this way thou didst make thyself the father of the Irish people, for whom thou prayest fervently to this day!

Rejoice; for countless disciples followed thee on the path of holiness!

Rejoice; among them all, blessed Brigid, for by thine unutterable love thou didst become the mother of all Ireland!

Rejoice; thou also, Holy David, wise bishop, for in Wales thou didst establish countless monasteries!

Rejoice; for on account of this the Welsh revere thee to this
day as their protector before God!

Rejoice; Holy Benedict, great struggler, for the land of Italy
was enlightened by thine unearthly life!

Rejoice; for through thy wonderful Rule thou didst become
a true father to all the monks of the West!

Rejoice; Holy Alexis, Man of God, for in the city of Rome
thou didst live in utter meekness!

Rejoice; for on account of thy many gifts the whole world
cherisheth thee as a great saint!

Rejoice; all ye Saints, that in the lands of the West confessed
the true faith!

KONTAKION VIII

THE ENEMY of our salvation could not bear that all the peoples of the
West, as with one voice, raised up songs of praise to the True God,
and therefore he set on them waves of savage and heathen peoples, who in
their cruelty passed all through fire and sword. But in those times of great
suffering, enlightened preachers rose up in the West, in nothing less than
the first Apostles. And through their burning zeal, they turned the
temptation of the enemy into heavenly blessing and brought the heathen
to Christ, teaching them to sing to Him as to One God: ALLELUIA!

OIKOS VIII

NOW LET us praise all those that among the Franks earned Heaven
by their struggles and through their zeal turned many back to Christ.
For shining with heavenly gifts, they enlightened the people and wisely
guided them to salvation; and therefore they are deigned to hear from the
mouths of all songs of praise like these:

Rejoice; Holy Remigius, wonderful archbishop, for thou
wast the first Apostle of the Franks!

Rejoice; for inflamed by holy zeal thou didst baptize Clovis, the King of the Franks, together with many heathen!

Rejoice; Holy Clotilde, holy woman, for through thy tears thou didst bring thy husband to Christ!

Rejoice; for together with Saints Radegund and Bathild, thou didst set all a true example of a Christian wife and Queen!

Rejoice; Holy Germanus, Bishop of Paris, for thy generosity made thee known as the father of the poor!

Rejoice; for thou didst shine forth before the whole world with thy great gentleness and kindness!

Rejoice; Holy Eligius, skilled smith, for thy love tamed the heathen hearts of stone!

Rejoice; for becoming Bishop of Noyon, thou didst turn countless savage Teutons back to Christ!

Rejoice; Holy Amandus, who in the Netherlands preached the Christian faith!

Rejoice; Holy Lambert, for together with thy disciple Hubert, thou too didst strive to enlighten these places!

Rejoice; Holy Leger, valiant bishop, for thou didst not waver in reproving the wrong-doings of the king and his subjects!

Rejoice; for on account of this thou wast tormented in all ways, and at the end received a martyr's death!

Rejoice; all ye Saints, that in the lands of the West confessed the true faith!

KONTAKION IX

SEEING themselves overwhelmed by the heathen throngs, the shepherds of the West wisely decided to go and conquer them for Christ. Therefore, they sent men enlightened by God and perfect in virtue, who through their valiant struggles defeated the darkness of heathenism and became fathers in Christ to many nations, together with whom they ceaselessly sang to God the song: ALLELUIA!

OIKOS IX

THROUGH Gregory, the wonderful Pope of Rome, and Augustine, the faithful monk, the English were the first of the Germanic peoples to be born to new life and offer to Christ a host of saints as a pure sacrifice. Now let us sing joyfully to them, as to those that made themselves worthy of the Kingdom of Heaven and the veneration of the whole world, saying to them thus:

> Rejoice; thou first, Holy Gregory, great Patriarch, for in perfect wisdom thou didst shepherd the lands of the West!

> Rejoice; for burning with zeal for Christ, thou didst strive to bring the heathen peoples to the Faith!

> Rejoice; for on account of this, thou didst send Saint Augustine to preach, and together with him, thou art to this day called the Apostle of the English!

> Rejoice; Holy Augustine, for thou didst bring the English nation to Christ, baptizing their king, Ethelbert!

> Rejoice; for becoming Archbishop of Canterbury, together with thy disciples thou wast the first to bring the light of Christ to the English land!

> Rejoice; Paulinus, Birinus and Felix, wonderful apostles, for ye became fathers in Christ of the English!

Rejoice; Sigebert, Edwin, and Oswald, martyr kings, who
  defended the Christian faith unto blood!

Rejoice; Aidan, Chad and Botolph, pious fathers, for in the
  English lands ye established monastic life!

Rejoice; Theodore, Wilfrid, and John, most wise bishops,
  for through you the English Church was filled with
  glory!

Rejoice; Audrey, Hilda and Mildred, holy nuns, for by your
  strivings ye outran by far many men!

Rejoice; among all the English saints, Cuthbert, great
  wonderworker, and Guthlac, father of the desert!

Rejoice; thou too, wise and Venerable Bede, for thou didst
  devote all thy life to the Holy Scriptures!

Rejoice; all ye Saints, that in the lands of the West confessed
  the true faith!

KONTAKION X

THE SPANISH lands also made themselves worthy of great preachers
and bishops, who by their unceasing struggles brought the heathen to
Christ and turned the heretics to the true faith, calling all to give glory and
praise to the True God and ever sing to Him in thanksgiving: ALLELUIA!

OIKOS X

NOW LET us rightly honour, as is meet, all those that in Spain
wondrously confessed the true faith of Christ our Saviour and for it
fought unto death. And let us offer them songs of praise, as to those that
scattered the darkness of lies and made the truth victorious, joyfully saying
to them thus:

Rejoice; Holy Martin, Archbishop of Braga, for through thy
  zeal thou didst bring the Sueves to the true faith!

Rejoice; for on account of this thou art to this day reckoned
as the enlightener and father of these places!

Rejoice; Holy Hermenegild, for thou wast the first of the
Visigoths to confess the Orthodox Faith!

Rejoice; for on account of this thou didst even suffer death,
setting at naught thy father, the heretical king!

Rejoice; Holy Leander, for through thy labours the Visigoths
abandoned the Arian heresy!

Rejoice; for becoming Bishop of Seville, thou didst wisely
strive for the best in thy flock!

Rejoice; for in this thou wast helped by thy brother and
sister, Saints Fulgentius and Florence!

Rejoice; thou too, Holy Isidore, for thou wast the fourth and
most honoured child of this holy family!

Rejoice; for thou didst succeed thy brother to the see of
Seville, proving to be an undeceiving guide on the path
of salvation!

Rejoice; for through thy countless writings thou didst
enlighten the world and to this day art revered as a
Father!

Rejoice; Holy Ildephonsus, Archbishop of Toledo, for thou
didst show thyself to be a true disciple of Saint Isidore
and a wise shepherd!

Rejoice; for burning with love for the Most Pure Mother of
God, thou didst defend in writing her eternal virginity!

Rejoice; all ye Saints, that in the lands of the West confessed
the true faith!

KONTAKION XI

THE LIGHT of Christ shone forth even in the unfriendly lands of the Teutons, for the God of glory called all the nations to Himself. Therefore, now let us sing to Him Who in His ineffable mercy redeemed mankind from corruption and let us worship Him as the Only God, saying: ALLELUIA!

OIKOS XI

NOW LET us praise, as is meet, the wondrous preachers that rose up from among the Irish and the English, who enlightened many peoples and through their wisdom and zeal showed themselves to be one in honour with the Holy Apostles, and let us sing to them, as to those that brought to Christ a great harvest of heathen people, saying to them thus:

Rejoice; thou first, Holy Columba, wonderful son of Eire,
for through thy zeal thou didst enlighten the lands of
the Scots!

Rejoice; for by founding the famed monastery of Iona,
thou didst become an Apostle and father to the
heathen Picts!

Rejoice; thou too, Holy Columban, for leaving Ireland, thou
didst become a fearless preacher to many nations!

Rejoice; for thou didst found many monasteries in the West,
setting in them a rule according to the teachings of the
desert fathers!

Rejoice; for fearlessly thou didst reprove the evil deeds of
unworthy bishops and kings, suffering for this
countless persecutions!

Rejoice; Holy Gall, for thou wast deigned to be a disciple of
Saint Columban and the beloved Apostle of the Swiss!

Rejoice; thou too, Holy Clement, most wise Englishman, for thou didst preach Christ among the savage heathen!

Rejoice; for on account of thy burning zeal, thou bearest to this day the title of Apostle of the Frisians!

Rejoice; Holy Boniface, for together with Saint Clement thou didst bring the Gospel to the lands of the Germans!

Rejoice; for through thee and thy holy disciples, God foreordained to bring to Himself all the German peoples!

Rejoice; for with the blessing of the holy Pope Zacharias, thou didst strive to correct the impieties of the Franks!

Rejoice; for thou didst crown thy holy labours with the crown of martyrdom, which thou didst receive in great old age!

Rejoice; all ye Saints, that in the lands of the West confessed the true faith!

KONTAKION XII

THE DREADED Northmen were the last fruit which the faithful people of the West brought to the True God. For being enlightened with the true faith, the Viking nations began to worship our Saviour Christ with zeal, singing to Him in a sweet voice: ALLELUIA!

OIKOS XII

NOW LET us honour with praises all those that shone forth in the West in the times near the end and through their struggles made themselves the heirs of Heaven. For some even suffered martyrdom for Christ, while others fearlessly preached Him among the heathen. Therefore, let even us offer them honour, as is meet, singing to them thus:

Rejoice; all ye that in the Iberian lands suffered death at the hands of the unfaithful Hagarenes!

Rejoice; among them, Eulogius and George, for together with many others ye hallowed the city of Cordoba by your blood!

Rejoice; all those that in the Irish and English lands suffered martyrdom at the hands of the savage Vikings!

Rejoice; for on account of your sacrifice, God turned the people that persecuted you to believe in Him!

Rejoice; among all the new martyrs, Edmund, glorious king, for through thy sufferings thou didst become the great defender and patron of the English land!

Rejoice; Holy Anschar, for thou wast the first to preach Christ among the heathen Danes!

Rejoice; for thou didst become Bishop of Hamburg and to this day art revered as the Apostle of the North!

Rejoice; thou too, Holy Olaf, valiant warrior, for being Viking by blood, thou didst offer thyself as a pure sacrifice to God!

Rejoice; for thou didst become the Christian King of Norway, slaughtered by the heathen for thine unwavering faith!

Rejoice; Holy Sigfrid, for through thy struggles thou didst enlighten the Swedish land and turn the heathen king to Christ!

Rejoice; Dunstan, Archbishop of Canterbury, for thy wisdom and kindness made thee the much beloved father of the whole English land!

Rejoice; for thou didst anoint as king Saint Edward, the
innocent martyr, whose relics bring comfort to
Orthodox Christians to this day!

Rejoice; all ye Saints, that in the lands of the West confessed
the true faith!

KONTAKION XIII

NOW LET us sing with songs of thanksgiving to God, Who called forth
His Saints from all over the Earth and gathered His beloved from
the ends of the world, to Him, Who is glorified in the Holy Trinity. For
through His chosen one, Saint John the Wonderworker, He hath revealed
to us the ancient saints of the West for our joy and comfort in these latter
days. For all these things, therefore, and for all His goodness towards us,
let us thank Him as our most beloved God, and let us worship Him with
voices of praise, saying to Him: ALLELUIA! *(Thrice)*

And again, Oikos I and Kontakion I are read.

OIKOS I

THE most holy name of our Saviour hath been glorified wondrously in
you, O saints of the West. For, beholding your holy life and deeds
for salvation, the peoples of the West learned how to worship the True
God and honour you with joy, saying:

Rejoice; apostles and martyrs, monks and bishops, for ye are
the praise and joy of all the West!

Rejoice; for ye above all are the most precious fruit of
these lands!

Rejoice; for your holy blood washed away all heathen
defilement!

Rejoice; for through teachings full of power ye delivered the
people from ignorance!

Rejoice; for in the darkness of those times ye shone forth
like most radiant beacons of light!

Rejoice; for before the whole world ye were shown to be
true guides to the path of salvation!

Rejoice; for in this way ye became fathers in Christ to all the
peoples of the West!

Rejoice; for even to this day ye pray unceasingly for us in the
heavens!

Rejoice; for ye above all are the strong hope of these places!

Rejoice; for ye are the boast of all the faithful of the West!

Rejoice; for ye teach us how to give true honour to God!

Rejoice; for ye call the whole West to repentance and turn
back to God!

Rejoice; all ye Saints, that in the lands of the West confessed
the true faith!

KONTAKION I

NOW let us praise, as is meet, all the saints that in times of old shone
forth in the lands of the West, enlightening these parts through their
sufferings and struggles. And let us sing to them, as to those that
unceasingly pray for us before God, saying:

Rejoice; all ye Saints, that in the lands of the West confessed
the true faith!

PRAYER TO ALL THE SAINTS THAT SHONE FORTH IN THE LANDS OF THE WEST

O ye saints of the West, that in times of old confessed the true faith of our Saviour Christ and for it fought even unto death, thus making yourselves worthy of heavenly glory and heirs of everlasting life! Now do we, your unworthy successors, fall to our knees before you, and humbly beg you: as ye have boldly interceded for us before the throne of God unto this day, so from this time on do ye pray, O our beloved saints, for all the lands of the West! Pray that the Merciful and Long-Suffering God grant them forgiveness of sins and correction of life, and turn them, through His judgements, to repentance and the true faith for which ye sacrificed yourselves.

Again we pray unto you, O saints, for all the right believing faithful of the West who have need of your help and mercy: protect us with your prayers from all the temptations that befall us; strengthen us in the true faith and grant us zeal to preach it; guard us from all the wickedness of enemies seen and unseen; and show us victorious before the unfaithful, for the glory of God and for your honour. That through you, O saints of the West, the true faith may once again shine forth in the West with power, as it shone forth in times of old, and that the light of Christ may enlighten all. And thus, O ye saints, who through Divine Providence have shown yourselves to us in these latter days, receive us also, as the workers of the eleventh hour, for your veneration. And pray for us, who unworthily sing unto you songs of praise, that our God, Who easily forgiveth, make us also partakers of heavenly bliss, granting us salvation, as the God Who is Good and loveth mankind. That thus, together with you, beloved saints of the West, we may sing unto Him and worship Him as the All-Merciful God, the Father, the Son, and the Holy Spirit, now and ever, and unto the ages of ages. AMEN.

AKATHIST TO ALL SAINTS OF NORTH AMERICA

KONTAKION I

WITH grateful hearts we sing praises in thine honour, O All Saints of North America. Ye gave thy lives to the Lord as an offering of love. Ye are the first fruits of Christ's bountiful harvest here in the New World. As faithful servants of thy Master, ye laboured in the Vineyard of His Holy Church. Through thy example, ye have shown us the joy of the Orthodox Way. As we assemble today to honour ye, we cry:

Rejoice; All Saints of North America!

OIKOS I

WE glorify the Lord Who hath glorified ye, O sanctified men, women, and children of these North American lands. We stand in awe before thy countless miracles revealed to us by Our Father in heaven. Together with the bodiless choirs, we offer to ye these words of loving praise:

Rejoice; O holy Father Tikhon, Patriarch of Moscow and
enlightener of North America!

Rejoice; O Hierarch Innocent, Alaskan missionary and
evangelizer of the Aleuts!

Rejoice; O blessed Raphael, first Bishop of Brooklyn and
faithful shepherd!

Rejoice; O holy Nicholas, confessor and teacher of
heavenly theology!

Rejoice; O venerable Herman elder and wonderworker
of Alaska!

Rejoice; O martyrs Juvenal and Peter, martyrs crowned
by God!

Rejoice; O righteous Jacob, pastor and teacher of your flock!

Rejoice; O John and Alexis, defenders of the
Orthodox Way!

Rejoice; All Saints of North America!

KONTAKION II

O HOLY New Martyrs of North America, we honour thy lives by recounting the many sufferings that led to thy holy deaths. Ye were faithful to the Lord to the very end, and have been crowned as faithful witnesses in the Kingdom of Heaven. Through thy victories, we are delivered from the snares of the evil one, so that we might sing: ALLELUIA!

OIKOS II

T HE Church of North America is renewed and purified through the shedding of thy blood, O Faithful Witnesses of Christ. Through thy sufferings, ye strengthen and enliven those who follow in thy footsteps down the hard and narrow way. Seeing ye clothed in white robes and glorified by the Lord of hosts, we sing to ye these words of loving praise:

Rejoice; O holy Tikhon, long-suffering confessor and
   Patriarch of Moscow!

Rejoice; O soldiers of Christ, who fought and persevered to
   the very end!

Rejoice; O New Martyrs, who triumphed over the prince
   of darkness!

Rejoice; O Father Alexander, passion-bearer of Moscow!

Rejoice; O heavenly patrons of the North American Church!

Rejoice; O holy Peter, shining star of the Aleut people!

Rejoice; O John, first martyr of the Bolshevik revolution!

Rejoice; O holy Juvenal, zealous preacher of Grace!

Rejoice; All Saints of North America!

KONTAKION III

A S ye guided thy people to the homeland of God's Kingdom, ye proved yourselves defenders of the faith entrusted to ye, O Confessors and Stewards of the North American Church. Having rightly directed the word of the truth, ye preserve us from the injury of false teachings. Ye gave yourselves to imprisonment, sufferings, and death — remaining faithful all the while to the One Who is Faithful and True. As we behold your steadfastness in times of affliction, we sing: ALLELUIA!

OIKOS III

THE great adversary and enemy of our souls never ceases his ferocious attacks against the Holy Church. Hating the light of the Father's Radiance that shines from thy lives, the children of the evil one condemned ye to prolonged captivity and death, O long-suffering ones. As your grateful children, we offer to ye these words of loving praise:

Rejoice; O Hierarch Tikhon, protector of the sacred
treasures of the Church!

Rejoice; O valiant preachers of the Wisdom, Word, and
Power of God!

Rejoice; O holy Nicholas, defender of thy people in times of
oppression!

Rejoice; O Comfort of those persecuted for the sake of
righteousness!

Rejoice; O inspired teachers of the royal way of Orthodox
theology!

Rejoice; O Father John, loyal priest and intercessor for
the faithful!

Rejoice; O divine guardians of the Tradition of the Holy
Apostles!

Rejoice; O faithful guides leading us on the path of salvation!

Rejoice; All Saints of North America!

KONTAKION IV

AS imitators of the Twelve Apostles, ye travelled to the North American continent in order to make disciples of its many peoples. Through your preaching, ye gave an Indication of the Way into the Kingdom of Heaven. Thy teachings have illumined us with

The Word of salvation. In this way, ye laboured to the very end, so that we might sing: ALLELUIA!

OIKOS IV

WITH love and zeal ye tilled the soil of the North American lands with the divine seed of the Gospel. The sowing of Christ's divine word was cultivated in the hearts of thy people through thy faithful ministry. Ye uprooted the tares of false teachings and brought forth a great harvest of faith here in the New World. Together with the Holy Apostles, we offer to ye these words of loving praise:

Rejoice; All Saints of North America!

OIKOS V

AFTER His resurrection, the glorified Son of God sent His Twelve Apostles to the ends of the earth in order to declare His name among all nations. In these latter days, the Lord hath sent ye, as Equals to the Apostles, in order to teach us the commandments of the Gospel. Following in thy footsteps, O Apostles and Evangelists of North America, we sing to ye these words of loving praise:

Rejoice; O Hierarch Tikhon, pioneer of Orthodoxy in North America!

Rejoice; O Father Innocent, missionary and master of languages!

Rejoice; O faithful stewards of the Divine Household of the Lord!

Rejoice; O guardians of the Mysteries of the Kingdom of God!

Rejoice; O shepherds, protecting your flock from the enemy!

Rejoice; O labourers in the Vineyard of Christ's Holy Church!

Rejoice; O Raphael, blessed teacher of Orthodox doctrine!

Rejoice; O zealous preachers of Christ's resurrection!

Rejoice; All Saints of North America!

KONTAKION VI

I N obedience to the will of God ye left thine ancestral homelands, O Holy Hierarchs of North America. In order to fulfil thine episcopal work ye sailed the great oceans and crossed vast continents. With diligence, ye sought after thy scattered flock and guided them to the shelter of the Lord's Church. As Loving Fathers, ye fed thy children with the teachings of the Gospel, so that we might sing: ALLELUIA!

OIKOS VI

O HOLY Hierarchs of North America, ye endured many wants and hardships in order to fulfil thine episcopal work here in this new land. Through thy lowliness, we have been exalted in Christ. Through thy poverty, we have become rich in the Spirit. As models of virtue, we sing unto ye these words of loving praise:

Rejoice; O holy bishops, intercessors before the throne
of Christ!

Rejoice; O Father Innocent, evangelizer of the Northern
peoples!

Rejoice; O Patriarch Tikhon defender of the Apostolic
Tradition!

Rejoice; O blessed Raphael, teacher of the American
peoples!

Rejoice; O Confessor Nicholas, spring of heavenly theology!

Rejoice; O teachers of the children of the heavenly Father!

Rejoice; O divine clarions of the Gospel of grace!

Rejoice; O faithful servants of the Holy Trinity!

Rejoice; All Saints of North America!

KONTAKION VII

G UIDED by the grace of the Holy Spirit, ye crossed the Pacific and
Atlantic Oceans on your way to the New World in order to fulfil
thine apostolic witness, O Holy Missionaries and Evangelists of North
America. Following the legacy of Saints Cyril and Methodius, ye
translated the Scriptures and liturgical services into the tongues of the local
peoples and established schools for the training of native clergy. All of this
ye have done, so that we might sing: ALLELUIA!

OIKOS VII

B URNING with the love of Christ, ye travelled across the span of North
America in order to nurture and edify the Church which God
obtained through the blood of His own Son. As inheritors of your fruitful
work, O Sanctified Hierarchs and Evangelists, we sing to ye these words of
loving praise:

Rejoice; O heroic imitators of the chosen Apostles Peter
and Paul!

Rejoice; O teachers of the first principles of the Gospel
of God!

Rejoice; O honourable models of righteousness and
holiness!

Rejoice; O trustworthy guides on the road to eternal life!

Rejoice; O noble messengers of the grace of Jesus Christ!

Rejoice; O good shepherds of the Church in America!

Rejoice; O zealous instructors of Orthodox theology!

Rejoice; O humble servants following the will of God!

Rejoice; All Saints of North America!

KONTAKION VIII

FOLLOWING the example of the Holy Fathers, ye dedicated thyselves to many spiritual labours and struggles, O blessed monastics and ascetics of the New World. Ye have revealed to us the fruits of true holiness thine obedience to the will of God has confirmed for us the promises of the Gospel. Thy poverty and humility have shone forth as examples for all the inhabitants of North America. Seeing ye clothed in glory and exalted with Christ, we sing: ALLELUIA!

OIKOS VIII

BY observing the commandments of the Gospel, ye showed the peoples of North America the path to righteousness and holiness, O Venerable and God-bearing monastics. Working together with the grace of God, we imitate thy meekness and purity of heart, so that we might sing these words of loving praise:

Rejoice; O Father Herman, founder of monasticism in the New World!

Rejoice; O venerable monastics, fountain of marvellous wonders!

Rejoice; O Champions of Orthodoxy here in the New World!

Rejoice; O conversers with the angels and the Theotokos!

Rejoice; O treasury of the Orthodox Church in America!

Rejoice; O wondrous ascetics, comfort of the afflicted!

Rejoice; O well-springs of holiness in North America!

Rejoice; O protectors of the poor and dispossessed!

Rejoice; All Saints of North America!

KONTAKION IX

FORSAKING the vanity of this world, O blessed ascetics of North America, ye became true disciples of the Divine Teacher by acquiring the gifts of the Holy Spirit. Ye fought the demons and overcame their power by the power of the sign of the Cross. Through self-denial and abstinence, ye have shone forth the inward beauty of holiness and righteousness. Emulating thy life of repentance, we sing unto God: ALLELUIA!

OIKOS IX

AS living vessels of the grace of Jesus Christ, ye sanctify this new land, O our venerable fathers and mothers of the North American continent. Ye offer to God a sacrifice of loving intercession for those who follow thy way as we assemble to honour your memory, we sing unto ye these words of loving praise:

Rejoice; O blessed ones, whose names are written in the Book of Life!

Rejoice; O valiant soldiers who fought the enemies of Christ!

Rejoice; O speedy defenders of those in need of justice!

Rejoice; O wondrous partakers of the heavenly manna!

Rejoice; O restoration of those fallen into grievous sins!

Rejoice; O marvellous fountain of healing for the sick!

Rejoice; O divine freedom from the insanity of evil!

Rejoice; O passionate lovers of virtue!

Rejoice; All Saints of North America!

KONTAKION X

THY BLAMELESS way of life is a source of amazement to the angels, O ye Righteous Ones — known and unknown — of North America. Assisted by the Holy Spirit, ye firmly established the Orthodox Faith in this new land. With patience and diligence, ye built upon a foundation laid long ago with Christ Himself as the cornerstone. Having received from ye the riches of faith, we sing unto God: ALLELUIA!

OIKOS X

DOING all things for the glory of God and the love of thy neighbour, ye fulfilled thy calling to holiness, O Righteous Ones of North America. Ye accomplished the tasks given to ye, according to the measure of grace given to ye by the Lord. Ye fished the great waters of the Alaskan North; ye tilled the fertile soils of the Canadian and Midwestern plains; ye laboured under harsh conditions in the mines and mills; ye toiled day and night in factories of the American cities, all so that we might sing unto ye these words of loving praise:

Rejoice; O faithful who took up your crosses and
    followed Christ!

Rejoice; O honoured citizens of the Kingdom of Heaven!

Rejoice; O royal priesthood of the New Jerusalem!

Rejoice; O holy nation of the Prince of Peace!

Rejoice; O chosen vessels of the Holy Spirit!

Rejoice; O pillars of Orthodoxy in America!

Rejoice; O Eternal City of the living God!

Rejoice; O pious teachers of the faith!

Rejoice; All Saints of North America!

KONTAKION XI

THE Wisdom, Word, and Power of God, begotten from His Father before the beginning of time, was incarnate in these latter days from His Holy Mother, the Theotokos, and Ever-Virgin Mary. Through the grace of the Spirit, O Blessed Ones of North America, ye thereby became partakers of the Divine Nature and have been perfected after the image of the One Who is the express image of His Divine Father. Together with ye, we sing unto God: ALLELUIA!

OIKOS XI

THE King of heaven and earth humbled himself by taking the form of a servant in order to become the least and the last of His brethren. In His never-ending love for man, He poured Himself out fully — so that we might be filled with all the fullness of His grace. Following His example, O ye Righteous Ones of North America, ye served the ones to whom ye were sent. Ye healed the sick, ye gave aid to the poor, ye sought out the lost, ye raised infants, ye guided the youth, and ye cared for the elderly, all so that we might sing to ye these words of loving praise:

Rejoice; O holy bishops, gracious adornments of the lands
    of North America!

Rejoice; O Hieromartyrs, benefactors of the faithful living in
    the New World!

Rejoice; O fervent evangelists, great preachers of the saving
    Word of God!

Rejoice; O patient confessors, illumination of those living
    in darkness!

Rejoice; O monastics, bright stars of the Northern heavens!

Rejoice; O blessed ascetics, wonder of the angelic hosts!

Rejoice; O venerable fathers, guides of the fallen!

Rejoice; O holy mothers, life of your children!

Rejoice; All Saints of North America!

KONTAKION XII

S URROUNDED by your heavenly glory, O Hierarchs, Martyrs, Apostles, Monastics and all righteous men and women of North America, known and unknown, we beseech ye — as your spiritual children — to intercede for us before Christ for the forgiveness of our sins. We worship the Lord Who has given ye to us as Heavenly Patrons and Guardians for the protection and salvation of our souls and bodies. Together with the Bodiless Hosts, we sing unto God: ALLELUIA!

OIKOS XII

W E celebrate thy great works, All Saints of North America. We offer thanks to Christ for the wondrous deeds ye have accomplished through Him for the enlightenment of all men, women, and children living in this new land. Together with God's elect, we sing unto ye these words of loving praise:

Rejoice; O divine exaltation of the Rocky Mountains, and
the Pacific West!

Rejoice; O gracious adornments of New England, and the
Atlantic states!

Rejoice; O joyful beacons of the Great Lakes, and the
Midwestern plains!

Rejoice; O heavenly constellation of the Canadian
Provinces!

Rejoice; O wondrous aurora of Alaska, and the Arctic North!

Rejoice; O shining stars of the North American continent!

Rejoice; O brilliant flowers of the South-western deserts!

Rejoice; O fragrant blossoms of the American South!

Rejoice; All Saints of North America!

KONTAKION XIII

O HOLY Luminaries of North America, look down upon us, thy sinful servants and accept this present supplication. Entreat the Lord Jesus Christ that He will continue to bestow upon us His many mercies. Be a refuge and a protection for us that we might be delivered from all physical and spiritual harm. Continue to guide us into the heavenly Kingdom, so that we might sing: ALLELUIA! *(Thrice.)*

And again, Oikos I and Kontakion I are read.

OIKOS I

W E glorify the Lord Who has glorified ye, O sanctified men, women, and children of these North American lands. We stand in awe before thy countless miracles revealed to us by Our Father in heaven. Together with the bodiless choirs, we offer to ye these words of loving praise:

> Rejoice; O holy Father Tikhon, Patriarch of Moscow and enlightener of North America!

> Rejoice; O Hierarch Innocent, Alaskan missionary and evangelizer of the Aleuts!

> Rejoice; O blessed Raphael, first Bishop of Brooklyn and faithful shepherd!

> Rejoice; O holy Nicholas, confessor and teacher of heavenly theology!

> Rejoice; O venerable Herman elder and wonderworker of Alaska!

> Rejoice; O martyrs Juvenal and Peter, martyrs crowned by God!

> Rejoice; O righteous Jacob, pastor and teacher of your flock!

Rejoice; O John and Alexis, defenders of the Orthodox Way!

Rejoice; All Saints of North America!

KONTAKION I

W ITH grateful hearts we sing praises in thine honour, O All Saints of North America. Ye gave thy lives to the Lord as an offering of love. Ye are the first fruits of Christ's bountiful harvest here in the New World. As faithful servants of thy Master, ye laboured in the Vineyard of His Holy Church. Through thy example, ye have shown us the joy of the Orthodox Way. As we assemble today to honour ye, we cry:

Rejoice; All Saints of North America!

PRAYER TO THE SAINTS OF NORTH AMERICA

O ALL-BLESSED and wise Saints of God, who have sanctified North America by thy holy deeds, leaving thy relics as seeds of the Orthodox Faith, and who now stand before the throne of God in ceaseless prayer for our land! We sinners make bold on this day to offer this hymn of praise. We exalt thy great and holy deeds, O spiritual warriors of Christ, who with patience and courage have vanquished the enemy completely, delivering us from his craft and cunning. We bless thy holy lives, ye lamps of God, who have shone with the light of faith and virtue and have illumined our minds and hearts to the knowledge of God. We glorify thy great miracles, O Flowers of Paradise, who have blossomed in our land, spreading the sweet fragrance of thy gifts and wonders. We praise thy love that reflects God's own love, O our defenders and intercessors, and trusting in thy help, we fall down before ye and cry: O Holy Enlighteners Innocent and Tikhon! Help us the faithful of North America to preserve steadfastly the Orthodox faith that ye have planted in us as a seed which, watered by divine rain, will bring forth fruit a hundredfold. Confirm the Church in North America by thy prayers, and gather the scattered sheep into one flock, preserving it safe from all harm. O Holy Father Herman of Alaska! Keep us from the delusions of this transitory life, that denying ourselves and taking up our cross, we may follow Christ, crucifying our flesh with its lusts and passions, and bearing each other's burdens. O Holy Martyrs Juvenal and Peter! Strengthen us in courageous perseverance even unto the shedding of our blood for the Orthodox faith, so that no adversity may separate us from the love of God, which is in Jesus Christ. All Saints, known and unknown, who have shown forth throughout the history of this land, remember our weakness and hardship, and by thy prayers beseech Christ our God, that we, having successfully crossed the fathomless depths of the sea of life, keeping unharmed the treasury of the faith, may reach the harbour of eternal salvation and live in the Kingdom of God on high together with ye and all who have served Him throughout all ages. Through the grace and compassion and love of mankind of our Lord and Saviour Jesus Christ, to Whom, together with the Eternal Father, and the Most Holy Spirit, be never-ending glory and worship by all creation, unto the ages of ages. AMEN.

AKATHIST TO SAINT CHAD OF LICHFIELD

KONTAKION I

A S a true shepherd of the flock of Christ, thou didst bring the Orthodox Christian faith to the land of Mercia. In following the example of the Holy Apostles, thou didst minister to thy flock, traversing the land on foot. Refusing earthly riches, thou didst proclaim that thou art not above the common man.

Rejoice; holy hierarch Chad, great wonderworker for all ages!

OIKOS I

C HAMPION of truth and teacher of spiritual awakening! Thrice blessed disciple of our great father Aidan, forever we shall call upon thine intercessions. Teach us to partake of thy greatness, O good shepherd of the Mercian land. Thy defence of the suffering is renowned, and shall be remembered forever in the hearts of all people:

Rejoice; great Apostle of the Mercian people!

Rejoice; grand Enlightener of the Midlands!

Rejoice; boast of Yorkshire, whose holiness is beholden
to thee!

Rejoice; thou who wast taught by a saint and didst in turn
instruct others to holiness!

Rejoice; new Aidan, frail in body but strong in spirit!

Rejoice; thou who didst teach the Wisdom of the Word,
that we may receive eternal life!

Rejoice; revered father so willing to offer hope and love!

Rejoice; thou who didst walk the straight and narrow path
to righteousness!

Rejoice; thou who proclaimest unto all the Good News that
"Christ is Risen!"

Rejoice; holy hierarch Chad, great wonderworker for all ages!

KONTAKION II

B EARING great qualities of both mind and spirit, the greatest of thy
fruits, was the ever presence of God in thee. All who approached
thee bore witness to it; therefore, may Christ grant us the steadfastness
to emulate thee in both word and deed, as we cry: ALLELUIA!

OIKOS II

F OLLOWING Christ's Command to "Go Forth," as a witness, thou
didst go forth and proclaim the Gospel with holy Egbert. Owing to
thy labours, many in Ireland found the True Faith of Jesus Christ, and
thus found refuge in His Holy Church:

Rejoice; new Patrick, apostolic are thine endeavours and
worthy is thy blessedness!

Rejoice; sing Brigit and Ita, "this grand isle is
hallowed again!"

Rejoice; new Kieran, sojourning on the plains of the
Emerald Isle!

Rejoice; for Finnian and Nathy adore thine Irish labours!

Rejoice; new Kevin, monk and solitary, robed in virtue!

Rejoice; Ireland crieth out, for her land was blessed by
thy works!

Rejoice; new Brendan, "sailing" on foot to new lands
preaching the Gospel of Christ!

Rejoice; new Columba, miracle-worker for a scattered flock!

Rejoice; for the saints of Ireland sound forth their
unchanging song!

Rejoice; holy hierarch Chad, great wonderworker for all ages!

KONTAKION III

AWARE of thy revered holiness as Abbot of Lastingham, the
Northumbrian king Oswy demanded thee as bishop for the See of
York. Unwilling to accept such a task, thou didst so only in obedience to
thy brethren. Thy humble-mindedness greatly shineth forth for all the
ages to bear witness, and thus we shall forever cry: ALLELUIA!

OIKOS III

O GREAT hierarch Chad, when thy episcopate was questioned by the
holy Theodore, thou didst relinquish it with great piety, calling thine
"unworthiness" and "only in obedience" as reason. So moved by such
humility, Theodore found in thee a true image of the High Priesthood,
and thus called upon thee to be bishop of Mercia. In thine emulation of
Christ, help us to emulate thee, O vessel of true Christian humility:

Rejoice; thou who did take up the Episcopal throne through
    obedience, only to relinquish it through obedience!

Rejoice; boast of men and adoration of kings!

Rejoice; thou who didst toil onward to new lands and
    new tasks!

Rejoice; for Theodore of Tarsus saw thy true worthiness!

Rejoice; keeper of the Faith of Christ the Lord!

Rejoice; first bishop of Lichfield, through thy works,
    miracles arose and wonders came to pass!

Rejoice; thou who didst bring the True Faith to whom God
    hath chosen!

Rejoice; true friend of Christ, exalted in heaven and on
    earth!

Rejoice; teacher of God's Truth kept undefiled within His
    Holy Church!

Rejoice; holy hierarch Chad, great wonderworker for all ages!

KONTAKION IV

THOU didst know well the wisdom of the Holy Fathers, that "there
is nothing here for us." Thou didst teach thy flock the fleeting
nature of this life, and the glory that is with God alone. Comfort us
now, for we are weak, and we look to thee as our model of renewal in
Him, singing: ALLELUIA!

OIKOS IV

O GREAT Enlightener of Mercia, after learning of the great martyrs
who perished under Diocletian on the plains of Lichfield; thou didst

honour their sacrifice by moving the Mercian See to the place of their martyrdom, thus proclaiming to all the glory of them who truly follow Christ the Lord!

Rejoice; great Archpastor, filled with love and kindness for all people!

Rejoice; celebrated witness to the heathen of Northumbria!

Rejoice; jewel of Lichfield and protector of all Mercia!

Rejoice; witness truly worthy of "God's Call!"

Rejoice; thou who didst show to all the glory of the martyrs of Lichfield!

Rejoice; humble bishop, meekly walking the earth!

Rejoice; pious elder, humility is thy virtue!

Rejoice; thou who didst serve the faithful with a singular love!

Rejoice; firm protector of thy people in flesh and in spirit!

Rejoice; holy hierarch Chad, great wonderworker for all ages!

KONTAKION V

ARCHPASTOR for only three years, thou didst emulate Christ in every manner. O bearer of the Heavenly Spirit, establishing churches and monasteries, and calling a great many to "put on Christ." We honour thee, O great wonderworker, and champion of Christ's Holy Church, singing: ALLELUIA!

OIKOS V

AS the Venerable Bede hath written, "in humility and self-denial... thou didst travel about, not on horseback, but on foot, after the manner of the Holy Apostles, preaching the Gospel in towns and open country, in cottages, villages, and palaces." Truly apostolic were thy labours, O Apostle of Mercia.   We look upon thee as a source of inspiration to all!

Rejoice; for the Holy Apostles sing thy praise!

Rejoice; thou who didst walk the earth preaching the Word
of God!

Rejoice; radiant wanderer of Christ's Church!

Rejoice; O "Nicholas of the Isles," image of meekness
whose love brought renown!

Rejoice; wise witness, traversing the Midlands with cheer and
Christian hospitality!

Rejoice; heavenly patron of Lichfield!

Rejoice; faithful companion of Christ on earth!

Rejoice; great Enlightener, for thy memory deserveth a place
in every heart!

Rejoice; through thy life and labours, the Church
accomplisheth Her Divine task!

Rejoice; holy hierarch Chad, great wonderworker for all ages!

KONTAKION VI

FOLLOWING the Apostle Paul's charge to "Pray without ceasing," thou didst seek solitude at the bottom of the well.   Gaining spiritual wisdom in unceasing prayer, thou didst obtain the greatest gift, beholding the Uncreated Light, and thus we sing: ALLELUIA!

OIKOS VI

WHILE hunting their quarry, the heathen sons of Wulfhere found thee praying in silence. So impressed by thy sight, a frail old man upon his knees, face glowing in prayer, they knelt before thee and asked thy blessing. True holiness did they find in earthly flesh, and asked to be baptized into Christ. Then the wicked Wulfhere, the Mercian King, having fallen into the hands of the evil one, wast filled with great anger and slew them both. Seeking the same for thee, he approached thy humble cell and bore witness to a great sight, a blinding light, the Uncreated Light that shone upon thee. We follow the cry of King Wulfhere, "holy hierarch Chad, have mercy on me!"

Rejoice; hallowed vessel of the Uncreated Light!

Rejoice; the power of the Holy Spirit came upon thee!

Rejoice; the wisdom of the Holy Fathers is championed
> by thee!

Rejoice; for the martyrs Wulfhad and Ruffin, sons of
> Wulfhere, sing thy praise!

Rejoice; the saints exult, for their knowledge is shown forth
> in thee!

Rejoice; for the toil of thy hands built houses of God!

Rejoice; spiritual father gifted with the Light of Christ!

Rejoice; teacher of the sanctified and bulwark of the truth!

Rejoice; dearly loved Mercia, land blessed with the milk
> and honey of grace!

Rejoice; holy hierarch Chad, great wonderworker for all ages!

KONTAKION VII

O MIRACLE-MAKER! Healing ailments of the flesh and pangs of the soul, proclaiming the Word of God on foot! Boast of God's elect and glorious intercessor! How can we who are sinful recall such great feats, when our own souls are filled with evil and mould? We cry to thee, beseech our Eternal Lord, the Holy, and Divine Word, to fill our iniquitous hearts with Christian love and virtue, singing: ALLELUIA!

OIKOS VII

G IVING help to the helpless, and hope to the afflicted, thy miracle-working relics bear the healing grace of God. He hath given thee the power to work wonders. In thee, His greatness is shone forth; thus, now and forever we join the angelic hosts in song, glorifying Our Father in the heavens:

Rejoice; O blessed miracle-maker of the Isles!

Rejoice; abundant grace shining forth from thy holy relics!

Rejoice; aid us towards the bond that thou hast with the Holy Spirit!

Rejoice; exalted healer of the spiritually sick!

Rejoice; thou who helpest us turn base desire toward noble purpose!

Rejoice; champion of truth and teacher of godliness!

Rejoice; Ireland singeth and Britain rejoiceth in thy ministering!

Rejoice; the saints of the Isles sound forth their unchanging song!

Rejoice; our Most Holy Lady Theotokos smileth upon thee!

Rejoice; holy hierarch Chad, great wonderworker for all ages!

KONTAKION VIII

O DIVINE and sacred temple of the Holy Spirit! We cry to thee, for our sorrow is great, and we are worthy of every judgement that befalleth us. But perchance if thou shouldst intercede on our behalf, we may be assuaged of suffering. We entreat thee, O holy hierarch, show us the way to joy and beauty, as we sing: ALLELUIA!

OIKOS VIII

DURING great tempests thou didst preach to thy people, "God doth thunder forth from the heavens, He doth rouse the faithful to look to the future judgement." "Examine your hearts, and do good, that ye may never be struck down!" O ye faithful, heed these great words, let us remember our iniquities, and let us sing:

Rejoice; father Chad, earthly teacher of Christ's most sacred mysteries!

Rejoice; unyielding pillar of Christian Orthodoxy!

Rejoice; wise elder, choosing truth above all else!

Rejoice; steadfast teacher, we hearken unto thy wisdom!

Rejoice; thou who didst help us to see the greater purpose beyond the cycles of life!

Rejoice; healer of those stained with wrath!

Rejoice; meek father, championing the divine truth!

Rejoice; for thy children seek thy heavenly intercession!

Rejoice; thou whose prayers are heard by the Eternal One!

Rejoice; holy hierarch Chad, great wonderworker for all ages!

KONTAKION IX

GIVING thyself to ecclesiastical truth and purity of doctrine, thou didst beseech the faithful to practice humility, self-denial and the continuous study of divine Scriptures, not only in word, but also in deed. Grace shineth forth from thee holy Chad, and thus we sing forever: ALLELUIA!

OIKOS IX

K NOWING full well God's will, thou didst remain unwavering in faith, a model of virtue for all Christians to emulate! Hearken unto our cry, when we call upon thee in our daily struggle with the enemy. We look upon thee as our inspiration, and pray that the angels may come unto us, as of old they came unto thee:

Rejoice; wise monk and bishop, who didst learn of the
    saving grace through unceasing prayer!

Rejoice; thou who didst find inner peace in the angelic habit!

Rejoice; for the Cherubim honour thee with song!

Rejoice; for the saint's marvel at thee!

Rejoice; new Anthony, monastic robed in the warmth of
    the Spirit!

Rejoice; for the Seraphim shine thy light to all mankind!

Rejoice; for our souls are enriched by thy prayer!

Rejoice; for the Angels chariot thy soul to Abraham's
    Bosom!

Rejoice; for thou hast found favour in the eyes of God!

Rejoice; holy hierarch Chad, great wonderworker for all ages!

KONTAKION X

W ITH the threat of the plague, thou didst choose to stand fast and remain with thy flock rather than flee, only to fall victim to the same suffering. O protector and defender of the infirm and afflicted! Thy body became a prison house of pain and torment. Thou didst give thy life for thy people, and thus forever receive a great reward in the heavens, a crown of victory, and thus we sing: ALLELUIA!

OIKOS X

SEEKING thy return to thy heavenly home, God sent His angels to bring thee unto Him. O wonder and valiant champion of the Church. Angels chariot thee, and men honour thee! Help us in our time of need, and beseech God to illumine our souls with His Divine Light:

Rejoice; clairvoyant elder who foresaw thine own repose!

Rejoice; valiant warrior and defender of thy flock!

Rejoice; teaching all the care of others!

Rejoice; righteous confessor, sacrificing thyself to be with thy flock!

Rejoice; holy Abba, western example of the eastern ideal!

Rejoice; strong rampart of the Orthodox Faith!

Rejoice; thou who didst recapture the Grace of God by burying the passions of the flesh!

Rejoice; instructing us to oneness with God through heartfelt prayer!

Rejoice; thou who didst urge us to become the "perfect man matured with the fullness of Christ!"

Rejoice; holy hierarch Chad, great wonderworker for all ages!

KONTAKION XI

THOU didst reveal true Christian love to thy people, O holy Archpastor, shepherding and caring for thy flock in both soul and body. A servant worthy of God's call! Thus, we join the angelic hosts in their song, "Glory to Thy Power, O Lord," crying: ALLELUIA!

OIKOS XI

THY faithful shall forever love and honour thee, O father, and hierarch Chad. When frightened and tortured by the evil one, we know full well that thy heavenly intercessions can break the bonds of the devil's assaults. O conqueror of demons and boast of Angels, let us sing with joy:

Rejoice; spiritual soldier of the unseen warfare!

Rejoice; thou who didst rise above the pull of shadow!

Rejoice; for demonic hosts are enraged by their weakness before thee!

Rejoice; advocate of the Light, who didst not cower before the darkness!

Rejoice; for evil recoileth at the mention of thy name!

Rejoice; for we hear thy sweet song to the Eternal Lord!

Rejoice; O saint of God, righteous keeper of the True Faith, present within the Church!

Rejoice; for God hath truly blessed thee, sweet bishop of the lost sheep!

Rejoice; for we, thy flock, call upon thee, "pray to God for us!"

Rejoice; holy hierarch Chad, great wonderworker for all ages!

KONTAKION XII

THE innocent and the just know well thy greatness, for many have come to thy tomb, seeking thy protection. We honour thee, O great warrior of Christ! We have witnessed thy wonders, do thou now help us in our suffering as thou didst help thy flock in Mercia. We beseech thy prayers, great confessor of the Church of Christ, in wiping away the many stains of sin; intercede on our behalf to God to forgive us our iniquities. And thus, we shall forever cry: ALLELUIA!

OIKOS XII

HOLY hierarchs Chad and Cedd, righteous priests Caelin and Cynebil, O thrice-blessed brothers of Christ, duly united in true Orthodox manner as ministers to do His Will! Ye are true models of brotherly love, rightly adorning His Holy Church. Hearken unto our prayers as we joyfully sing:

Rejoice; sainted brethren of Christ's Church on earth!

Rejoice; for ye were tutored in holiness by the great Aidan of Lindisfarne!

Rejoice; tabernacles of the Divine Spirit in Northumbria!

Rejoice; precious pearls in pagan lands blessed by your works!

Rejoice; saints of the West, so too glorified in the East!

Rejoice; for ye truly carried out the command to "be thy brother's keeper!"

Rejoice; shining forth in the West like unto Basil, Gregory, and Peter, the great brothers of the East!

Rejoice; holy hierarch Cedd, great bishop of London!

Rejoice; holy Caelin and Cynebil, righteous priests in the north!

Rejoice; holy hierarch Chad, great wonderworker for all ages!

KONTAKION XIII

O HOLY bearer of the Uncreated Light, blessed through unceasing prayer in the Name of Jesus Christ. Divine example of true Christian humility, great Apostle of Mercia, as Archpastor thou didst proclaim the Gospel of Christ. O spiritual warrior and champion of the Church in the West, as a converser with heavenly hosts, thou wast carried up to the heavenly courts with angelic song. O holy hierarch and Confessor Chad may our souls forever cry: ALLELUIA! *(Thrice.)*

And again, Oikos I and Kontakion I are read.

OIKOS I

CHAMPION of truth and teacher of spiritual awakening! Thrice blessed disciple of our great father Aidan, forever we shall call upon thine intercessions. Teach us to partake of thy greatness, O good shepherd of the Mercian land. Thy defence of the suffering is renowned, and shall be remembered forever in the hearts of all people:

Rejoice; great Apostle of the Mercian people!

Rejoice; grand Enlightener of the Midlands!

Rejoice; boast of Yorkshire, whose holiness is beholden
    to thee!

Rejoice; thou who wast taught by a saint and didst in turn
    instruct others to holiness!

Rejoice; new Aidan, frail in body but strong in spirit!

Rejoice; thou who didst teach the Wisdom of the Word,
    that we may receive eternal life!

Rejoice; revered father so willing to offer hope and love!

Rejoice; thou who didst walk the straight and narrow path to
    righteousness!

Rejoice; thou who proclaimest unto all the Good News that
    "Christ is Risen!"

Rejoice; holy hierarch Chad, great wonderworker for all ages!

KONTAKION I

As a true shepherd of the flock of Christ, thou didst bring the Orthodox Christian faith to the land of Mercia. In following the example of the Holy Apostles, thou didst minister to thy flock, traversing the land on foot. Refusing earthly riches, thou didst proclaim that thou art not above the common man.

Rejoice; holy hierarch Chad, great wonderworker for all ages!

PRAYER TO SAINT CHAD OF LICHFIELD

O JESUS Christ God, the Divine Logos, we beseech Thee that we may be deemed worthy to recall the works of Thy great wonderworker and hierarch Chad. We pray that we may find grace through his great piety, humility, unceasing prayer, fasting and obedience to his brethren. We seek his counsel and intercessions before Thy glorious Throne. We ask Thee, our God, to grant us humility, love, and steadfastness in faith and teaching. Bestow good thoughts and intentions upon us and upon our brothers and sisters, and especially upon our enemies who wrong us. Help us in times of need to call upon holy Chad's humility to Saint Theodore. As a model of obedience, holy Chad relinquished the See of York, feeling unworthy of such an honour, and so was rewarded with a great See in Mercia and, more, precious humility. Help us, O Almighty God, to emulate humble Chad and preserve us from selfish and vain thoughts. Help us never to forget those that suffer, the downtrodden and the unfortunate. Be a hand for us, when in humility, we step aside for others. Keep us, for the sins of pride, vanity and lust are hard to battle and conquer, and only through Thee are they truly defeated. May we learn to love one another in Thee, O Christ, and may we strive for concord through Thee with those before us and around us. May we put aside all earthly cares and come to the knowledge of Thine Eternal Truth. Thou art the Divine Architect Who didst shape this vast universe and Whose power is limitless. We humbly beg Thee, forgive us our sins, for Thy power is great and we are weak. Remember humble Chad's prayers for our sake, and have mercy on us in Thy dread

Judgement. For Thine is the kingdom, and the power, and the glory, of the Father, and of the Son, and of the Holy Spirit, always, now and ever, and unto the ages of ages. AMEN.

AKATHIST TO SAINT CUTHBERT OF LINDISFARNE

KONTAKION I

O CUTHBERT, the great and admirable warrior who shineth forth with thy many merits: now the Lord shineth through thee in thine eternal reward, for thou crushest the fires of the flesh. With thy heart didst thou scorn all passing things in thy duty and love for Christ, and in thy labour didst not scorn the Lord's commandments, for in thy generosity and eagerness thou didst flow with the Light of Christ, opening an everlasting stream of grace where none had been found before. O thou, who broughtest forth an abundant harvest in rocky earth, do thou ever pray to the Thrice-Holy Lord that our souls may be saved.

OIKOS I

A S an infant thou didst play as a child, O holy Cuthbert, and wast reproved by thy friend for thine indulgence at play, urging thee to exercise watchfulness over mind and body. For he upbraided thee by the Holy Spirit: Why dost thou persist in doing what is contrary to thy nature and rank, most holy bishop? The Lord hast marked thee to instil virtue into thine elders! Thereby didst he prophecy thine illustrious life to come, and fulfilled the words of the Holy Scripture, for out of the mouths of babes hast the Lord perfected the praise of His saints:

Rejoice; thou whom the Lord admonished with the words
of a child!

Rejoice; thou who heeded the words of His angel, and was
thereby healed!

Rejoice; thou whose eyes were opened at thy priestly call!

Rejoice; thou whose eyes beheld the angel of God!

Rejoice; thou who was made whole by a soldier of Christ!

Rejoice; thou whom like Judas Maccabeus beheld an
angelic soldier!

Rejoice; thou whose childish prayers were mocked by an
earthly brood!

Rejoice; thou whose prayers were accepted by the heavenly
hosts!

Rejoice; thou whose boyish weakness was despised by those
in trouble at sea!

Rejoice; thou whose manly prayers preserved souls on
storm-tossed waters!

Rejoice; thou whose youthful piety caused men to burn
inwardly with shame at their impiety!

Rejoice; thou whose praise never ceased to flow from
their mouths!

Rejoice; O Holy Wonderworker Cuthbert!

KONTAKION II

THY holy prayers were heard freely in heaven, O holy one, since thou
didst rid thyself of the chains of this life: for as thou didst pray to
deliver faithful men from the sea as did Moses of old, so too didst thou
despise the curses of the pagans who refused to turn away from the
darkness that had swallowed them; now thou prayest for us as thou didst
pray for their deliverance of old, that we may be saved from the jaws of
darkness and cry aloud: ALLELUIA!

OIKOS II

UPON seeing the holy soul of Aidan carried by angels to heaven, thou
didst set to thanking God and exhorting thy companions: Know
thine own wretchedness, which blindeth us with sleep before the glory
of God! O brethren, what marvels I have seen! The gate of Heaven
opened, and an angelic band bearing the soul of God's holy one. Whilst
we remain in darkness, he is taken to the Heavenly Light! Whilst
we remain on earth, he treadeth the path to Heaven! Just as holy Cuthbert
didst enflame the hearts of all with heavenly zeal, let us now call out to
him with joyous hearts:

Rejoice; O holy father who wast fed with bread from
Heaven!

Rejoice; O holy one who feedeth us through thy holiness
of life!

Rejoice; O keeper of the holy fasts!

Rejoice; O faster, fed for the sake of thy piety!

Rejoice; O new Elias, who refused hospitality from a widow!

Rejoice; O pious one whose Host dwelleth among the
  Heavenly hosts!

Rejoice; thou who saith to God, I was fasting for love
  of Thee!

Rejoice; thou who with thy beast wast fed, and who
  thereby blessed the Name of the Lord!

Rejoice; O thou who from nothing is granted the
  heavenly food!

Rejoice; O new prophet who testifieth to the fruits of fasting!

Rejoice; O holy one who treadeth the paths of the Lord!

Rejoice; O righteous saints whose paths led thee to the
  glory on high!

Rejoice; O Holy Wonderworker Cuthbert!

KONTAKION III

THOU didst approach the Holy Isle mounted on thy steed, and laying
down thy spear and reins thou didst take up the monastic
life. Crossing the waters on dry land as did Moses of old, thou didst leave
the worldly Egypt behind as the waters came together. Pious Boisil
greeted thee with the words of the Lord to Nathaniel: Behold an Israelite
indeed, in whom there is no guile! And foreseeing thy progress on
the ladder of the monastic life, he persuaded the abbot to bless thee
to place thy foot on the lowest rung. Thus, thou didst then begin in all
things to ascend to the heights of ascetic ways, that we may now raise our
voices to God and cry: ALLELUIA!

OIKOS III

AS the steward of hospitality at Ripon, thou didst welcome strangers as
thy loving charge, and like Abraham didst welcome unwittingly an
angel sent to test thy devotion, washing his feet as a true emulator of
Christ. Urging the angelic one to wait on thee for his morning bread, thou

wast instead given by him spiritual food: for on thy return thou didst find no footprint in the snow, but the fragrance of holiness awaiting at the door for thee. Then Cuthbert cried, Now I know it was an angel, come not to be fed but to feed. He hath brought the bread that cannot be brought forth on earth, whiter than the lilies, sweeter than roses, more delicious than honey! It is no wonder that he refused earthly food when he can enjoy in Heaven the bread of eternal life! Thus, the miracle moved the saint to greater zeal, calling us all to cry to the Lord of All:

Rejoice; thou who didst resort to prayer when thy elder
  was cast down!

Rejoice; thou whose prayers raised him up whole again!

Rejoice; thou who seest God's strength made perfect
  in weakness!

Rejoice; thou who didst seek strength in the Theologian's
  Gospel!

Rejoice; thou who didst pore over the Gospel at the
  deathbed of thy friend!

Rejoice; thou who didst pour out tears at his passing from
  this life!

Rejoice; thou who didst lament for the cares of this
  fleeting world!

Rejoice; thou who wouldst run from them to an island on
  the ocean!

Rejoice; thou who sawest flight from the world as a treasure
  to be desired!

Rejoice; thou who sawest in worldly cares the passions
  that only fly away with death!

Rejoice; thou spiritual son of a prophet!

Rejoice; thou spiritual father of thy Holy Isle!

Rejoice; O Holy Wonderworker Cuthbert!

KONTAKION IV

THOU didst follow in the footsteps of thy spiritual father, taking up his mantle and the spiritual care of his flock, preaching the Word zealously, seeking the conversion of all, calling the lost back from idolatry as the prophets of old! Thou didst labour day and night to find the lost, hidden in hills and caves of the earth, and they in turn gathered round thee to witness thine angelic countenance, and to hear thy holy words that they might sing: ALLELUIA!

OIKOS IV

REVERENCE could not master a brother driven by the curiosity of the first Adam, desiring to see the nightly wonders of holy Cuthbert on the shores of the sea: he witnessed there the ministrations of dumb animals to the holy one as he spent his night in prayer, seeking fellowship with the New Adam, Our Lord. The holy one bade him tell no-one of the miracle until the Second Coming of Christ, a vow which he there made before the holy one, silently crying from the depths of his soul:

Rejoice; holy saint, tasting Paradise on earth!

Rejoice; holy one, converser with beasts as our first ancestors
      in Eden!

Rejoice; thou who offerest thy prayers on the ocean shore!

Rejoice; thou in whom the ocean of Grace overwhelmeth
      the shores of the flesh!

Rejoice; thou who didst shine forth the Light of Heaven!

Rejoice; beacon to those sailing the stormy waters of life!

Rejoice; blessed friend of the Lord!

Rejoice; blessed husbandman of the Lord's creation!

Rejoice; blessed carer of human souls!

Rejoice; blessed companion to man and beast!

Rejoice; foreshadowing of renewed nature!

Rejoice; sanctified nature in the fallen world!

Rejoice; O Holy Wonderworker Cuthbert!

KONTAKION VI

WONDROUS is God in His saints, Who glorifieth them as they were in the first days in Paradise! For as then Adam enjoyed a peaceable kingdom betwixt the beasts and man, so didst Thou vouchsafe to Thy servant Cuthbert, who in his preaching hungered for bread from heaven, and like the prophet Elias was fed by the birds from the heavens! O holy father, thou didst honour the Lord's words that the labourer should not be without his wages, and didst share thy meat with the winged servant who brought it, as a type of the Communion between the Lord and His Creation, and an image of the manna sent by the Lord to His New Israel who ever singeth to Him: ALLELUIA!

OIKOS VI

THE sons of men beheld in the upstretched hands of holy Cuthbert the power of the hand of God, for He Who calmeth the fires of the passions by the prayers of His holy one calmed the fires of the evil one, both real and illusory, and didst turn the hearts of men from distraction, to do homage to the True God, crying with one voice:

Rejoice; stream that causeth the fires of the demons to cease!

Rejoice; water that washeth clean the eyes of the spiritually blind!

Rejoice; thou who quenchest the delusions of the mind!

Rejoice; thou who enlightenest the eyes of the faithful!

Rejoice; thou who dost deliver from the mire of earthly
delusion!

Rejoice; thou who dost rescue from the flames of sin!

Rejoice; thou who dost teach the hearts of those with
ears to hear!

Rejoice; thou who dost reconcile the senseless to the Lord!

Rejoice; thou who didst calm the fears of thy mother!

Rejoice; thou who didst work miracles by the power of
the Son!

Rejoice; thou who didst work wonders like the fathers
of old!

Rejoice; thou who didst shine like a new flame before
thy kinsmen!

Rejoice; O Holy Wonderworker Cuthbert!

KONTAKION VI

THE sheriff sent word to the holy one: she whom I love perisheth in the captivity of the demons; only speak the word, and she shall receive healing in the spirit and release from the flesh. But the holy one replied: blessed is he that cometh in the name of the Lord! And returning thence, loosed her by the touch of his bridle from the chains of demonic captivity, loosing from her lips the joyful cry: ALLELUIA!

OIKOS VI

ON the Holy Isle shining forth the illumination of Truth, thou didst dispel the darkness of the demons, for unable to bear thy holiness, their strength failed, and those who were divided by darkness were united by enlightenment in brotherhood, and cried aloud in joy:

Rejoice; unity of monastics!

Rejoice; divider from the ways of sin!

Rejoice; thou who hast trampled upon the unrepentant
hearts of men!

Rejoice; thou who hast censured the rebellious spirit
of disunity!

Rejoice; gentle tide which drowned the sins of repentant
hearts!

Rejoice; island of silence refreshing those athirst for Christ!

Rejoice; beacon guiding those on the stormy sea of life!

Rejoice; protector of the faithful in thy psalmody!

Rejoice; succour of the common people!

Rejoice; restorer of the suffering from all manner
of affliction!

Rejoice; house of prayer unseen by the eyes of the world!

Rejoice; thou who laid the One Foundation in the island of
thy heart!

Rejoice; O Holy Wonderworker Cuthbert!

KONTAKION VII

WHEN holy Cuthbert was nigh unto departing from the sight of
men, the birds of the air presented to him repentance: for when
in their pride they stole from him grain and straw, they humbled
themselves with offerings of fat and prostrations. Wherefore he marvelled
at the mercies of God toward His creatures, crying aloud: ALLELUIA!

OIKOS VII

NEW was the countenance God's servant Cuthbert showed to the
brethren, when he joined with them each year at the Passion of

Christ: for he preserved the gift of meekness undiminished in his heart, and by prayer brought forth a wellspring of humility, springing up on the dry land of Farne, that seeing this marvel, all might cry out:

> Rejoice; thou who by prayer turnest solid rock to a watery
> > fountain!

> Rejoice; constant stream of prayer, neither diminished
> > nor lost!

> Rejoice; clear pool reflecting the servitude of Christ!

> Rejoice; thou who showest forth the ministry of the
> > Apostles!

> Rejoice; joyful feet carrying forth the Gospel!

> Rejoice; soles worn thin on the road of preaching!

> Rejoice; guide of monks to prayerfulness!

> Rejoice; thou who didst redeem thy brethren by unceasing
> > prostrations!

> Rejoice; supplication before the merciful God!

> Rejoice; forgiveness won by prayer and fasting!

> Rejoice; thou whose window was open to all thy brethren
> > in need!

> Rejoice; recluse who closed the doors of thy heart to
> > the passions!

> Rejoice; O Holy Wonderworker Cuthbert!

KONTAKION VIII

As Solomon of old received the offerings of the tribes of Israel for raising up the Holy Temple of God, so too did the Creation serve holy Cuthbert, for in raising up a hut to house him in prayer and supplication to Christ, he received timber from the seas themselves, though his brethren failed to provide it. For in such strange ways does the Lord reconcile those estranged from Him, that they might cry with grateful hearts: ALLELUIA!

OIKOS VIII

WHOLLY present in the counsel of the saints is the grace of the Holy Spirit, while in no way absent from their ascetic struggle, for these labours bring forth holiness of life, whose fruit is sweetness for all who taste of it, thereby yearning all the more to know the sweetness of Him Who was born of the Virgin, and to sing such words as these:

Rejoice; thou who by Divine providence pourest forth
abundant healings!

Rejoice; thou whose miracles draw the faithful to Christ!

Rejoice; thou who in thy life didst heal thy sister by the touch
of thy relic!

Rejoice; thou whose relics are given by God for veneration
in the present age!

Rejoice; thou earthly Cherubim!

Rejoice; thou flesh-bearing Seraphim!

Rejoice; thou who dost restore broken flesh to
completeness!

Rejoice; thou who yokest together dust of earth and
godliness!

Rejoice; thou who by prayer healest the sickness of
transgressions!

Rejoice; thou who by supplications grantest the taste of
Paradise!

Rejoice; cincture, binding the wounds of the lovers of Christ!

Rejoice; thou hope in eternal healings!

Rejoice; O Holy Wonderworker Cuthbert!

KONTAKION IX

ALL angel-kind was amazed as Thy servant Cuthbert, O Lord, who like an angel in the flesh saw things to come as if they were wholly present with him; for he beheld the inaccessible foreknowledge of God, making it accessible to all, speaking with boldness and hearing from all: ALLELUIA!

OIKOS IX

ORATORS most eloquent fall dumb before the prophecies of Thy saints; for they are at a loss to explain how Thou couldst raise up royal heirs where there were no offspring, or how Thou couldst call forth from solitude the holy to rule with wisdom over Thy flock. But as for us, marvelling at the mysteries Thou hast revealed in prophecy through Thy saints, we cry with faith:

Rejoice; vessel of the prophecies of God!

Rejoice; treasury of the secrets of His providence!

Rejoice; thou who revealest the foolishness of kings!

Rejoice; thou who provest their ambitions frail as
  spiders' webs!

Rejoice; for unbelievers are confounded!

Rejoice; for the boastings of the faithless are faded away!

Rejoice; thou who didst bow thy heart to the will of God!

Rejoice; thou who didst accept thy bishopric when kings and
  bishops bowed before thee!

Rejoice; thou whose prophecy drew a king from across
  the sea!

Rejoice; thou whose news blessed thy people with a humble
  sovereign!

Rejoice; worthy helmsman of Christ's Church on the
  Holy Isle!

Rejoice; haven by thy prayers for those who fare on the sea
  of life!

Rejoice; O Holy Wonderworker Cuthbert!

KONTAKION X

WISHING to do God's will, like a new Elias, thou didst see the
chariot of thy soul ready to rise to heaven; and, though God's
providence was revealed to thee the prayer of thy friend Herbert that was
heard by God; for by his intercessions He called thee both to thy repose at
like time, that the Lord Himself might hear thy cry: ALLELUIA!

OIKOS X

THOU art a rampart for those who doubt wakefulness beyond the
grave, O holy Cuthbert; for the Maker of heaven and earth revealed
to thee at table the vision of things beyond this world: the soul of a pious
servant of God, borne heavenward by the angels. By thy testimony, O
holy one, thou dost prepare us for the journey of our soul to judgement,
and teachest all to cry out to thee:

Rejoice; pillar of holiness!

Rejoice; gate of visions of heaven!

Rejoice; revealer of spiritual revelations!

Rejoice; bestower of Divine consolations!

Rejoice; for thou didst convict those drowning in the mire
  of shame!

Rejoice; for thou didst admonish the unbelieving in mind!

Rejoice; for thou didst bring to nought the doubts of
  the faithless!

Rejoice; for thou didst strengthen the hope of the faithful!

Rejoice; confirmation of the judgements of God!

Rejoice; thou who wouldst join the souls of the just to
  the Lord!

Rejoice; holy father of the repentant!

Rejoice; witness of the angelic escorts of holy souls!

Rejoice; O Holy Wonderworker Cuthbert!

KONTAKION XI

DEFEATED is every hymn that striveth to reckon the multitude of miracles worked through thee, O holy Cuthbert; for even should we offer thee, O blessed father, hymns of praise numberless as the waves of the sea, we should still have done nothing worthy of the great abundance of mercies poured out on us who cry to thee: ALLELUIA!

OIKOS XI

AS a brilliant staff of healing shining to those in sickness and despair, we behold the holy Cuthbert, for he cultivated a life of prayer, and by it healed suffering souls; still he reacheth out his arm with mercy, and blessing us, is honoured by these our cries:

Rejoice; thou who dost bear the Cup of Life!

Rejoice; thou who dost overturn the chalice of death!

Rejoice; holy one, anointing mankind with healing!

Rejoice; blessed one, deliverer of ailing souls!

Rejoice; for thou hast caused new hope of life to dawn!

Rejoice; for thou hast caused Christ's ever-flowing river of healings to gush forth!

Rejoice; thou who didst restore a dying son to his mother!

Rejoice; thou who didst wash away the odour of sickness!

Rejoice; dispenser of the Bread of Life!

Rejoice; bearer of the Wine-cup pouring forth salvation!

Rejoice; sweet-scented fragrance of deliverance from the plague of death!

Rejoice; life-bringing healer to those in despair!

Rejoice; O Holy Wonderworker Cuthbert!

KONTAKION XII

WISHING to show forth His grace, He that healeth the infirmities of men granted great healing to His servant Cuthbert, who having on his death bed staunched the ailment of his brother, heareth from all: ALLELUIA!

OIKOS XII

WHILST hymning the Lord Christ, we all sing praises to His servant Cuthbert, as a dwelling-place of the Lord's grace; for the Lord Who foreseeth all things and healeth all infirmities was present with him, and He glorified His servant in both life and death, and taught all to praise him thus:

Rejoice; dwelling-place of grace in thy tomb!

Rejoice; thou who rested within the Holy of Holies!

Rejoice; preacher of brotherly love to thy brethren!

Rejoice; inexhaustible treasury of healing!

Rejoice; restorer of the servants of kings!

Rejoice; sustainer of thy brother priests!

Rejoice; unshakeable tower of Lindisfarne!

Rejoice; impregnable bulwark of Durham!

Rejoice; thou through whom soil is raised to holiness!

Rejoice; thou through whom storms are cast down!

Rejoice; healer of mortal flesh!

Rejoice; salvation of a multitude of souls!

Rejoice; O Holy Wonderworker Cuthbert!

KONTAKION XIII

O GLORIOUS saint who didst hallow thy island home with thy healings, that it might receive thy holy relics at thy repose, free us from every calamity and disease of body and soul, and deliver from every torment those who cry with one voice: ALLELUIA! *(Thrice.)*

And again, Oikos I and Kontakion I are read.

OIKOS I

A S an infant thou didst play as a child, O holy Cuthbert, and wast reproved by thy friend for thine indulgence at play, urging thee to exercise watchfulness over mind and body. For he upbraided thee by the Holy Spirit: Why dost thou persist in doing what is contrary to thy nature and rank, most holy bishop? The Lord hast marked thee to instil virtue into thine elders! Thereby did he prophecy thine illustrious life to come, and fulfilled the words of the Holy Scripture, for out of the mouths of babes hast the Lord perfected the praise of His saints:

Rejoice; thou whom the Lord admonished with the words
of a child!

Rejoice; thou who heeded the words of His angel, and was thereby healed!

Rejoice; thou whose eyes were opened at thy priestly call!

Rejoice; thou whose eyes beheld the angel of God!

Rejoice; thou who was made whole by a soldier of Christ!

Rejoice; thou whom like Judas Maccabeus beheld an angelic soldier!

Rejoice; thou whose childish prayers were mocked by an earthly brood!

Rejoice; thou whose prayers were accepted by the heavenly hosts!

Rejoice; thou whose boyish weakness was despised by those in trouble at sea!

Rejoice; thou whose manly prayers preserved souls on storm-tossed waters!

Rejoice; thou whose youthful piety caused men to burn inwardly with shame at their impiety!

Rejoice; thou whose praise never ceased to flow from their mouths!

Rejoice; O Holy Wonderworker Cuthbert!

KONTAKION I

O CUTHBERT, the great and admirable warrior who shineth forth with thy many merits: now the Lord shineth through thee in thine eternal reward, for thou crushest the fires of the flesh. With thy heart didst thou scorn all passing things in thy duty and love for Christ, and in thy labour didst not scorn the Lord's commandments, for in thy generosity and eagerness thou didst flow with the Light of Christ, opening an everlasting stream of grace where none had been found before.   O thou, who broughtest forth an abundant harvest in rocky earth, do thou ever pray to the Thrice-Holy Lord that our souls may be saved.

PRAYER TO SAINT CUTHBERT

Holy Father Cuthbert, Pray to God for us!

O LORD, Thou Who alone preservest us unfailing in divine love and oneness of mind, grant that we may live in concord with all the servants of Christ's holy Church, and show patience to us who seek hospitality in the household of faith.   Preserve us from entanglement with those who have forsaken the Faith, deliver us from schisms and heresies, grant that we may learn the teachings of our Fathers, and live by them. Strengthen us to carry out the rule of life which Thou in Thy mercy hast seen fit to grant us through the witness and prayers of thy holy servant Cuthbert and all Thy saints, for Thou art holy, always, now and ever, and unto the ages of ages. AMEN.

ANOTHER PRAYER TO SAINT CUTHBERT

(Said on the Feast Day of St. Cuthbert - 20ᵗʰ March)

Holy Father Cuthbert, Pray to God for us!

O LORD our God, it is truly meet and just, right and availing to our salvation, that we should at all times, and in all places, give thanks unto Thee, Father Almighty, Everlasting God, upon this day of the departure to Christ of our most holy Father Cuthbert, who first became an example in daily life, in temperate and most chaste conduct, and afterwards took up the monastic yoke, nourished only by the love of God, who did not seek to shepherd Thy Church, but rather was invited to do so by Thy Divine Providence, and the counsel of the churches. He had ever fought manfully and mightily against flesh and blood, and the rulers of this realm, seizing victory with the helm of hope for salvation, the breastplate of righteousness, the shield of faith, and the sword of the Word of God; through him Thou didst make manifest many miracles, and grant him before time a vision of his repose: Therefore, O Lord, We entreat Thee through the intercessions of our holy Father Cuthbert, that we may be counted worthy to reach the haven of joy and the heavenly realms of Thee, before Whom stand the countless choirs of Angels and Archangels, singing the Thrice Holy hymn. For Thou art a merciful God, and unto Thee do we send up glory, to the Father, and to the Son, and to the Holy Spirit, now and ever, and unto the ages of ages. AMEN.

AKATHIST TO SAINT GUTHLAC OF CROWLAND

Tone VIII

KONTAKION I

CHOSEN ascetic and superb servant of Christ, who poured out in the Fenland wilderness inexhaustible streams of inspiration and a multitude of miracles. We praise thee with love and call out to thee:

> Rejoice; O holy Guthlac, champion of Christ and guide of
> all the faithful!

OIKOS I

AS an angel in the flesh thou wast shown forth in the Fenland waste by the grace of God Who ever careth for men. Seeing the beauty of thy virtues, we thy children now cry out to thee:

Rejoice; thou who didst live in virtue for thy youth!

Rejoice; thou who didst ever live in fear of God and do His holy will!

Rejoice; thou who didst manifest the grace of God in numberless virtues!

Rejoice; thou who didst cast out demons from the possessed!

Rejoice; thou who wast filled with love for thy fellow-men and didst labour for their salvation!

Rejoice; thou who dost bring joy to all who pray to thee in faith and love!

Rejoice; O holy Guthlac, champion of Christ and guide of all the faithful!

KONTAKION II

S EEING the abundance and variety of thy virtues, O holy Father, we see in thee a living source of God's wonders and benefits. Thou dost refresh with love and miracles all who cry in faith to God: ALLELUIA!

OIKOS II

B EING filled with love, thou didst lay aside the armour of thine earthly king, O Father, and arming thyself with the spiritual weapons of faith and prayer, thou didst enlist as a true warrior of Christ, and we call out to thee in admiration:

Rejoice; firm stronghold of Orthodox Truth!

Rejoice; precious vessel of the gifts of the Holy Spirit!

Rejoice; champion of the King of Heaven!

Rejoice; great faster and doer of God's commandments!

Rejoice; severe ascetic who gavest thyself no repose!

Rejoice; enlightener of a host of monks!

Rejoice; O holy Guthlac, champion of Christ and guide of
all the faithful!

KONTAKION III

SEEKING the path of true asceticism, thou didst cross the Fenland waters with thy faithful disciples, and alighting on the wilderness of Crowland Isle, thou didst plant there a haven, wherein with vigils and fasting thou didst labour in the service of God to Whom we cry out: ALLELUIA!

OIKOS III

Dwellers in Heaven should be praising thee, and not we on earth, for our words are feeble beside thy deeds. Yet offering to God what we have, we cry out to thee thus:

Rejoice; thou who didst water the Fenland waste with thy
tears of compunction!

Rejoice; thou who didst enlighten many by thy holy labours!

Rejoice; thou who wast revered by the fish and birds of
the air!

Rejoice; bright luminary beloved by all!

Rejoice; model of spiritual meekness!

Rejoice; giver of comfort to those in need!

Rejoice; O holy Guthlac, champion of Christ and guide of
all the faithful!

KONTAKION IV

B EWILDERED by thy deeds of piety and love, we know not how to praise thee worthily, O holy Father Guthlac. Thou didst gather round thee a following of monks and ascetics who inspired by thy spiritual struggles and preaching of the Gospel, sought to follow thee in the service of God, to Whom we cry out: ALLELUIA!

OIKOS IV

T HE English people beheld thy life and marvelled at God's mercies manifested in that watery wasteland. And so we also, crossing the waters of this life, cry out marvelling to thee:

Rejoice; enlightener of those in the pagan darkness!

Rejoice; thou who didst dedicate thy habitation to the Holy Apostle Bartholomew!

Rejoice; thou who didst emulate his apostolic zeal and preaching!

Rejoice; loving chastiser of those who had gone astray!

Rejoice; speedy comfort to those who repented of their sins!

Rejoice; vanquisher of demons with the three-fold scourge of Divine virtue!

Rejoice; O holy Guthlac, champion of Christ and guide of all the faithful!

KONTAKION VI

T HOU didst feed the fish and birds and all manner of wild creatures with the crumbs of thy frugal sustenance, O blessed Guthlac, and thou didst nourish kings and prelates with thy humble words of enlightenment and prophetic wisdom, wherefore with them do we cry out in wonder to God: ALLELUIA!

OIKOS VI

DWELLING in an empty tomb for thy cell, thou wast ever mindful of death, and spending thy days and nights in singing psalms and keeping vigil, thou wast granted to converse with Angels, and with them we cry out to thee:

Rejoice; thou who wast a minister to all God's creatures!

Rejoice; thou who provided by thy prayers for all in need!

Rejoice; inexhaustible bread for the hungry!

Rejoice; thou healer of those in sickness!

Rejoice; quick uplifting for those who had fallen!

Rejoice; thou who restored sight to the blind!

Rejoice; O holy Guthlac, champion of Christ and guide of
all the faithful!

KONTAKION VI

BEING granted to read the minds and hearts of men as though gazing through a glass, thou didst call to repentance, O Guthlac, thy disciple who was tempted to slay thee, and he, like many whose thoughts and temptations thou didst reveal, fell before God in true contrition and cried: ALLELUIA!

OIKOS VI

HEARING of thy fame and miracles, many sought out thy humble solitude, O Father Guthlac, and besought thee to deliver them from slavery to sin and we also beseech thee to pray for us that we may live in peace and quiet, saving our souls as we gratefully cry out to thee:

Rejoice; helper of those who call upon thee in faith!

Rejoice; thou who deliverest from death and the
  enslavement of evil!

Rejoice; thou who preservest from lies and violence!

Rejoice; preserver of the innocent from bonds!

Rejoice; thou who foilest the attacks of the unrighteous!

Rejoice; destroyer of falsehood and exalter of truth!

Rejoice; O holy Guthlac, champion of Christ and guide of
  all the faithful!

KONTAKION VII

THOU didst gather round thee a band of holy hermits, whose names
we venerate with thine; Tatwin thy first disciple, Egbert, Cissa and
Bettelin, Etheldrytha the former Queen, and Pega thy righteous sister.
Now with these good Saints thou dost pray for us to God as we on earth
cry out to Him: ALLELUIA!

OIKOS VII

O FERVENT venerator of the Holy Saints of the West, thou wast
manifested as one of them, exhorting thy flock to preserve and
emulate the Orthodox Faith that they confessed, and astonishing the
English race by thy holy life. Now preserve us in that same Faith as we cry
out to thee:

Rejoice; new Martin by thy miracles and ascetic feats!

Rejoice; new Germanus by thy confession of the
  Orthodox Faith!

Rejoice; new Hilary by thy divine theology!

Rejoice; new Gregory by thine apostolic labour for
  the English!

Rejoice; new Felix by thy gentle love and monastic fervour!

Rejoice; new Bartholomew by thy preaching of the Gospel!

Rejoice; O holy Guthlac, champion of Christ and guide of
all the faithful!

KONTAKION VIII

AT the end of thy life, O holy Guthlac, thou was granted to
know the time of thy death, and having received Christ in
the Divine Mysteries at Paschaltide, thou didst prepare thy soul
for Heaven. Now marvelling at thy faith and saintly virtue, we all cry
out to God: ALLELUIA!

OIKOS VIII

O LABOURER of Christ's vineyard who knew no rest even at the end
of thy much toiling life, help us now in our labours as we strive to be
faithful to Christ, crying out in praise to thee:

Rejoice; thou who didst endure to the end and so attain
salvation!

Rejoice; thou who wast deemed worthy to give up thy soul at
the Feast of Christ's Resurrection!

Rejoice; thou who didst keep thy faith and courage when
tempted with inner desolation!

Rejoice; thou who didst toil for thy disciples and those who
sought thee for guidance!

Rejoice; thou whose soul did soar to Heaven like a bird
on the wing!

Rejoice; thou who workest wonders for those who come to
thy Shrine with faith and love!

Rejoice; O holy Guthlac, champion of Christ and guide of
all the faithful!

KONTAKION IX

A LL Angel-kind made glad at thy soul's flight to their heavenly home, marvelling at the wonders thou didst work on earth through the action of the Holy Spirit, to Whom we sing: ALLELUIA!

OIKOS IX

O RATORS find it impossible to describe thy life of holiness with their many and eloquent words, O holy Guthlac, for thou didst become an island for the power of the ineffable God amidst a sea of sin. Yet unable to fall silent at the wonder shining through the ages to our age of feeble faith, we glorify thee singing:

Rejoice; divine palace from where the counsel of the Good
King is given!

Rejoice; small and humble abode containing the spacious
beauty of Angels' mansions!

Rejoice; thou who didst gain a house not made with hands,
eternal in the heavens!

Rejoice; infirmary wherein all manner of diseases are
divinely healed!

Rejoice; closet wherein thy holy labour of prayer was
hidden!

Rejoice; blessed temple of the Holy Spirit!

Rejoice; O holy Guthlac, champion of Christ and guide of
all the faithful!

KONTAKION X

W ISHING to save the world, the Saviour of all raised up a new Saint for the English people, and through him has called us out of the dark recesses of sin. Hearing this call to repentance, we his unworthy children in turn cry out to God: ALLELUIA!

OIKOS X

THOU art a wall sheltering us from adversity, O Father Guthlac, for through thy heavenly intercessions we are delivered from the attacks of demonic passions and from afflictions which beset us on earth. Before thy firm support of prayer, we cry with faith:

Rejoice; firm comfort to those in affliction!

Rejoice; strength to those in temptation!

Rejoice; God-revealed advice to those in doubt
and confusion!

Rejoice; refreshing water to those perishing in the heat
of sorrow!

Rejoice; loving father to the lonely and abandoned!

Rejoice; holy teacher of those who seek thy Truth!

Rejoice; O holy Guthlac, champion of Christ and guide
of all the faithful!

KONTAKION XI

THY life was a hymn to the Most Holy Trinity and worthy emulation of thy chosen protector, the Apostle Bartholomew, surpassing others in thought, word and deed, O most blessed Guthlac. For with much wisdom thou didst discern and teach the precepts of the True Faith, teaching us to sing with faith, hope and love to the One God in Trinity: ALLELUIA!

OIKOS XI

WE see thee as a radiant lamp of Orthodoxy amidst the darkness of ignorance and error, O God-chosen ascetic and guide of the faithful, our Father Guthlac. For even after thy repose thou dost speak the Truth to the ignorant and shine as a light to those who seek guidance and to all who cry out to thee:

Rejoice; radiance of Divine Wisdom to those in ignorance!

Rejoice; rainbow of quiet joys to the meek!

Rejoice; thunder to stubborn sinners!

Rejoice; lightning of the zeal of God!

Rejoice; rain of God's dogmas!

Rejoice; shower of inspired thoughts!

Rejoice; O holy Guthlac, champion of Christ and guide of
all the faithful!

KONTAKION XII

G RACE was poured forth on the English land through a holy ascetic
and his God-pleasing followers. Beholding this grace come forth
from one who dwelt in our land, let us receive it with reverence and
thanksgiving, crying out to God: ALLELUIA!

OIKOS XII

S INGING in praise to God, the heavenly choir of Saints maketh glad that
He hath not forsaken the fallen and unbelieving world but hath
manifested His almighty power in thee, His meek and humble servant. O
blessed Guthlac, with all the Saints greet and honour thee:

Rejoice; star of righteousness shining in Heaven's
firmament!

Rejoice; vanquisher of demons with the scourge of the
Name of the Trinity!

Rejoice; second Jonah warning of all the wages of sin!

Rejoice; new Baptist drawing all to a life of prayer and
repentance!

Rejoice; new Paul suffering to preach the Gospel in the spirit of truth!

Rejoice; new Bartholomew whose miracles instil in us faith and awe!

Rejoice; O holy Guthlac, champion of Christ and guide of all the faithful!

KONTAKION XIII

O OUR holy and most wondrous Father Guthlac, consolation for all the sorrowing, accept now our prayerful offering, that through thy prayers to our Lord, we may be spared Gehenna and by thy God-pleasing intercession, we may cry out eternally: ALLELUIA! *(Thrice.)*

And again, Oikos I and Kontakion I are read.

OIKOS I

A S an angel in the flesh thou wast shown forth in the Fenland waste by the grace of God Who ever careth for men. Seeing the beauty of thy virtues, we thy children now cry out to thee:

Rejoice; thou who didst live in virtue for thy youth!

Rejoice; thou who didst ever live in fear of God and do His holy will!

Rejoice; thou who didst manifest the grace of God in numberless virtues!

Rejoice; thou who didst cast out demons from the possessed!

Rejoice; thou who wast filled with love for thy fellow-men and didst labour for their salvation!

Rejoice; thou who dost bring joy to all who pray to thee in faith and love!

Rejoice; O holy Guthlac, champion of Christ and guide of
all the faithful!

KONTAKION I

CHOSEN ascetic and superb servant of Christ, who poured out in the
Fenland wilderness inexhaustible streams of inspiration and a
multitude of miracles. We praise thee with love and call out to thee:

Rejoice; O holy Guthlac, champion of Christ and guide of
all the faithful!

PRAYER TO SAINT GUTHLAC OF CROWLAND.

O BELOVED Father Guthlac, whilst on earth thou didst see the future
as if present, distant things as if near, the hearts and minds of men
as if they were thine own. We know that in this thou wast enlightened by
God, with Whom thou wast ever in the mystical communion of prayer,
and with Whom thou abidest eternally. As once, Thou didst hear the
petitions of thy followers and those who flocked to thee even before they
could speak to thee, so now hear our prayers, and bring them before the
Lord. Thou hast gone over to the life everlasting, unto the other world,
yet thou art in truth not far from us, for Heaven is closer to us than our
own souls. Show us who are troubled and cast down in sin the same
compassion that thou didst once show to those who sought thee out in thy
Fenland solitude. Give to us who have fallen into sin, confusion and
despair, the same stern, yet loving instruction that thou didst once give to
thy chosen flock. In thee, we see the living likeness of our Maker, the
living spirit of the Gospel, a second Apostle Bartholomew, and the
foundation of our Faith. In the pure life that thou didst live, we see a
model of virtue, a source of instruction and inspiration to those struggling
in the ascetic life. Beholding the grace bestowed upon thee, we know that
God has not forsaken his people. It is rather we that have fallen from
Him, and so must regain the likeness of Divinity as thou hast done.
Through thine intercession, O blessed one, grant that we may increase our
striving toward our heavenly homeland, setting our affections on things

above, toiling in prayer and virtue, waging war against the attacks of our fallen nature. Call on the mercy of God, that we may one day join thee in His Kingdom. For our deepest wish is to live forever with Him, the Father, and the Son, and the Holy Spirit, now and ever, and unto the ages of ages. AMEN.

AKATHIST TO SAINT XENIA
OF ST. PETERSBURG

KONTAKION I

O HOLY and blessed Mother Xenia, chosen favourite and fool for the sake of Christ, who elected to undergo the struggle of patience and the suffering of affliction, we who honour thy holy memory offer thee hymns of praise. Help us against our enemies, visible and invisible, that we may cry unto thee:

Rejoice; O blessed Xenia, who ever intercedeth for our souls!

OIKOS I

A FTER the death of thy husband, O blessed Mother, thou sought the life of the angels and rejected the beauty of this world and all that is in it — the lust of the eyes, the lust of the flesh, and the pride of life; and thou acquired the understanding of Christ. Wherefore, thou heareth these praises which we offer unto thee:

Rejoice; for thou wast the peer of Andrew, the fool for the sake of Christ!

Rejoice; for thou renounced thine own name, referring to thyself as dead!

Rejoice; for thou assumed foolishness and took the name of thy husband, Andrew!

Rejoice; for thou called thyself by a man's name, renouncing woman's weakness!

Rejoice; because for the sake of Christ thou accepted voluntary poverty!

Rejoice; for thou distributed all thy substance to good people and to the poor!

Rejoice; for by thy foolishness thou hath taught us to reject the vain wisdom of this age!

Rejoice; good comforter of all who have recourse to thee in prayer!

Rejoice; for thou wast full of wisdom transcending the world!

Rejoice; for thou preferred mockery and ridicule to earthly glory!

Rejoice; for thou hath been glorified by God!

Rejoice; speedy helper in time of trouble and despair!

Rejoice; O blessed Xenia, who ever intercedeth for our souls!

KONTAKION II

PERCEIVING thy manner of life as strange, for thou spurned thy home and all worldly riches, thy kinsmen in the flesh thought thee deranged; but the people of Saint Petersburg, seeing thy humility, lack of acquisitiveness, and voluntary poverty, sang unto God: ALLELUIA!

OIKOS II

O BLESSED Xenia, thou hid the understanding given thee by God under an apparent mindlessness; and amid the vanity of the great city, thou lived like a desert-dweller, unceasingly offering thy prayers up to God. And, marvelling at thy manner of life, we cry out to thee in praise:

Rejoice; for thou took upon thy shoulder the heavy cross of foolishness which God hadst given thee!

Rejoice; O blessed one who bore it without hesitation!

Rejoice; for thou hid the radiance of grace under an assumed insanity!

Rejoice; for thy foolishness wast most wise!

Rejoice; for through extreme humility and feats of prayer thou acquired the gift of clairvoyance!

Rejoice; for thou showed forth this gift for the benefit and salvation of the suffering!

Rejoice; for thou beheld the sufferings of the people clairvoyantly, as from afar!

Rejoice; for thy prayers brought relief to those in pain and distress!

Rejoice; for thou prophesied to the good woman the birth of a son!

Rejoice; for thou entreated God, that He grant that woman
a child!

Rejoice; for thou hurrieth to entreat the Lord on behalf of
thy neighbours!

Rejoice; for thou hath taught all to flee to God in prayer!

Rejoice; O blessed Xenia, who ever intercedeth for our souls!

KONTAKION III

B Y the power given thee by God from on high, thou manfully endured
burning heat and bitter cold, crucifying thy flesh, and the passions,
and lusts. Wherefore, enlightened by the Holy Spirit, thou cried out
unceasingly unto God: ALLELUIA!

OIKOS III

W ITH the sky as thy roof, and the earth as thy bed, O blessed one;
thou spurned the comfort of the flesh for the sake of the
Kingdom of God. And we, beholding thy manner of life, cry out to thee
with compunction:

Rejoice; for thou gave thy earthly home to the people!

Rejoice; for thou sought, and received the shelter of heaven!

Rejoice; for thou possessed nothing that was earthly, but
enriched all spiritually!

Rejoice; O treasure house of the gifts of heaven!

Rejoice; for thou accounted every material thing as nothing!

Rejoice; for thou were thus freed from every loss!

Rejoice; for thou endured hunger and cold in ragged clothing!

Rejoice; for by thy life thou teacheth us endurance!

Rejoice; for thou showed forth the love of God for all!

Rejoice; for thou hath been adorned with the fruits of piety!

Rejoice; for thou showed the world patience and
guilelessness!

Rejoice; O our fervent intercessor before the throne of the
Most High!

Rejoice; O blessed Xenia, who ever intercedeth for our souls!

KONTAKION IV

THE tempest of life which assailed Saint Petersburg thou weathered by meekness and guilelessness, O blessed Mother, and thou acquired dispassion toward this corrupt world; therefore, thou sing unto God: ALLELUIA!

OIKOS IV

HEARING of thee, that, having endured a multitude of afflictions for Christ's sake, thou comfort the sorrowful, strengthen the weak, and guide the lost to the straight path, the suffering hasten to thy aid, singing unto thee:

Rejoice; for thou loved the path of Christ with all your heart!

Rejoice; for thou joyfully bore the Cross of Christ!

Rejoice; for thou endured every offense offered thee by the
world, the flesh, and the devil!

Rejoice; for thou thus emulated the ascetics of the desert!

Rejoice; for thou wast full to overflowing with the gifts
of God!

Rejoice; for thou freely bestow spiritual gifts upon those
in need!

Rejoice; for thou showed love for thy neighbours!

Rejoice; for thou offered consolation to the suffering!

Rejoice; for thou shed unceasing tears of repentance!

Rejoice; for thou wipeth away the tears of those who weep!

Rejoice; for thou sought neither comfort nor warmth
for thyself!

Rejoice; for thou wast wondrously warmed by the grace of
the Holy Spirit!

Rejoice; O blessed Xenia, who ever intercedeth for our souls!

KONTAKION VI

THY HOLINESS, O blessed Xenia, was like a divinely guided star illumining the sky of Saint Petersburg; for unto all perishing in the madness of sin thou showed the path of salvation, calling all to repentance, that they might cry out to God: ALLELUIA!

OIKOS VI

SEEING thy feats of prayer and thy endurance of heat and cold, pious folk sought to alleviate thy sufferings, offering thee clothing and food; but thou distributed all these things to the poor, desiring to maintain thy struggle. And we, marvelling at thy voluntary poverty, cry out to thee thus:

Rejoice; for thou willingly endured burning heat and freezing
cold the sake of Christ!

Rejoice; for thou wast warmed by the indwelling of the
Holy Spirit!

Rejoice; for thou remained continually in prayer!

Rejoice; for thou never tire in interceding for mankind!

Rejoice; for by all-night vigils in prayer thou preserved Saint
    Petersburg from misfortunes!

Rejoice; for many times thou averted from it the wrath
    of God!

Rejoice; for every day of the year thou prayed at night in
    a field!

Rejoice; for by thy fervent tears thou warmed the cold earth!

Rejoice; for thou tasted the sweetness of paradise in poverty
    of spirit!

Rejoice; for in this sweetness thou left behind all
    earthly things!

Rejoice; for thou abide wholly in God!

Rejoice; for thou delight in the bridal banquet of thy Master!

Rejoice; O blessed Xenia, who ever intercedeth for our souls!

KONTAKION VI

A LL who have been delivered by thee from different ailments,
misfortunes and sorrows — the rich and the poor, the old and the
young — proclaim the holiness of thy life, O blessed one of God;
therefore, and glorifying thee, we cry out unto God: ALLELUIA!

OIKOS VI

T HE GLORY of thy struggles shone forth, O blessed Mother, when
at night thou secretly carried stones for those who were erecting
the Church of the Smolensk Icon of the Mother of God, lightening
the tasks of the builders; and mindful of this, we sinners cry out to thee
such things as these:

Rejoice; for thou teacheth us to perform virtuous deeds in
    secret!

Rejoice; for thou call all to feats of piety!

Rejoice; for thou aided those who were building the
churches of God!

Rejoice; for thou loved the holiness of the Church!

Rejoice; for thou labour for the Lord of the vineyard!

Rejoice; for thou ease our labours on the path of salvation!

Rejoice; for thou continually call upon the name of the Lord!

Rejoice; O speedy helper of those who have recourse
unto thee!

Rejoice; for thou hath found rest in Christ thy Master!

Rejoice; O good comforter of all the sorrowful!

Rejoice; for thou sanctified thy city by thy painful footsteps!

Rejoice; O heavenly aid of the city of Saint Petersburg!

Rejoice; O blessed Xenia, who ever intercedeth for our souls!

KONTAKION VII

D ESIRING to deliver from sorrow the mourning physician who had
buried his wife, thou commanded a certain maiden to hasten to
Okhta, there to take him as her husband and to console him. And they
did as thou said, singing unto God in joy: ALLELUIA!

OIKOS VII

A NEW WONDER thou revealed in thy prayer, O blessed Mother,
when thou said unto a pious woman: "Take a five-kopek piece, and
it will go out!" thus prophesying that fire would strike her house; and at thy
supplication the flame of the fire was extinguished. Therefore, mindful of
these things, we cry out praises unto thee:

Rejoice; for thou unceasingly grieved over thy sins!

Rejoice; for thou extinguish the sorrows of the people!

Rejoice; for thou bore suffering in body and soul!

Rejoice; for before God thou show forth boldness for the suffering!

Rejoice; O inextinguishable lamp burning brightly in prayer to God!

Rejoice; O our intercessor amid misfortunes and perils!

Rejoice; for thou saveth from perdition those beset by the passions!

Rejoice; for thou turneth pious virgins away from marriage with unbelievers!

Rejoice; for thou crucified thy flesh with constant mortification!

Rejoice; for thou deliver from despair those who have been wounded by a curse!

Rejoice; for thy defender was the Most High!

Rejoice; O speedy defender at an unjust trial!

Rejoice; O blessed Xenia, who ever intercedeth for our souls!

KONTAKION VIII

A S A HOMELESS wanderer thou trod the path of thy life in the capital city of Russia, bearing afflictions and reproaches with great patience; and, abiding now in the heavenly Jerusalem, in joy thou singeth unto God: ALLELUIA!

OIKOS VIII

THOU WAST all things to all, O blessed Xenia — comfort for the sorrowful, protection and defines for the weak, joy for the grieving, clothing for the poor, healing for the sick; therefore, we cry out unto thee:

Rejoice; for thou dwelleth in the mansions on high!

Rejoice; for thou prayeth there for us sinners!

Rejoice; O good one, who show us a model of service to God!

Rejoice; O provider of our every need!

Rejoice; O protectress of the persecuted and oppressed!

Rejoice; for thou, by thy supplications, help the Orthodox people!

Rejoice; for thou endured much affliction and grief!

Rejoice; for thou defend the afflicted who pray unto thee!

Rejoice; for thou rebuke those who abuse their fellows!

Rejoice; for thou put to shame unbelievers and those who babble!

Rejoice; for thou wast clothed in rags and tatters!

Rejoice; for God hath adorned thee with the splendid raiment of righteousness!

Rejoice; O blessed Xenia, who ever intercedeth for our souls!

KONTAKION IX

O BLESSED MOTHER, thou endured all illness, bodily poverty, hunger and thirst, and the reproach of iniquitous people who considered thee to be insane; yet, praying to the Lord, thou continually cried out to Him: ALLELUIA!

OIKOS IX

EVEN the most eloquent of orators are unable to understand how by thy foolishness thou reproved the madness of this world, and by thy weakness thou put the mighty and wise to shame, for they do not know the power and wisdom of God which are in thee; but we, receiving thy aid, sing to you such things as these:

Rejoice; O bearer of the divine Spirit!

Rejoice; for with the Apostle Paul thou boasted in
    thy weakness!

Rejoice; for thou reproved the world by thy feigned
    foolishness!

Rejoice; for thou spurned the glamour of this world for the
    sake of salvation!

Rejoice; for thou disdained the beautiful things of this earth!

Rejoice; for thou loved the good things of heaven with all
    thy heart!

Rejoice; for thou wast attentive unto the inner voice of
    the Lord!

Rejoice; for thou calleth us to the path of salvation!

Rejoice; O dread denouncer of drunkenness as a sin!

Rejoice; for thou wast renowned for your kindness and love!

Rejoice; O holy protectress of the Orthodox family!

Rejoice; for in Christ thou found comfort for thy sorrows!

Rejoice; O blessed Xenia, who ever intercedeth for our souls!

KONTAKION X

DESIRING to save thy soul, thou crucified thy flesh with its passions and lusts; and, utterly denying thyself, thou set thy cross upon thy shoulder and followed after Christ with all thy heart, singing unto Him: ALLELUIA!

OIKOS X

THOU art a firm rampart and an unassailable refuge for those who pray unto thee, O Mother Xenia; therefore, by thy supplications help us against our enemies, visible and invisible, that we may cry unto thee:

Rejoice; for thou worked diligently in the garden of Christ!

Rejoice; for thou moveth us to spiritual labour!

Rejoice; for through steadfastness of faith thou escaped the devil's snares!

Rejoice; for thou delivereth us from the snares of the enemy!

Rejoice; for thou offered thyself unto God like incense in a censer!

Rejoice; for thou bringeth the peace of God into the hearts of the people!

Rejoice; for thou shed rays of Christian love upon all!

Rejoice; for thou extinguish the spirit of malice in the hearts of the oppressed!

Rejoice; for thou impartrth blessing unto good children!

Rejoice; for by mystic supplication thou heal their ailments!

Rejoice; for through foolishness thou attained heavenly wisdom!

Rejoice; for thou hath shown forth the wisdom of God to the
afflicted world!

Rejoice; O blessed Xenia, who ever intercedeth for our souls!

KONTAKION XI

THOSE who have been saved from misfortunes, sorrows and all
dangers offer thee hymns of praise, O blessed Xenia, and with thee
joyously sing unto God: ALLELUIA!

OIKOS XI

THY LIFE, O holy Mother, has been shown to be a radiant light
illumining the people amid the darkness of this life; for thou hath
delivered those who have fallen into the mire of sin and directed their path
to the light of Christ. Therefore, we cry out unto thee:

Rejoice; O favourite of Christ, who while in the world lived
above the world!

Rejoice; for thou enlighten the Orthodox with the light
of God!

Rejoice; for thou by your many labours acquired great grace!

Rejoice; for thou shone forth with the grace of God in the
darkness of sin!

Rejoice; for thou set your hope upon the Almighty!

Rejoice; for on the path of salvation thou giveth a helping
hand to the desperate!

Rejoice; for thou wast clad in the brilliant robe of
unwavering faith!

Rejoice; for thou strengthen those who are weak in the Faith!

Rejoice; for thou wast renowned for your kindness and love!

Rejoice; for thou put to shame the spirits of malice!

Rejoice; for thy ways were those of an ascetic of
the wilderness!

Rejoice; for by thy manner of life thee amazed the angels!

Rejoice; O blessed Xenia, who ever intercedeth for our souls!

KONTAKION XII

THOU pour forth grace in abundance upon those who honour thy memory and flee to thy protection, O blessed Xenia; therefore, upon us who pray unto thee, do thou also pour forth streams of healing from God, that we may cry out unto Him: ALLELUIA!

OIKOS XIII

HYMNING thy many wonders, O blessed Mother, we praise thee, and entreat thee with all our heart: Forsake not us sinners amid our grievous circumstances, but beseech the Lord of hosts, that we fall not away from our Orthodox Faith, but that, strengthened in it by thy prayers, we may cry out unto thee:

Rejoice; for thou teacheth us to have sympathy for the suffering!

Rejoice; for thou bearest our infirmities with all thy heart!

Rejoice; for thou instruct us to crucify the flesh, together
with the passions and lusts!

Rejoice; for thou cometh to our aid amid every spiritual battle!

Rejoice; for thou heareth our every supplication!

Rejoice; O intercessor and protectress of those who honour
thy memory!

Rejoice; for thou who travelled the path of tribulation!

Rejoice; for thou thereby obtained everlasting salvation!

Rejoice; for thou giveth joy to those who hasten to your tomb!

Rejoice; for thou art a speedy helper in every misfortune!

Rejoice; for thy light hath shone forth before all!

Rejoice; for thou ever mediate the salvation of thy people!

Rejoice; O blessed Xenia, who ever intercedeth for our souls!

KONTAKION XIII

O HOLY and blessed Mother Xenia, who bore a heavy cross during thy lifetime: Accept from us sinners this entreaty offered unto thee. By thy supplications, protect us from the assaults of the spirits of darkness and from all who plot evils against us. Beseech our most compassionate God, that He grant us power and might, that we may bear our own crosses and, following Christ, may go forth, singing with you to Him: ALLELUIA! *(Thrice.)*

And again, Oikos I and Kontakion I are read.

OIKOS I

A FTER the death of thy husband, O blessed Mother, thou sought the life of the angels and rejected the beauty of this world and all that is in it — the lust of the eyes, the lust of the flesh, and the pride of life; and thou acquired the understanding of Christ. Wherefore, thou heareth these praises which we offer unto thee:

Rejoice; for thou wast the peer of Andrew, the fool for the sake of Christ!

Rejoice; for thou renounced thine own name, referring to thyself as dead!

Rejoice; for thou assumed foolishness and took the name of thy husband, Andrew!

Rejoice; for thou called thyself by a man's name, renouncing woman's weakness!

Rejoice; because for the sake of Christ thou accepted voluntary poverty!

Rejoice; for thou distributed all thy substance to good people and to the poor!

Rejoice; for by thy foolishness thou hath taught us to reject the vain wisdom of this age!

Rejoice; good comforter of all who have recourse to thee in prayer!

Rejoice; for thou wast full of wisdom transcending the world!

Rejoice; for thou preferred mockery and ridicule to earthly glory!

Rejoice; for thou hath been glorified by God!

Rejoice; speedy helper in time of trouble and despair!

Rejoice; O blessed Xenia, who ever intercedeth for our souls!

KONTAKION I

O HOLY and blessed Mother Xenia, chosen favourite and fool for the sake of Christ, who elected to undergo the struggle of patience and the suffering of affliction, we who honour thy holy memory offer thee hymns of praise. Help us against our enemies, visible and invisible, that we may cry unto thee:

Rejoice; O blessed Xenia, who ever intercedeth for our souls!

PRAYERS TO SAINT XENIA OF ST. PETERSBURG

PRAYER I

O BLESSED wanderer Xenia, heir to the Kingdom of the Father, who was homeless on the earth and most simple in the manner of thy life! Like those who in the past fell down before your tomb, so do we, who have recourse unto thee, now ask: Pray that, as the Lord says, our steps may be guided rightly toward the doing of His commandments, and that the soul-corrupting iniquity sown by the godless may not prevail over our generation. O thou who hid thyself from the wise of this age, yet were known to God, ask humility, meekness and the pledge of love for our hearts, faith in prayer, hope in repentance, strength in labours, the mercy of healing in sickness, and restoration of our whole life from this time forward, that, blessing thee, we may with compunction confess the Father, the Son, and the Holy Spirit, the consubstantial and indivisible Trinity, unto the ages of ages. AMEN.

PRAYER II

O HOLY and most blessed mother Xenia, who lived under the protection of the Most High and were strengthened by the Mother of God, and who endured hunger and thirst, cold and burning heat, oppression and persecution: Thou hath received from God the gift of clairvoyance and the power to work miracles, and thou rest under the shelter of the Almighty. The Holy Church now glorifies thee as a fragrant blossom. Praying before thy holy icon, we ask thee, as one who is alive and with us: Accept our petitions, and offer them up before the throne of the loving Father of heaven; and, since thou hath boldness before Him, for those who have recourse unto thee ask eternal salvation, compassionate blessing upon our good works and undertakings, and deliverance from all misfortunes and sorrows. In thy holy supplications before our most merciful Saviour, intercede for us, the unworthy and sinful. O holy and blessed Mother Xenia, help our children to receive illumination by the light of holy baptism and the seal of the gift of the Holy Spirit; raise our youths and maidens in faith, honesty, and the fear of God, and grant them success in their studies; heal the infirm; send down love and concord upon families; account monastics worthy to fight the good fight and protect them from oppression; make our pastors steadfast in the might of the Holy Spirit; preserve the Orthodox faithful in peace and tranquillity; and pray for those who at the hour of their death are deprived of the communion of the Holy Mysteries of Christ. Thou art our trust and hope, speedily hearkening to us and delivering us, unto thee do we send up thanks, and with thee do we glorify the Father, the Son, and the Holy Spirit, now and ever, and the unto ages of ages. AMEN.

THE ORDER FOR READING CANONS AND AKATHISTS WHEN ALONE

Before commencing any rule of prayer, and at its completion, the following reverences are made (prostrations or bows), called "The Seven Bow Beginning."

O GOD, be merciful to me, a sinner. *(Bow)*

O GOD, cleanse me, a sinner, and have mercy on me. *(Bow)*

HAVING created me, O Lord, have mercy on me. *(Bow)*

I HAVE sinned immeasurably, O Lord, forgive me. *(Bow)*

MY SOVEREIGN, most holy Mother of God, save me,
　　a sinner. *(Bow)*

O ANGEL, my holy Guardian, protect me from all
　　evil. *(Bow)*

HOLY Apostle (or martyr, or father) *(Name)* pray to
　　God for me. *(Bow)*

Then:

THROUGH the prayers of our holy fathers, O Lord Jesus
　　Christ, our God, have mercy on us. AMEN.

GLORY to Thee, our God, glory to Thee.

O HEAVENLY King, The Comforter, the Spirit of Truth, Who art everywhere present and fillest all things, Treasury of blessings and Giver of life: Come and abide in us, and cleanse us of every impurity, and save our souls, O Good One.

HOLY God, Holy Mighty, Holy Immortal, have mercy
　　on us. *(Thrice.)*

GLORY to the Father, and to the Son, and to the Holy Spirit,
both now and ever, and unto the ages of ages. AMEN.

O MOST Holy Trinity, have mercy on us.

O LORD, blot out our sins.

O MASTER, pardon our iniquities.

O HOLY ONE, visit and heal our infirmities for Thy
name's sake.

LORD, have mercy. *(Thrice.)*

GLORY to the Father, and to the Son, and to the Holy Spirit,
both now and ever, and unto the ages of ages. AMEN.

OUR FATHER, Who art in heaven, hallowed be Thy name. Thy
kingdom come, Thy will be done, on earth as it is in heaven. Give
us this day our daily bread, and forgive us our debts, as we forgive our
debtors; and lead us not into temptation, but deliver us from the evil one.

LORD, have mercy. *(Twelve Times.)*

GLORY to the Father, and to the Son, and to the Holy Spirit,
both now and ever, and unto the ages of ages. AMEN.

O COME let us worship God our King. *(Bow)*

O COME let us worship and fall down before Christ our
King and God. *(Bow)*

O COME let us worship and fall down before Christ Himself,
our King and God. *(Bow)*

PSALM 50

HAVE mercy on me, O God, according to Thy great mercy; and
according to the multitude of Thy compassions blot out my
transgression. Wash me thoroughly from mine iniquity, and cleanse me
from my sin.

For I know mine iniquity, and my sin is ever before me. Against Thee only have I sinned and done this evil before Thee, that Thou mightest be justified in Thy words, and prevail when Thou art judged.

For behold, I was conceived in iniquities, and in sins did my mother bear me. For behold, Thou hast loved truth; the hidden and secret things of Thy wisdom hast Thou made manifest unto me.

Thou shalt sprinkle me with hyssop, and I shall be made clean; Thou shalt wash me, and I shall be made whiter than snow.

Thou shalt make me hear joy and gladness; the bones that have been humbled will rejoice.

Turn Thy face away from my sins, and blot out all mine iniquities.

Create in me a clean heart, O God, and renew a right spirit within me.

Cast me not away from Thy presence, and take not Thy Holy Spirit from me.

Restore unto me the joy of Thy salvation, and with Thy governing Spirit establish me.

I shall teach transgressors Thy ways, and the ungodly shall turn back unto Thee.

Deliver me from blood-guiltiness. O God, Thou God of my salvation; my tongue shall rejoice in Thy righteousness.

O Lord, Thou shalt open my lips, and my mouth shall declare Thy praise.

For if Thou hadst desired sacrifice, I had given it; with whole-burnt offerings Thou shalt not be pleased.

A sacrifice unto God is a broken spirit; a heart that is broken and humbled God will not despise.

Do good, O Lord, in Thy good pleasure unto Sion, and let the walls of Jerusalem be builded.

Then shalt Thou be pleased with a sacrifice of righteousness, with oblation and whole-burnt offerings.

Then shall they offer bullocks upon Thine altar.

THE SYMBOL OF THE ORTHODOX FAITH

I BELIEVE in one God, the Father Almighty, Maker of heaven and earth, and of all things visible and invisible.

And in one Lord Jesus Christ, the only-begotten Son of God; begotten of the Father before all ages; Light from Light, True God from True God, begotten, not made, of one essence with the Father, through Whom all things were made: Who for us men, and for our salvation, came down from Heaven, and was incarnate by the Holy Spirit and the Virgin Mary, and became Man: And was crucified for us under Pontius Pilate, and suffered and was buried: And He rose on the third day according to the Scriptures: And ascended into Heaven, and sitteth at the right hand of the Father. And shall come again, with glory, to judge both the living and the dead; Whose kingdom shall have no end.

And in the Holy Spirit, the Lord, the Giver of Life; Who proceedeth from the Father; Who with the Father and the Son together is worshipped and glorified; Who spake by the Prophets.

And in One, Holy, Catholic and Apostolic Church. I confess one Baptism for the remission of sins. I look for the Resurrection of the Dead; And the life of the Age to come. AMEN.

Then the Canons and Akathists are read as follows:

- If one Canon or Akathist is to be read, it is read straight through.

- If more than one Canon is to be read, the first Song of the first Canon is read. If the Refrain before the final or last two Troparia is Glory... Now ... , it is replaced by the Refrain of the Canon and "Most Holy Mother of God, save us" (the latter comes before a Troparion to the Virgin). The first Song of the second Canon is read, beginning with the Refrain (the Eirmos of the first Canon only is read), etc. Glory... and Now... are used only as Refrains before the last two Troparia (or last Troparion) of the final Canon to be read. Then the third Song of the first Canon, beginning with the Eirmos, etc. After the third Song: Lord have mercy (Thrice), Glory... Now... Sedalions. When there is more than one Canon, the Kontakion(s) of the second and any additional ones are read after the Sedalions. Glory... Now... is read before the final verses. Then Songs IV, VI, and VI are read. After Song VI: Lord, have mercy (Thrice), Glory... Now ... Kontakion of the first Canon. Then Songs VII, VIII, and IX are read.

- If an Akathist is read with the Canon(s), it is included after Song VI. All Kontakions of the Canon(s) are read after Song III in this case.

  o After Song IX:

  o It is truly meet to bless thee...

  o Trisagion to Our Father ...

  o Have mercy on us... and the rest of the Prayers Before Sleep.

  o If no other prayers are to be read, the closing is as follows:

    ▪ It is truly meet to bless thee...

    ▪ Prayer(s) following the Canon (s).

    ▪ Trisagion to Our Father...

    ▪ Lord, have mercy. (Thrice)

    ▪ Glory... Now...

- More Honourable than the Cherubim...

- Through the prayers of our holy fathers, O Lord Jesus Christ, our God, have mercy on us. Amen.

Those who are preparing for Holy Communion are obliged to read three Canons and one Akathist the evening before. Usually read are the Canons to the Saviour, the Mother of God, and the Guardian Angel (in that order), and either an Akathist to the Saviour or to the Mother of God. Those who desire to carry out this evening rule of prayer daily receive great spiritual benefit from doing so.

ACKNOWLEDGEMENTS

I wish to thank my son Iain for his love, enthusiasm, encouragement, and support; also, my dear friends Jennifer, Margaret, and Mary Lou for their encouragement and support — and for helping me stay sane during the creation of this volume and my other projects.

Special thanks to Kolina for explaining Photoshop® in a way that made sense.

Special commendation, as always, to the extraordinarily wonderful staff at Starbucks Store 11649 for their smiles, keeping me well caffeinated and allowing me to spend endless hours there working on this project.

Through the intersessions of all of the Saints may
God grant each of you many years.

Printed in Great Britain
by Amazon

14457008R00284